Financial Statement Analysis

Financial Statement Analysis

Nikhar Agarwal

RANDOM PUBLICATIONS
NEW DELHI (INDIA)

Financial Statement Analysis

ISBN 978-93-5111-231-0

Published in 2014 in India by

RANDOM PUBLICATIONS

4376-A/4B, Gali Murari Lal, Ansari Road
New Delhi-110 002
Phone : +91-11-43580356, +91-11-23289044
e-mail: randomexports@gmail.com, sales@randompublications.com, info@randompublications.com
Reprinted 2019

Type Setting by : Keystoneprintads, Delhi-110051
Digitally Printed at : Replika Press Pvt. Ltd.

Preface

Financial statement analysis is the process of understanding the risk and profitability of a firm through analysis of reported financial information, by using different accounting tools and techniques. Financial statement analysis consists of reformulating reported financial statements, analysis, and adjustments of measurement errors, and financial ratio analysis on the basis of reformulated and adjusted financial statements. Financial statement analysis is the foundation for evaluating and pricing credit risk and for doing fundamental company valuation. Financial statement analysis typically starts with reformulating the reported financial information.

In relation to the income statement, one common reformulation is to divide reported items into recurring or normal items and non-recurring or special items. In this way, earnings could be separated into normal or core earnings and transitory earnings. The idea is that normal earnings are more permanent and hence more relevant for prediction and valuation. Normal earnings are also separated into net operational profit after taxes (NOPAT) and net financial costs. The balance sheet is grouped, for example, in net operating assets (NOA), net financial debt, and equity. Analysis and adjustment of measurement errors question the quality of the reported accounting numbers.

The reported numbers can for example be a bad or noisy representation of invested capital, for example in terms of NOA, which means that the return on net operating assets (RNOA) will be a noisy measure of the underlying profitability. Expensing of R&D is an example when such investment expenditures are expected to yield future economic benefits, suggesting that R&D creates assets which should have been capitalized in the balance sheet. Financial ratio analysis should be based on regrouped and adjusted financial statements. Two types of ratio analysis are performed: analysis of risk and analysis of profitability: In spite of financial statement analysis being a highly useful tool, it also features some limitations, including comparability of financial data and the need to look beyond ratios. Although comparisons between two companies can provide valuable clues about a company's financial health, alas, the differences between companies' accounting methods make it, sometimes, difficult to compare the data of the two. Besides, many a times, sufficient data are on hand in the form of foot notes to the financial statements so as to restate data to a comparable basis. Or else, the analyst should remember the lack of data comparability before reaching any clear-cut conclusion. However, even with this limitation, comparisons between the key ratios of two companies along with industry averages often propose avenues for further investigation.

To summarize, financial statement analysis is concerned with analyzing the balance sheet and the income statement of a business to interpret the business and financial ratios of a business for financial representations, business evaluation, in addition to financial forecasting.

I thank all members of my team who have helped in the preparation of the book. My special thanks go to "Random Publications" who have published the book.

– *Nikhar Agarwal*

Contents

1

Introduction to Financial Management

CONCEPT

Financial management entails planning for the future of a person or a business enterprise to ensure a positive cash flow. It includes the administration and maintenance of financial assets. Besides, financial management covers the process of identifying and managing risks.

The primary concern of financial management is the assessment rather than the techniques of financial quantification. A financial manager looks at the available data to judge the performance of enterprises. Managerial finance is an interdisciplinary approach that borrows from both managerial accounting and corporate finance. Some experts refer to financial management as the science of money management. The primary usage of this term is in the world of financing business activities. However, financial management is important at all levels of human existence because every entity needs to look after its finances.

LEVELS OF FINANCIAL MANAGEMENT

Broadly speaking, the process of financial management takes place at two levels. At the individual level, financial management involves tailoring expenses according to the financial resources of an individual. Individuals with surplus cash or access to funding invest their money to make up for the impact of taxation and inflation. Else, they spend it on discretionary items. They need to be able to take the financial decisions that are intended to benefit them in the long run and help them achieve their financial goals.

From an organizational point of view, the process of financial management is associated with financial planning and financial control. Financial planning seeks to quantify various financial resources available and plan the size and timing of expenditures. Financial control refers to monitoring cash flow. Inflow is the amount of money coming into a particular company, while outflow is a record of the expenditure being made by the company. Managing this movement of funds in relation to the budget is essential for a business. At the corporate level, the main aim of the process of managing finances is to achieve the various goals a company sets at a given point of time. Businesses also seek to generate substantial amounts of profits, following a particular set of financial processes.

Financial managers aim to boost the levels of resources at their disposal. Besides, they control the functioning on money put in by external investors. Providing investors with sufficient amount of returns on their investments is one of the goals that every company tries to achieve. Efficient financial management ensures that this becomes possible.

Strong financial management in the business arena requires managers to be able to:

- Interpret financial reports including income statements, Profits and Loss or PandL, cash flow statements and balance sheet statements
- Improve the allocation of working capital within business operations
- Review and fine tune financial budgeting, and revenue and cost forecasting
- Look at the funding options for business expansion, including both long and short term financing
- Review the financial health of the company or business unit using ratio analyses, such as the gearing ratio, profit per employee and weighted cost of capital
- Understand the various techniques using in project and asset valuations
- Apply critical financial decision making techniques to assess whether to proceed with an investmtn
- Understand valuations frameworks for businesses, portfolios and intangible assets.

MANAGERIAL FINANCE

Managerial finance is the branch of the finance that concerns itself with the managerial significance of finance techniques. It is focused on assessment rather than technique. The difference between a managerial and a technical approach can be seen in the questions one might ask of annual reports. One concerned with technique would be primarily interested in measurement. They would ask: are moneys being assigned to the right categories? Were generally accepted accounting principles GAAP followed? One concerned with management though would want to know what the figures mean.

- They might compare the returns to other businesses in their industry and ask: are we performing better or worse than our peers? If so, what is the source of the problem? Do we have the same profit margins? If not why? Do we have the same expenses? Are we paying more for something than our peers?
- They may look at changes in asset balances looking for red flags that indicate problems with bill collection or bad debt.

- They will analyse working capital to anticipate future cash flow problems.

Managerial finance is an interdisciplinary approach that borrows from both managerial accounting and corporate finance. Sound financial management creates value and organisational agility through the allocation of scarce resources amongst competing business opportunities. It is an aid to the implementation and monitoring of business strategies and helps achieve business objectives.

MANAGERIAL ACCOUNTING ROLE

Managers also need to look at how resources are allocated within an organization. They need to know what each activity costs and why. These questions require managerial accounting techniques such as activity based costing. Managers also need to anticipate future expenses. To get a better understanding of the accuracy of the budgeting process, they may use variable budgeting.

ROLE OF CORPORATE FINANCE

Managerial finance is also interested in determining the best way to use money to improve future opportunities to earn money and minimize the impact of financial shocks.

To accomplish these goals managerial finance uses the following techniques borrowed from Corporate finance:

- Valuation
- Portfolio theory
- Hedging
- Capital structure

CORPORATE FINANCE

Corporate finance is an area of finance dealing with financial decisions business enterprises make and the tools and analysis used to make these decisions. The primary goal of corporate finance is to maximize corporate value while managing the firm's financial risks. Although it is in principle different from managerial finance which studies the financial decisions of all firms, rather than corporations alone, the main concepts in the study of corporate finance are applicable to the financial problems of all kinds of firms.

The discipline can be divided into long-term and short-term decisions and techniques. Capital investment decisions are long-term choices about which projects receive investment, whether to finance that investment with equity or debt, and when or whether to pay dividends to shareholders. On the other hand, the short term decisions can be grouped under the heading "Working capital management". This subject deals with the short-term balance of current assets and current liabilities; the focus here is on managing cash, inventories, and short-term borrowing and lending.

The terms corporate finance and corporate financier are also associated with investment banking. The typical role of an investment bank is to evaluate the company's financial needs and raise the appropriate type of capital that best fits those needs.

CAPITAL INVESTMENT DECISIONS

Capital investment decisions are long-term corporate finance decisions relating to fixed assets and capital structure. Decisions are based on several inter-related criteria.

- Corporate management seeks to maximize the value of the firm by investing in projects which yield a positive net present value when valued using an appropriate discount rate.
- These projects must also be financed appropriately.
- If no such opportunities exist, maximizing shareholder value dictates that management must return excess cash to shareholders.

Capital investment decisions thus comprise an investment decision, a financing decision, and a dividend decision.

The Investment Decision

Management must allocate limited resources between competing opportunities in a process known as capital budgeting. Making this capital allocation decision requires estimating the value of each opportunity or project, which is a function of the size, timing and predictability of future cash flows.

Project Valuation

In general, each project's value will be estimated using a discounted cash flow valuation, and the opportunity with the highest value, as measured by the resultant net present value will be selected. This requires estimating the size and timing of all of the incremental cash flows resulting from the project. Such future cash flows are then discounted to determine their *present value*. These present values are then summed, and this sum net of the initial investment outlay is the NPV. The NPV is greatly affected by the discount rate. Thus, identifying the proper discount rate - often termed, the project "hurdle rate" - is critical to making an appropriate decision. The hurdle rate is the minimum acceptable return on an investment—i.e. the project appropriate discount rate.

The hurdle rate should reflect the riskiness of the investment, typically measured by volatility of cash flows, and must take into account the financing mix. Managers use models such as the CAPM or the APT to estimate a discount rate appropriate for a particular project, and use the weighted average cost of capital to reflect the financing mix selected.

In conjunction with NPV, there are several other measures used as selection criteria in corporate finance. These are visible from the DCF and include discounted payback period, IRR, Modified IRR, equivalent annuity, capital efficiency, and ROI. Alternatives to NPV include MVA/EVA and APV.

Valuing Flexibility

In many cases, for example RandD projects, a project may open paths of action to the company, but this reality will not typically be captured in a strict NPV approach. Management will therefore employ tools which place an explicit value on these options. So, whereas in a DCF valuation the most likely or average or scenario specific cash flows are discounted, here the"flexibile and staged nature" of the investment is modelled, and hence"all" potential payoffs are considered. The difference between the two valuations is the"value of flexibility" inherent in the project.

The two most common tools are Decision Tree Analysis and Real options analysis; they may often be used interchangeably:

- DTA values flexibility by incorporating possible events and consequent management decisions. In the decision tree, each management decision in response to an"event" generates a"branch" or"path" which the company could follow; the probabilities of each event are determined or specified by management.
  Once the tree is constructed:
  - "All" possible events and their resultant paths are visible to management;
  - Given this"knowledge" of the events that could follow, management chooses the actions corresponding to the highest value path probability weighted;
  - Then, assuming rational decision making, this path is taken as representative of project value.
- ROA is usually used when the value of a project is contingent on the value of some other asset or underlying variable.
  Here:
  - Using financial option theory as a framework, the decision to be taken is identified as corresponding to either a call option or a put option;
  - An appropriate valuation technique is then employed - usually a variant on the Binomial options model or a bespoke simulation model, while Black Scholes type formulae are used less often.
  - The"true" value of the project is then the NPV of the"most likely" scenario plus the option value.

Quantifying Uncertainty

Given the uncertainty inherent in project forecasting and valuation, analysts will wish to assess the sensitivity of project NPV to the various inputs to the DCF model. In a typical sensitivity analysis the analyst will vary one key factor while holding all other inputs constant, ceteris paribus.

The sensitivity of NPV to a change in that factor is then observed, and is calculated as a"slope": ΔNPV/Δfactor. For example, the analyst will determine NPV at various growth rates in annual revenue as specified, and then determine the sensitivity using this formula. Often, several variables may be of interest, and their various combinations produce a"value-surface", where NPV is then a function of several variables. Using a related technique, analysts also run scenario based forecasts of NPV. Here, a scenario comprises a particular outcome for economy-wide,"global" factors as well as for company-specific factors. As an example, the analyst may specify specific growth scenarios, where all key inputs are adjusted so as to be consistent with the growth assumptions, and calculate the NPV for each.

Note that for scenario based analysis, the various combinations of inputs must be internally consistent, whereas for the sensitivity approach these need not be so. An application of this methodology is to determine an"unbiased" NPV, where management determines a probability for each scenario - the NPV for the project is then the probability-weighted average of the various scenarios. A further advancement is to construct stochastic or probabilistic financial models - as opposed to the traditional static and deterministic models. For this purpose, the most common method is to use Monte Carlo simulation to analyse the project's NPV. This method was introduced to finance by David B. Hertz in 1964, although has only recently become common: today analysts are even able to run simulations in spreadsheet based DCF models, typically using an add-in, such as Crystal Ball. Using simulation, the cash flow components that are impacted by uncertainty are simulated, mathematically reflecting their"random characteristics". Here, in contrast to the scenario approach, the simulation produces several thousand random but possible outcomes, or"trials".

The output is then a histogram of project NPV, and the average NPV of the potential investment - as well as its volatility and other sensitivities - is then observed. This histogram provides information not visible from the static DCF: for example, it allows for an estimate of the probability that a project has a net present value greater than zero. Continuing the example: instead of assigning three discrete values to revenue growth, and to the other relevant variables, the analyst would assign an appropriate probability distribution to each variable, and, where possible, specify the observed or supposed correlation between the variables. These distributions would then be"sampled" repeatedly - incorporating this correlation - so as to generate several thousand scenarios, with corresponding valuations, which are then used to generate the NPV histogram. The resultant statistics will be a more accurate mirror of the project's"randomness" than the variance observed under the scenario based approach.

The Financing Decision

Achieving the goals of corporate finance requires that any corporate investment be financed appropriately. Since both hurdle rate and cash flows will be affected, the financing mix can impact the valuation. Management must therefore identify the "optimal mix" of financing—the capital structure that results in maximum value.

The sources of financing will, generically, comprise some combination of debt and equity financing. Financing a project through debt results in a liability or obligation that must be serviced, thus entailing cash flow implications independent of the project's degree of success.

Equity financing is less risky with respect to cash flow commitments, but results in a dilution of ownership, control and earnings. The *cost of equity* is also typically higher than the *cost of debt* and so equity financing may result in an increased hurdle rate which may offset any reduction in cash flow risk.

Management must also attempt to match the financing mix to the asset being financed as closely as possible, in terms of both timing and cash flows.

One of the main theories of how firms make their financing decisions is the Pecking Order Theory, which suggests that firms avoid external financing while they have internal financing available and avoid new equity financing while they can engage in new debt financing at reasonably low interest rates. Another major theory is the Trade-Off Theory in which firms are assumed to trade-off the tax benefits of debt with the bankruptcy costs of debt when making their decisions. An emerging area in finance theory is right-financing whereby investment banks and corporations can enhance investment return and company value over time by determining the right investment objectives, policy framework, institutional structure, source of financing and expenditure framework within a given economy and under given market conditions.

One last theory about this decision is the Market timing hypothesis which states that firms look for the cheaper type of financing regardless of their current levels of internal resources, debt and equity.

The Dividend Decision

Whether to issue dividends, and what amount, is calculated mainly on the basis of the company's unappropriated profit and its earning prospects for the coming year. If there are no NPV positive opportunities, i.e. projects where returns exceed the hurdle rate, then management must return excess cash to investors. These *free cash flows* comprise cash remaining after all business expenses have been met.

This is the general case, however there are exceptions. For example, investors in a "Growth stock", expect that the company will, almost by definition, retain earnings so as to fund growth internally. In other cases, even though an opportunity is currently NPV negative, management may consider "investment flexibility"/potential payoffs and decide to retain cash flows.Management must also decide on the form of the dividend distribution, generally as cash dividends or via a share buyback. Various factors may be taken into consideration: where shareholders must pay tax on dividends, firms may elect to retain earnings or to perform a stock buyback, in both cases increasing the value of shares outstanding. Alternatively, some companies will pay "dividends" from stock rather than in cash. Today, it is generally accepted that dividend policy is value neutral.

WORKING CAPITAL MANAGEMENT

Decisions relating to working capital and short term financing are referred to as working capital management. *These involve managing the relationship between a firm's short-term assets and its short-term liabilities.*

The goal of Corporate Finance is the maximization of firm value. In the context of long term, capital investment decisions, firm value is enhanced through appropriately selecting and funding NPV positive investments. These investments, in turn, have implications in terms of cash flow and cost of capital.

The goal of Working capital management is therefore to ensure that the firm is able to operate, and that it has sufficient cash flow to service long term debt, and to satisfy both maturing short-term debt and upcoming operational expenses. In so doing, firm value is enhanced when, and if, the return on capital exceeds the cost of capital.

Decision Criteria

Working capital is the amount of capital which is readily available to an organization. That is, working capital is the difference between resources in cash or readily convertible into cash and cash requirements. As a result, the decisions relating to working capital are always current, i.e. short term, decisions. In addition to time horizon, working capital decisions differ from capital investment decisions in terms of discounting and profitability considerations; they are also "reversible" to some extent..

Working capital management decisions are therefore not taken on the same basis as long term decisions, and working capital management applies different criteria in decision making: the main considerations are:

- Cash flow/liquidity and
- Profitability/return on capital.
- The most widely used measure of cash flow is the net operating cycle, or cash conversion cycle. This represents the time difference between cash payment for raw materials and cash collection for sales. The cash conversion cycle indicates the firm's ability to convert its resources into cash. Because this number effectively corresponds to the time that the firm's cash is tied up in operations and unavailable for other activities, management generally aims at a low net count.
- In this context, the most useful measure of profitability is Return

on capital. The result is shown as a percentage, determined by dividing relevant income for the 12 months by capital employed; Return on equity shows this result for the firm's shareholders. Firm value is enhanced when, and if, the return on capital, exceeds the cost of capital. ROC measures are therefore useful as a management tool, in that they link short-term policy with long-term decision making.

Management of Working Capital

Management will use a combination of policies and techniques for the management of working capital. These policies aim at managing the *current assets* and the short term financing, such that cash flows and returns are acceptable.

- Cash management. Identify the cash balance which allows for the business to meet day to day expenses, but reduces cash holding costs.
- Inventory management. Identify the level of inventory which allows for uninterrupted production but reduces the investment in raw materials - and minimizes reordering costs - and hence increases cash flow; Just In Time; Economic order quantity; Economic production quantity.
- Debtors management. Identify the appropriate credit policy, i.e. credit terms which will attract customers, such that any impact on cash flows and the cash conversion cycle will be offset by increased revenue and hence Return on Capital.
- Short term financing. Identify the appropriate source of financing, given the cash conversion cycle: the inventory is ideally financed by credit granted by the supplier; however, it may be necessary to utilize a bank loan or to "convert debtors to cash" through "factoring".

FINANCIAL RISK MANAGEMENT

Risk management is the process of measuring risk and then developing and implementing strategies to manage that risk. Financial risk management focuses on risks that can be managed using traded financial instruments. Financial risk management will also play an important role in cash management. This area is related to corporate finance in two ways.

Firstly, firm exposure to business risk is a direct result of previous Investment and Financing decisions. Secondly, both disciplines share the goal of enhancing, or preserving, firm value. All large corporations have risk management teams, and small firms practice informal, if not formal, risk management. Derivatives are the instruments most commonly used in financial risk management. Because unique derivative contracts tend to be costly to create and monitor, the most cost-effective financial risk management methods usually involve derivatives that trade on well-established financial markets. These standard derivative instruments include options, futures contracts, forward contracts, and swaps.

RELATIONSHIP WITH OTHER AREAS IN FINANCE

Investment Banking

Use of the term "corporate finance" varies considerably across the world. In the United States it is used to describe activities, decisions and techniques that deal with many aspects of a company's finances and capital.

In the United Kingdom and Commonwealth countries, the terms "corporate finance" and "corporate financier" tend to be associated with investment banking - i.e. with transactions in which capital is raised for the corporation.

Personal and Public Finance

Corporate finance utilizes tools from almost all areas of finance. Some of the tools developed by and for corporations have broad application to entities other than corporations, for example, to partnerships, sole proprietorships, not-for-profit organizations, governments, mutual funds, and personal wealth management. But in other cases their application is very limited outside of the corporate finance arena.

Because corporations deal in quantities of money much greater than individuals, the analysis has developed into a discipline of its own. It can be differentiated from personal finance and public finance.

EVOLUTION OF FINANCIAL MANAGEMENT

There is an assumption that inadequate financial management practices are contributors to turbulence in the small firm sector; yet there have been few investigations into the factors that influence an owner-manager's approach and the processes involved in the evolution of strategy and associated learning in this area. Previous studies have adopted a comparative static approach that is survey-based; we argue that these studies can only give limited insights.

We adopt a comparative case study methodology to develop an evolutionary process view of financial management in small firms. Despite the increased attention paid to owner-managers in the small firms sector, we know comparatively little about the process of financial management and how small firms learn and adjust strategy and decision-making in this area.

We attempt to shed some light on the process issues within small firms from qualitative evidence collected as part of a programme of case study research with entrepreneurs and owner-managers. We discuss case evidence and focus on how owner-managers reach financial management decisions, how they learn and adjust behaviour within the entrepreneurship process.

SCOPE OF FINANCIAL MANAGEMENT

Scope of financial management is vast and important to business. It is involve in all level of management and all fields of human activities. We can prove that without good financial management, no organization can be alive. Organization is helpful for people and wants welfare of public.

But, it need fund, money and cash and for getting it, it uses techniques of financial management. So financial management makes his place everywhere. Never understand it as the name of book but it is practical science to support business to live respectful life in society.

We can divide financial management scope into three major parts:

- *Financial Management in New Companies*: A new company spends large amount on production and marketing but it should ignore proper use of its fund. Financial management's gateway is new company and if new company ignores financial management study, it means it is ignoring cash, inventory, debtors and fixed assets management. Past study reveals that big organization or companies did not trade even one year and before one year they took their baggage and became liquidated. Why? Because, given debt was demanded from these companies by creditors. By answering no, court had liquidated them. So, if you are starting new company, become regular readers of financial management.
- *Financial Management in Old Companies*: Old company can survive in long run, if it is capable to pay debt timely, to pay salary on time and to pay other daily expenses. Because old company has good reputation in financial market, so financial management's some part like working capital management is very significant. Old company should try to increase growth rate by using new techniques of financial management.
- *Financial Management in NGO*: In this material age, every work is becoming business. Only NGO are working not for profit aim. Its aim is not to earn money but here is also question of its existence. Like survive of company, NGO can live only and only after proper management of its cost and management of cost can be taught only in financial management. So, NGO are also under the scope of financial management. Every NGO wants to provide free services long time. Without, use the techniques of financial management, NGO starts misuse the scarce sources of public. After revealing this fact, public may reduce to donate to NGO, so NGO should be aware about financial management.

OBJECTIVES OF FINANCIAL MANAGEMENT

PROVIDE SUPPORT FOR DECISION MAKING

Financial management provides managers with the information and knowledge they need to support operational decisions and to understand the financial implications of decisions before they are made. It also enables managers to monitor their decisions for any potential financial implications and for lessons to be learned from experience, and to adapt or react as needed.

ENSURE THE AVAILABILITY OF TIMELY, RELEVANT AND RELIABLE FINANCIAL AND NON-FINANCIAL INFORMATION

Financial management gives managers the information that either forms the basis for calculating financial information, or is used for management control and accountability purposes.

MANAGE RISKS

Financial management enables an organization to identify, assess and consider the financial consequences of events that could compromise its ability to achieve its goals and objectives and/or result in significant loss of resources. Financial management is an important component of risk management and needs to be considered with the full range of business risks, such as operational and strategic risks as well as social, legal, political and environmental risks.

USE RESOURCES EFFICIENTLY, EFFECTIVELY AND ECONOMICALLY

Financial management is necessary to ensure that an organization has enough resources to carry out its operations, and that it uses these resources with due regard to economy, efficiency and effectiveness.

STRENGTHEN ACCOUNTABILITY

Financial management is essential for an organization to understand and demonstrate how it has used the financial resources entrusted to it and what it has accomplished with them.

PROVIDE A SUPPORTIVE CONTROL ENVIRONMENT

Financial management contributes to promoting an organizational climate that fosters the achievement of financial management objectives - a climate that includes commitment from senior management, shared values and ethics, communication and organizational learning.

COMPLY WITH AUTHORITIES AND SAFEGUARD ASSETS

Financial management is essential to ensuring that an organization carries out its transactions in accordance with applicable legislation, regulations and executive orders; that spending limits are observed; and that transactions are authorized. It also provides an organization with a system of controls for assets, liabilities, revenues and expenditures. These controls help to protect against fraud, financial negligence, violation of financial rules or principles and losses of assets or public money.

GOAL CONFLICTS AND AGENCY PROBLEMS

INTRODUCTION

The importance of establishing goals for financial regulators is recognized by the Basel Committee on Banking Supervision.

The first sentence of the Committee's first principle states:

- An effective system of banking supervision will have clear responsibilities and objectives for each agency involved in the supervision of banking organizations.

The Core Principle goes on to state the following:

- Each such agency should possess operational independence and adequate resources. A suitable legal framework for banking supervision is also necessary, including provisions relating to authorisation of banking organisations and their ongoing supervision; powers to address compliance with laws as well as safety and soundness concerns; and legal protection for supervisors. Arrangements for sharing information between supervisors and protecting the confidentiality of such information should be in place.

Effective design of a regulatory system to ensure financial stability typically includes specification of a set of regulations to ensure that institutions operate in a safe and sound manner, a system of prudential supervision of depository institutions either vested in the central bank or some other regulator, and a system of safety nets in the form of a lender of last resort function coupled with either an explicit or implicit deposit insurance scheme. However, the regulatory systems can often be plagued by agency problems and potential goal conflicts, especially since regulations and financial structures dynamically evolve over time, which may interfere with the objectives of ensuring safety and soundness.1 Clearly, regulatory design and agency problems have been important contributors to financial crises in the U.S., such as the collapse of the Ohio state deposit insurance fund, and more recently the collapse of the Rhode Island credit union insurance funds, not to mention the problems that contributed to the collapse of the FSLIC. Similar issues have been equally important in the rest of the world as well.2 Witness the many incidents of financial crises that have occurred in even the last few years - often at great costs to taxpayers. Because of the importance of a sound, well-functioning financial system to achieving economic growth and improving societal welfare through the promotion of efficient allocation of resources, the potential for goal conflicts and agency problems to arise should be considered in designing a financial regulatory and supervisory system. Moreover, an effective design would consider not only current issues but also be incentive compatible and timeconsistent to address new problems as they arise.

The Economic and Financial Committee of the European Union recently concluded that"...the existing regulatory and supervisory arrangements in Europe provide a coherent and flexible basis for safeguarding financial stability, but recommended that their practical functioning needs enhancement." Furthermore, the Committee put forward the general principle that"...private institutions should be involved as much as possible in both crisis prevention and, if this fails, in crisis management. Each financial institution is responsible for its own safety and soundness. If financial losses occur, the firm's shareholders should bear the costs and its management should suffer the consequences."3 While such pronouncements sound good, without also providing explicit mechanisms detailing how the private sector will be involved, little has been accomplished, especially if the loss control incentives of the regulators and financial institutions are misaligned.

It has been widely recognized both in the US and elsewhere that goal conflicts and agency problems exist which may frustrate the effective functioning of these loss control arrangements. Without more explicit consideration of these issues in designing a financial regulatory structure, it may be difficult to assure that, should a crisis arise, it will be handled efficiently or that the public will be adequately protected from losses.

Employing the framework in Wall and Eisenbeis, first discusses the nature of these conflicts and then considers whether the structure being put in place for the European Monetary Union raises special considerations that have not yet been addressed and may impact the ability to achieve the objectives put forth by the Basel Committee. In particular, there is an attempt to isolate key features of the"new" system that may be vulnerable to conflicts or problems. In the process, the experience of the US is relied upon to the extent that there are relevant parallels that may provide useful insights as to the potential vulnerabilities in the European design.

Subsequent sections first define and discuss the nature of the goal and agency conflicts. The paper then turns to ways that they typically are resolved in a democratic system. Finally, sections turn to design features that would help mitigate the problems and their application to the European Monetary Union.

AGENCY PROBLEMS AND GOAL CONFLICTS

The issues surrounding the appropriate way to structure financial regulatory agencies and how to apportion their responsibilities are long standing but are seldom dealt with in a systematic way before a crisis arises. In the United States, Congress tends to address financial regulatory problems in a sequential and evolving way. It usually responds to weakness or design flaws exposed by financial crises or emerging competitive inequities spawned by innovations of financial institutions designed to take advantage of regulatory arbitrage.4 When problems appear, Congress often puts regulatory solutions in place in a piecemeal fashion without regard to secondary consequences of subsequent market responses. But more important for this discussion, while at least temporarily solving one problem, the solutions may result in conflicts and imprecise or overlapping mandates to different regulatory bodies that carry with them another set of problems. For example, a staff report of the U.S. Senate Committee on Governmental Affairs notes that "Where several agencies are involved i n a particular regulatory function there is the possibility of omissions, inconsistencies and conflicting policy."

Horvitz stresses the importance of this problem to financial services by pointing out that Congress has assigned multiple goals to the financial service regulators. Each of the three major federal banking agencies – the Office of the Comptroller of the Currency, the Federal Reserve System and Federal Deposit Insurance Corporation has a different mix of goals. The OCC, for example, charters and regulates national banks. The FDIC provides federal deposit insurance and supervises state chartered banks that aren't members of the Federal Reserve System and certain thrift institutions. The Federal Reserve not only conducts monetary policy but also serves as the lender-of-lastresort and the supervisor of both state chartered member banks and bank holding companies. Because of this differing mix of responsibilities and goals, policies may be applied or implemented differently and jurisdictional conflicts arise between the regulatory agencies over the form, substance, and implementation of regulations.

One clear example of such a goal conflict existed many years ago between the US banking agencies' safety and soundness responsibilities and their requirement to enforce the securities laws when applied to banks. The banking agencies long perceived that providing disclosures to investors of the financial condition of a bank might in some instances trigger a run on the bank to the detriment of depositors and result in potential losses to the deposit insurance fund. This problem was particularly critical to the FDIC that perceived its primary mission to protect the deposit insurance fund, even if it came at the expense of shareholders.

For this reason, the FDIC resisted for many years the disclosure of financial information – even a basic income statement - out of fear that accurate information might trigger a run on financial intuitions it was responsible for, even if the information was relevant to investors. It wasn't until the bank holding company form of organization became the dominant form of banking organization, whose disclosure requirements were administered by the SEC, New York Stock Exchange, other securities exchanges and not the banking agencies, that financial institutions were required to expand their financial disclosures.

Of course now, we would regard such information as not only relevant to investors, but also important to achieving market discipline, which was an anathema in earlier regulatory regimes.

An additional layer of potential conflicts among the regulators exists beyond just those at the federal level because each of the 51 states not only charter banks and thrift institutions but also promulgate rules and regulations governing their operations and activities within their home states. They also provide overlapping supervision of these institutions. State and federal regulations are not necessarily harmonized and can be conflicting.

For example, there is currently a dispute brewing between many state regulators and the OCC who has pre-empted state banking agency enforcement actions for national banks as well as the application of state laws pertaining to mortgage lender/broker licensing laws, escrow account laws, credit score disclosure laws, and antipredatory lending laws by national banks.5 As a result, many larger institutions, especially those with significant multi-state operations are now opting for national over state charters.

The resulting loss of constituents – that is, institutions to supervise and regulate by state banking regulators not only threatens the agencies' raison d'etra but also depletes their financial base. State regulators typically rely upon examination fees for their funding, a feature of regulatory design that is also fraught with potential conflicts of interest. This trend away from state charters is clearly an example of regulatory arbitrage.

More generally, in the financial regulatory arena, there are several affected parties with stakes in the outcome. These include the Congress and other legislative bodies, the public, regulated and non-regulated financial institutions, shareholders and financial institution customers, and the regulatory agencies themselves.

Each of these different parties interact with each other in a dynamically evolving economy in a dialectical process described by Kane. There are many examples where conflicts arise from agency problems, such as the case where the FSLIC used the provision of tax benefits to induce acquirers to take over failed SandLs. These inducements may have helped protect the FSLIC fund, but shifted risk to the US taxpayer who ultimately ended up paying over 150 billion dollars to resolve the thrift crisis in the late 70s and early 1980s. It has also been illustrated how the assignment of different and possibly conflicting goals to regulatory agencies may lead to problems. In many cases the conflicts can be resolved i n a consistent fashion in the public arena only by congressional action or compromise between the agencies. When goal conflicts are resolved external to the agencies, this is termed external conflict resolution.

In some cases, these conflicts could be reduced or eliminated by assigning jurisdiction for the conflicting goals to a single agency. However, in most important instances, assigning jurisdiction to a single agency does not eliminate the conflict, rather, it merely transforms the way that the conflicts are resolved, as was the case with the conflict described earlier for the FDIC between the interest of the insurance fund and the interests of investors. Resolving goal conflicts administratively means that the decision will be conditioned by agency's perception and interpretation of the primacy of its responsibilities and mandates. And the resulting outcomes may not necessarily reflect those that would arise if the conflicts were resolved in the political arena. When the resolution process is de facto delegated to a single agency to solve, this process is called internal conflict resolution.

While the concerns about financial regulatory structure noted by Horvitz have long existed, the problem has become more acute in recent years. Financial firms have used advances in information processing and financial technology to exploit legal loopholes and to offer ever more products that are functionally equivalent to those offered by differently regulated financial services firms. The result has been that competing institutions offering essentially identical products are subject to different rules, regulations, and regulatory burdens that differentially impact firms' profits and competitiveness in markets. To exploit these differences, institutions now routinely seek the most favourable regulatory climate in which to operate for the products they offer. As a consequence, policies adopted by one regulator intended to achieve a specific public policy goal often have the unintended consequence of shifting market shares either to financial services firms regulated by another agency with different goals or to unregulated firms who perceive a competitive advantage and enter the market.

The range of policy areas with possible goals that may be subject to possible conflicts includes: consumer protection, monetary policy, community development, investor protection, market transparency, safety and soundness, ensuring the safety net, reducing systemic risk, and antitrust. The potential problems associated with conflicting regulatory goals are almost certain to increase whenever financial innovations arise to arbitrage regulations or financial modernization legislation is passed to modify the legal barriers separating different types of financial services firms. The question is to how best resolve the conflicts.

A FRAMEWORK FOR OPTIMAL RESOLUTION OF AGENCY AND GOAL CONFLICTS

At the highest level, design of optimal policies to resolve conflicting policy goals requires policymakers to have information on the trade-offs among the available alternatives to achieve their policy goals. Selection of the best combination of policies and methods for their implementation depends on social preferences and requires knowledge of and the ability to measure utility that is aggregated across all of the individuals in society. Because the aggregate social welfare function depends on preferences of the members of society, its parametres are surely not known nor are they directly observable.

In the absence of knowledge of the social welfare function, revealed preference exercised through the political process can be used as an indirect mechanism to infer the appropriate goal tradeoffs. To this end a presumption of a representative democracy is that the elected members of the legislature are a microcosm of society whose views and preferences reflect those of society at large. But since voters cannot directly control their legislator's actions, the elected official is essentially the voters' agent.7 Moreover, these representatives are able to listen to and balance competing special interests.

This process reveals preferences for different policy outcomes. For this reason, legislators are better suited to make policy judgments than is a bureaucratic agency, for example, which often has a narrower set of goals and priorities. Because the legislature is explicitly structured so as to reflect society's views and preferences, it could be argued that all goal conflicts should be resolved by the legislature.

But the myriad of issues and lack of time makes reliance upon the legislature to essentially micromanage disputes among competing interests in a timely fashion in financial markets infeasible. One option would be for parties with special interests in particular regulatory outcomes to appeal to the legislature each time there is need for a new regulatory policy or a change in regulation. The legislature would then be faced with two costly choices. One would be to attempt ex ante to gather information and write legislation that covers all contingencies— a task that would generally be prohibitively costly and difficult, and another would be to plan regularly to write new legislation to cover changing circumstances. The alternative would be to legislate a general framework for regulatory decision making and delegates, subject to judicial oversight, to regulatory agencies the responsibility to make case by case decisions and to write specific regulations to achieve specified policy objectives.

This, of course, is the option most often selected by the US Congress. For example, in passing the Bank Holding Company Amendments of 1970, there was great debate over what activities would and would not be permitted to banking organizations through the holding company form. In the end, instead of putting forth a laundry list of permissible activities, it listed several activities that presumptively would be permissible and then delegated to the Board of Governors of the Federal Reserve System the authority to decide what activities would be permissible. The Congress also specified the criteria that the Board would use – that permissible activities would be "... so closely related to banking or managing or controlling banks as to be a proper incident thereto..."8 This delegation to the Board has resulted in new activities being authorized over time and illustrates how delegation to an agency can work.

There has been little need for the US congress to intervene in the authorization of new banking activities. Having said this, some criticism has been levied that the Board has not been pro-active enough in authorizing new activities in a timely fashion. Agency problems also arise within legislative bodies because of the need to conserve members' time, which is the scarce resource. The committee system, with oversight responsibility over related sets of issues, not only economizes on time through specialization but also creates the potential for members of the oversight and funding committees to obtain control rents from regulatory agencies and their constituencies. Members who are particularly interested in a set of economic goals may be able to exercise substantial influence over an agency's choice of priorities. Indeed, these members may be able to induce the agency to establish priorities among the goals in cases where there is almost no chance the full legislature would agree to such priorities.

This ability to influence agencies provides a further incentive for the committee writing legislation to delegate goal conflicts to a regulatory agency especially when that agency will be subject to the committee's jurisdiction in the future. Blinder offers another reason for delegation of more decisions to government agencies, related to the fact that agencies tend to have longer time horizons than legislators.9 US congressmen for example, must stand for election every two years, and thus need to demonstrate to their constituents that they have been productive on their behalf before the next election. By definition, this means that they prefer solutions to problems that generate immediately perceivable results or that avoid imposing short term costs on their constituents. In contrast, those regulators who serve at the pleasure of the President likely will have the option of staying in their positions for at least four years, while other regulatory appointees, such as the Comptroller of the Currency serve six year terms and members of the Board of Governors of the Federal Reserve serve fourteen year terms. These longer term serving regulators can afford to take a longer view when assessing regulatory alternatives and this might result in more socially desirable decision making.

Regulatory agencies play two important roles in setting public policy:

- They provide legislative bodies with information about the set of efficient policies,
- They implement the resolution of conflicting goals delegated to them. One consideration is the relative efficiency of different agency structures in producing information.

If economies of scope exist in gathering information across different types of financial services, especially when institutions are headquartered in one locality but operate across borders, then internalizing goal conflicts may enhance the efficiency of information production. Alternatively, there may be diseconomies of scope such that information is more efficiently produced by agencies that specialize in particular problems or industries. This issue may be especially important in situations where regulation is decentralized, as in the EMU, but there is great need for information sharing across jurisdictions when institutions operate across borders.

POTENTIAL AGENCY PROBLEMS AND GOAL CONFLICTS WITHIN THE EUROPEAN MONETARY UNION

There are many areas where the potential for agency problems and goal conflicts may arise within the structure of the regulation of financial institutions within the EMU.

Faced with these conflicts, authorities are faced with three choices:

- Rely upon legislation to hardwire the choices and tradeoffs.
- Assign the resolution of conflicts to a single agency and rely upon internal resolution of conflicts by the agency itself.
- Assign conflicting goals to different regulatory agencies so that conflict resolution is externalized and ultimately left to the political process.

As a practical matter, the EU did not have the luxury of a clean slate as far as banking supervisory structure is concerned. While the EU did create a central bank, existing financial systems and legal/regulatory structures have been too different to permit the creation of a single banking regulatory agency. Thus, in practice, the choice of goal conflict resolution had to rely upon quasi-legislative solutions. In this case the European Commission, which is the body formally charged with originating and drafting legislative proposals to the Council and the European Parliament, delegated through directives to individual member countries and their respective regulatory and supervisory agencies the responsibility to design their own regimes.

The intent of the European Union was to create a single market for goods and services, including financial services to foster economic growth and to enhance consumer welfare through increased competition. Under the agreements, a so-called "single passport" was agreed to which allowed any financial institution chartered in one member country to operate freely in other member countries. However, having established this principle, the question then was how to shape the regulatory structure?12 Historical practice had been to rely upon the host country to regulate how firms doing business within its borders would conduct their business.

The problem with this in the EU was the concern that the host country would potentially structure regulation in ways that would disadvantage the foreign firms in competing with domestic institutions.13 But this would be inconsistent with the single market objective, and this was made more imperative with the introduction of the EURO.

The alternative selected was to rely upon the home country to provide regulation, supervision and deposit insurance for the depository institutions that they chartered.14 Furthermore, over the longer run, regulatory competition would likely come into play facilitating the evolution of a single market. Individual country self interest in promoting and their institutions would also be an inducement to compete via deregulation of financial services.

Countries offering more attractive charter options or accommodative regulatory regimes would expect to see their institutions gain market share in the EU. The logical consequence of allowing home country regulation would, as the result of regulatory competition, be a less regulated and homogeneous market place. One consequence of leaving regulation and supervision to the home country is that the member countries in the EU have adopted different structures for financial institution supervision and regulation. Some have split supervision and regulation according to function while others have consolidated supervision and regulation into a single agency.

In some instances the central bank is involved and in other countries it is not. Hence, if faced with the same supervisory or regulatory issue, agencies with different mix of functions will potentially choose different sets of policy tradeoffs depending upon their mix of responsibilities and their individual statutory mandates.15 Some will face external resolution while others will be faced with internal resolution of conflicts. Policies will also differ across countries to the extent that internal goal conflict resolution is required as compared with external goal resolution.

These differing tradeoffs will result in different policies and will set up many opportunities for individual institutions to pit the countries' agencies against each other and will foster regulatory arbitrage on the part of financial institutions to seek a competitive advantage.16 Relying upon regulatory competition to level the playing field carries with it the risk of a race to the bottom and more lax supervision as far as safety and soundness is concerned. The EU has attempted to address this problem by setting minimum supervisory standards to be universally applicable through directives and agreements. In effect, the attempt is at least to set a lower bound as far as safety and soundness risks are concerned.

One of the more important of these directives sets policy towards capital adequacy through the Capital Adequacy Directive, which led to the Basel I capital standards for EU supervisors to follow. Basel I has now been refined by the Basel Bank Supervisors Committee now known as Basel II. Unfortunately, concentration of supervisory efforts on capital standards substitutes supervisory judgment for marketbased risk weights to determine if an institution has sufficient capital. Wall and Eisenbeis argue that this focus is misplaced and misdirects supervisory attention from prompt corrective action and least cost resolution of troubled institution.

While the EU has attempted to set minimum regulatory standards and promote cooperation and information sharing among the individual country supervisors, there is no EU-wide supervisor responsible for resolving the failures of institutions, and hence any goal conflicts that may arise should a major institution experience financial difficulty must rely upon external resolution of those conflicts. With no national supervisor to make the goal tradeoffs, it will likely be left to the European Commission or some similar body to resolve conflicts as they arise.

The kinds of conflicts and implications for financial stability are significant and may become more so as the EU evolves. The financial system will become more integrated and more countries with different economic and financial systems at different stages of development are joining the EU. The remainder of this paper will focus on three critical areas where the goal conflicts are likely to be most important: the design of deposit insurance system, the apportionment of supervisory responsibilities between home and host country regulators, and the structure of bankruptcy resolution in the event that institutions get into financial difficulties.

The Structure of Deposit Insurance within the EMU

The desired structure for deposit insurance in the EU was sketched out in the EU's Deposit Guarantee Directive that went into effect in 1995. The DGD endorses a decentralized approach to deposit insurance, despite the fact that depository institutions are authorized to operate within any of the member countries, and delegates to the member countries the responsibility to provide coverage to the depositors in the banks headquartered within the country. Additionally, it is the responsibility of the home country's central bank to serve as the lender of last resort in cases that don't involve EUwide systemic risk issues. The broad-based systemic lender of last resort function is left to the European Central Bank.

In effect, the system bifurcates the responsibilities for controlling banking risk between the micro-risk associated with the operation of single institutions from the macro-risk associated with contagion risk or risk that spreads from one institution to another regardless of where the institutions are headquartered.

The DGD specifies the general features that an acceptable deposit insurance system should have. The most specific features being that the system should provide deposit insurance coverage of 20 thousand Euros, should exclude coverage of inter-bank deposits, and may exclude other liabilities at the discretion of the national government. Co-insurance of liabilities is permitted but not required. Coverage of depositors in branches in countries other than the home country is the responsibility of the home country.

Interestingly, there is a provision that permits the branches of a multinational bank to opt to provide top coverage up to those branch depositors through the host country's deposit insurance scheme, when that coverage would be "better" than that provided by the home country's plan. Finally, it is also instructive in terms of what deposit insurance features are not prescribed. These include funding of the plans, pricing of coverage, who should operate the plan how troubled institutions should be handled, what too-big-to-fail policies might or might not be pursued, or how conflicts would be resolved where two deposit insurance funds might be affected by failure of an institution with top up coverage.

In establishing the minimal requirements for deposit insurance schemes, the attempt was obviously to balance the fact that some EU members already had deposit insurance plans in place and generally, most of the key provisions and features of there programmes were different. There was no one obviously optimal structure for deposit insurance plans, and presumably the best that could be hoped for was that the schemes would be harmonized over time. The potential for cross-boarder conflicts appeared minimal since there were few truly multinational institutions in the EU.

As might be expected, those plans that were put in place in order to comply with the DGD varied substantially from those already in place. Finally, responsibility for supervision and risk monitoring is apportioned differently across the system and within the different countries.

Going forward, however, the patchwork set of deposit insurance schemes, when coupled with the bifurcated approach to controlling systemic risk, seems fraught with the potential for agency and conflicts of interest problems.

These arise from several sources including:

- Uncertainties about the funding of the deposit insurance plans,
- Differences in deposit insurance coverage and pricing of coverage,
- Reliance upon the home country, as opposed to host country responsibility, should institutions get into financial difficulties,
- Differences in treatment with respect to the lender-of-last-resort function,
- Differences in approaches to bankruptcy and priority of claims in troubled institutions and
- Differences in EMU vs non-EMU participants.

Based upon the long history within the United States with multiple decentralized deposit insurance schemes and a fragmented bank regulatory and supervisory structure, there is a very great risk that the system being put in place in the EU will be fraught with conflicts and regulatory competition and that will not be robust to financial crises. Much of the difficulty flows from a fundamental misunderstanding of the role of deposit insurance, the nature of the guarantees being given, and the relationship between deposit insurance systems and the central bank's lender of last resort function in controlling systemic risk.

TIME VALUE OF MONEY

The time value of money is the value of money figuring in a given amount of interest earned over a given amount of time.

For example, 100 dollars of today's money invested for one year and earning 5 per cent interest will be worth 105 dollars after one year. Therefore, 100 dollars paid now or 105 dollars paid exactly one year from now both have the same value to the recipient who assumes 5 per cent interest; using time value of money terminology, 100 dollars invested for one year at 5 per cent interest has a future value of 105 dollars. This notion dates at least to Martín de Azpilcueta of the School of Salamanca. The method also allows the valuation of a likely stream of income in the future, in such a way that the annual incomes are discounted and then added together, thus providing a lump-sum"present value" of the entire income stream.

All of the standard calculations for time value of money derive from the most basic algebraic expression for the present value of a future sum,"discounted" to the present by an amount equal to the time value of money. For example, a sum of FV to be received in one year is discounted to give a sum of PV at present:

$$PV = FV - r \cdot PV = FV/(1+r).$$

Some standard calculations based on the time value of money are:

- *Present value*: The current worth of a future sum of money or stream of cash flows given a specified rate of return. Future cash flows are discounted at the discount rate, and the higher the discount rate, the lower the present value of the future cash flows. Determining the appropriate discount rate is the key to properly valuing future cash flows, whether they be earnings or obligations.
- *Present value of an annuity*: An annuity is a series of equal payments or receipts that occur at evenly spaced intervals. Leases and rental payments are examples. The payments or receipts occur at the end of each period for an ordinary annuity while they occur at the beginning of each period for an annuity due.
- Present value of a perpetuity is an infinite and constant stream of identical cash flows.
- Future value is the value of an asset or cash at a specified date in the future that is equivalent in value to a specified sum today.
- Future value of an annuity is the future value of a stream of payments, assuming the payments are invested at a given rate of interest.

CALCULATIONS

The solutions may be found using the formulas, a financial calculator or a spreadsheet. The formulas are programmed into most financial calculators and several spreadsheet functions.

For any of the equations below, the formula may also be rearranged to determine one of the other unknowns. In the case of the standard annuity formula, however, there is no closed-form algebraic solution for the interest rate.

These equations are frequently combined for particular uses. For example, bonds can be readily priced using these equations. A typical coupon bond is composed of two types of payments: a stream of coupon payments similar to an annuity, and a lump-sum return of capital at the end of the bond's maturity - that is, a future payment. The two formulas can be combined to determine the present value of the bond.

An important note is that the interest rate i is the interest rate for the relevant period. For an annuity that makes one payment per year, i will be the annual interest rate. For an income or payment stream with a different payment schedule, the interest rate must be converted into the relevant periodic interest rate. For example, a monthly rate for a mortgage with monthly payments requires that the interest rate be divided by 12 The rate of return in the calculations can be either the variable solved for, or a predefined variable that measures a discount rate, interest, inflation, rate of return, cost of equity, cost of debt or any number of other analogous concepts. The choice of the appropriate rate is critical to the exercise, and the use of an incorrect discount rate will make the results meaningless. For calculations involving annuities, you must decide whether the payments are made at the end of each period or at the beginning of each period. If you are using a financial calculator or a spreadsheet, you can usually set it for either calculation. The following formulas are for an ordinary annuity. If you want the answer for the Present Value of an annuity due simply multiply the PV of an ordinary annuity by (1 + i).

FORMULA

Present Value of a Future Sum

The present value formula is the core formula for the time value of money; each of the other formulae is derived from this formula. For example, the annuity formula is the sum of a series of present value calculations.

The present value (PV) formula has four variables, each of which can be solved for:

$$PV = \frac{FV}{(1+i)^n}$$

- PV is the value at time=0
- FV is the value at time=n
- i is the rate at which the amount will be compounded each period
- n is the number of periods

The cumulative present value of future cash flows can be calculated by summing the contributions of FV_t, the value of cash flow at time=t

$$PV = \sum_{t=0}^{n} \frac{FV_t}{(1+i)^t}$$

Note that this series can be summed for a given value of n, or when n is ∞. This is a very general formula, which leads to several important special cases given below.

Present Value of an Annuity for n Payment Periods

In this case the cash flow values remain the same throughout the n periods. The present value of an annuity formula has four variables, each of which can be solved for:

$$PV(A) = \frac{A}{i} \cdot \left[1 - \frac{1}{(1+i)^n}\right]$$

- PV(A) is the value of the annuity at time=0
- A is the value of the individual payments in each compounding period
- i equals the interest rate that would be compounded for each period of time
- n is the number of payment periods.

To get the PV of an annuity due, multiply the equation by (1 + *i*).

Present Value of a Growing Annuity

In this case each cash flow grows by a factor of (1+g). Similar to the formula for an annuity, the present value of a growing annuity (PVGA) uses the same variables with the addition of *g* as the rate of growth of the annuity (A is the annuity payment in the first period). This is a calculation that is rarely provided for on financial calculators.

Where i '≠ g:

$$PV = \frac{A}{(i-g)}\left[1 - \left(\frac{1+g}{1+i}\right)^n\right]$$

To get the PV of a growing annuity due, multiply the equation by (1 + *i*).
Where i = g:

$$PV = \frac{A \times n}{1+i}$$

Present Value of a Perpetuity

When n → ∞, the PV of a perpetuity (a perpetual annuity) formula becomes simple division.

$$PV(P) = \frac{A}{i}$$

Present Value of a Growing Perpetuity

When the perpetual annuity payment grows at a fixed rate (g) the value is theoretically determined according to the following formula. In practice, there are few securities with precise characteristics, and the application of this valuation approach is subject to various qualifications and modifications.

Most importantly, it is rare to find a growing perpetual annuity with fixed rates of growth and true perpetual cash flow generation. Despite these qualifications, the general approach may be used in valuations of real estate, equities, and other assets.

$$PVGP = \frac{A}{(i-g)}$$

This is the well known Gordon Growth model used for stock valuation.

Future Value of a Present Sum

The future value (FV) formula is similar and uses the same variables.

$$FV = PV \cdot (1+i)^n$$

Future Value of an Annuity

The future value of an annuity (FVA) formula has four variables, each of which can be solved for:

$$FV(A) = A \cdot \frac{(1+i)^n - 1}{i}$$

- *FV(A)* is the value of the annuity at time = *n*
- *A* is the value of the individual payments in each compounding period
- *i* is the interest rate that would be compounded for each period of time
- *n* is the number of payment periods

Future Value of a Growing Annuity

The future value of a growing annuity (FVA) formula has five variables, each of which can be solved for:

Where i '≠ g:

$$FV(A) = A \cdot \frac{(1+i)^n - (1+g)^n}{i-g}$$

Where i = g:

$$FV(A) = A \cdot n(1+i)^{n-1}$$

- *FV(A)* is the value of the annuity at time = *n*
- *A* is the value of initial payment paid at time 1
- *i* is the interest rate that would be compounded for each period of time
- *g* is the growing rate that would be compounded for each period of time
- *n* is the number of payment periods.

DERIVATIONS

Annuity Derivation

The formula for the present value of a regular stream of future payments is derived from a sum of the formula for future value of a single future payment, as below, where C is the payment amount and n the period. A single payment C at future time m has the following future value at future time n:

$$FV = C(1+i)^{n-m}$$

Summing over all payments from time 1 to time n, then reversing the order of terms and substituting $k = n - m$:

$$FV = \sum_{m=1}^{n} C(1+i)^{n-m} = \sum_{k=0}^{n-1} C(1+i)^{k}$$

Note that this is a geometric series, with the initial value being $a = C$, the multiplicative factor being $1 + i$, with n terms. Applying the formula for geometric series, we get,

$$FVA = \frac{C\left(1-(1+i)^{n}\right)}{1-(1+i)} = \frac{C\left((1+i)^{n}-1\right)}{i}$$

The present value of the annuity (PVA) is obtained by simply dividing by $(1 + i)^n$:

$$PVA = \frac{FVA}{(1+i)^{n}} = \frac{C}{i}\left(1-\frac{1}{(1+i)^{n}}\right)$$

Another simple and intuitive way to derive the future value of an annuity is to consider an endowment, whose interest is paid as the annuity, and whose principal remains constant.

The principal of this hypothetical endowment can be computed as that whose interest equals the annuity payment amount:

$$\text{Principal} \times i = C$$

$$\text{Principal} = C/i + \text{goal}$$

Note that no money enters or leaves the combined system of endowment principal + accumulated annuity payments, and thus the future value of this system can be computed simply via the future value formula:

$$FV = PV(1 + i)^n$$

Initially, before any payments, the present value of the system is just the endowment principal ($PV = C/i$). At the end, the future value is the endowment principal plus the future value of the total annuity payments ($FV = C/i + FVA$). Plugging this back into the equation:

$$\frac{C}{i} + FVA = \frac{C}{i}(1+i)^{n}$$

$$FVA = \frac{C}{i}\left[(1+i)^{n}-1\right]$$

Perpetuity Derivation

Without showing the formal derivation here, the perpetuity formula is derived from the annuity formula.

Specifically, the term:

$$\left(1-\frac{1}{(1+i)^n}\right)$$

can be seen to approach the value of 1 as n grows larger. At infinity, it is equal to 1, leaving,

$$\left(\frac{C}{i}\right)$$

as the only term remaining.

DIFFERENTIAL EQUATIONS

Ordinary and partial differential equations —equations involving derivatives and one variables are ubiquitous in more advanced treatments of financial mathematics. While time value of money can be understood without using the framework of differential equations, the added sophistication sheds additional light on time value, and provides a simple introduction before considering more complicated and less familiar situations. This exposition follows. The fundamental change that the differential equation perspective brings is that, rather than computing a number one computes a function. This function may then be analysed – how does its value change over time – or compared with other functions.

Formally, the statement that "value decreases over time" is given by defining the linear differential operator $\mathcal{L}$ as:

$$\mathcal{L} = -\partial_t + r(t).$$

This states that values decreases (–) over time (∂_t) at the discount rate ($r(t)$). Applied to a function it yields:

$$\mathcal{L} = -\partial_t + r(t).$$

For an instrument whose payment stream is described by $f(t)$, the value $V(t)$ satisfies the inhomogeneous first-order ODE $\mathcal{L}V = f$ this encodes the fact that when any cash flow occurs, the value of the instrument changes by the value of the cash flow.

The standard technique tool in the analysis of ODEs is the use of Green's functions, from which other solutions can be built. In terms of time value of money, the Green's function is the value of a bond paying $1 at a single point in time u – the value of any other stream of cash flows can then be obtained by taking combinations of this basic cash flow. In mathematical terms, this instantaneous cash flow is modeled as a delta function $\delta_u(t) := \delta(t - u)$. The Green's function for the value at time t of a $1 cash flow at time u is,

$$b(t;u) := H(u-t)\cdot\exp\left(-\int_t^u r(v)\,dv\right)$$

where H is the Heaviside step function – the notation "$;u$" is to emphasize that u is a *parametre* (fixed in any instance – the time when the cash flow will occur), while t is a *variable* (time). In other words, future cash flows are exponentially discounted (exp) by the sum (integral, $\int_t^u$) of the future discount rates $\int$ (for future, *r*(*v*) for discount rates), while past cash flows are worth 0 (*H*(*u* " *t*) = 1 if *t* < *u*,0 if *t* > *u*), because they have already occurred. Note that the value *at* the moment of a cash flow is not well-defined – there is a discontinuity at that point, and one can use a convention (assume cash flows have already occurred, or not already occurred), or simply not define the value at that point.

In case the discount rate is constant, $r(v) \equiv r$ this simplifies to,

$$b(t;u) = H(u-t) \cdot e^{-(u-t)r} = \begin{cases} e^{-(u-t)r} & t<u \\ 0 & t>u, \end{cases}$$

where (*u* " *t*) is "time remaining until cash flow".

Thus for a stream of cash flows *f*(*u*) ending by time *T* (which can be set to $T = +\infty$ for no time horizon) the value at time *t*, *V*(*t*;*T*) is given by combining the values of these individual cash flows:

$$V(t;T) = \int_t^T f(u) b(tl;u) du.$$

This formalizes time value of money to future values of cash flows with varying discount rates, and is the basis of many formulas in financial mathematics, such as the Black–Scholes formula with varying interest rates.

BOND VALUATION

Bond valuation is the process of determining the fair price of a bond. As with any security or capital investment, the theoretical fair value of a bond is the present value of the stream of cash flows it is expected to generate.

Hence, the value of a bond is determined by discounting the bond's expected cash flows to the present using the appropriate discount rate. Determining this rate in practice - i.e. "pricing" the bond - is done with reference to other instruments. Once the price or value has been calculated, the sensitivity of the price can then be estimated; the various yields, which relate the price of the bond to its coupons, can also be determined. When the bond includes embedded options, the valuation is more specialized and combines option pricing with the cash flow based approach.

Depending on the option as embedded, the option price as calculated is either added to or subtracted from the price of the "straight" portion. This total is then the value of the bond; the various yields can then be calculated for the total price.

CONCEPT

The fair price of a straight bond is determined by discounting its expected cash flows at the appropriate discount rate. The formula applied is as follows:

Present Value Relationship

- *Cash flows*:
  - The periodic coupon payments C, each of which is made n times every year
  - The par or face value F, which is payable at maturity of the bond after T years. In some of the bonds, their Maturity Redemption Price might be more than par value, in this case the F is actually the Redemption Price.
- *Discount rate*: the required yield or rate of return r
  - r is the market interest rate for bonds with similar terms and risk ratings
  - m is the number of coupons to be paid over the remaining lifetime of the bond, i.e. n times T.
  - u is (1 + r) i.e. an interest accumulation factor over one coupon period

Bond Price,

$$= P_c = \sum_{t=1}^{m} \frac{C}{u^t} + \frac{F}{(1+r)^T}.$$

Since the price is the present value of the cash flows, there is an inverse relationship between price and discount rate: the higher the discount rate the lower the value of the bond.

Clean and Dirty Price

When the bond is not valued precisely on a coupon date, the present value relationship, will incorporate accrued interest: i.e. any interest due to the owner of the bond since the previous coupon date. The price of a bond which includes this accrued interest is known as the "dirty price"; the "clean price" is the price excluding any interest that has accrued. The value returned by the formula is thus the dirty price.

Clean prices are generally more stable over time than dirty prices. This is because clean prices change for economic reasons whereas dirty prices change day to day depending on where the current date is in relation to the coupon dates, in addition to any economic reasons.

It is market practice to quote bonds on a clean-price basis. When a bond settles the accrued interest is added to the value based on the clean price to reflect the full market value.

BOND PRICING

The present value relationship reflects the theoretical approach to determining the value of a bond. In practice though, the bond's price is determined with reference to other, more liquid instruments. The two main approaches are as follows:

Relative Price Approach

Under this approach, the bond will be priced relative to a benchmark, usually a government security. Here, the yield to maturity on the bond is determined based on the bond's Credit rating relative to a government security with similar maturity or duration. The better the quality of the bond, the smaller the spread between its required return and the YTM of the benchmark. This required return is then used to discount the bond cash flows as to obtain the price.

Arbitrage-free Pricing Approach

Under this approach, the bond price will reflect its arbitrage-free price. Here, each cash flow is separately discounted at the same rate as a zero-coupon bond corresponding to the coupon date, and of equivalent credit worthiness. Here, in general, we apply the rational pricing logic relating to "Assets with identical cash flows".

In detail:

- The bond's coupon dates and coupon amounts are known with certainty.
- Therefore some multiple (or fraction) of zero-coupon bonds, each corresponding to the bond's coupon dates, can be specified so as to produce identical cash flows to the bond. (3) Thus the bond price today must be equal to the sum of each of its cash flows discounted at the discount rate implied by the value of the corresponding ZCB.
- Were this not the case, the abitrageur could finance his purchase of whichever of the bond or the sum of the various government securities was cheaper, by short selling the other, and meeting his cash flow commitments using the coupons or maturing zeroes as appropriate.
- Then his "risk free", arbitrage profit would be the difference between the two values.

YIELD AND PRICE RELATIONSHIPS

Once the price or value has been calculated, various yields - which relate the price of the bond to its coupons - can then be determined.

Yield to Maturity

The yield to maturity is the discount rate which returns the market price of the bond; it is identical to r in the equation. YTM is thus the internal rate of return of an investment in the bond made at the observed price. Since YTM can be used to price a bond, bond prices are often quoted in terms of YTM.

To achieve a return equal to YTM, i.e. where it is the required return on the bond, the bond owner must:

- Buy the bond at price P_0,

- Hold the bond until maturity, and
- Redeem the bond at par.

Coupon Yield

The coupon yield is simply the coupon payment (C) as a percentage of the face value (F).

Coupon yield = C/F

Coupon yield is also called nominal yield.

Current Yield

The current yield is simply the coupon payment (C) as a percentage of the (*current*) bond price (P).

Current yield = C/P_0.

Relationship

The concept of current yield is closely related to other bond concepts, including yield to maturity, and coupon yield.

The relationship between yield to maturity and the coupon rate is as follows:

- When a bond sells at a discount, YTM > current yield > coupon yield.
- When a bond sells at a premium, coupon yield > current yield > YTM.
- When a bond sells at par, YTM = current yield = coupon yield amt

PRICE SENSITIVITY

The sensitivity of a bond's market price to interest rate movements is measured by its duration, and, additionally, by its convexity.

Duration is a linear measure of how the price of a bond changes in response to interest rate changes. It is approximately equal to the percentage change in price for a given change in yield, and may be thought of as the elasticity of the bond's price with respect to interest rates. For example, for small interest rate changes, the duration is the approximate percentage by which the value of the bond will fall for a 1% per annum increase in market interest rate. So a 15-year bond with a duration of 7 would fall approximately 7% in value if the interest rate increased by 1% per annum. Convexity is a measure of the "curvature" of price changes, and is thus a complement to duration. The necessity for this additional measure arises since duration is a linear measure, whereas, in reality, as interest rates change, the price is a convex function of interest rates. Continuing the example, for a more accurate estimate of sensitivity, the convexity score would be added to the value of 7 for duration.

EXTENSIONS: MORE SOPHISTICATED BOND PRICING MODELS

- Bond pricing under CIR model

- Bond pricing under Hull-White model
- Bond pricing under HJM framework
- Bond pricing under Chen model

STOCK VALUATION

Valuing stocks involves four basic issues:

- The characteristics of the stock as a financial security
- The financial and business prospects of the issuer of the stock
- The relative valuation of the particular stock versus other stocks,
- The valuation of financial securities in general and the stock market in particular.

"Stock pickers" focus on the characteristics of the particular stock as a financial security and the financial and business prospects of the particular issuer. They believe that they should value the stock and analyse the prospects for the issuer independent of market and economic changes. With their focus on individual securities, they believe that they are"buying companies" that will prosper over a longer period of time and reward investors because of their success. Value investors try to buy"good companies at cheap prices" when these companies are out of favour with other less disciplined and more faddish investors. Growth investors strive to find companies with business strategies and products that will allow them to achieve high levels of growth. Both value and growth investors try to ignore the future path of the market or economy.

They are confident that the prospects for the individual securities they are buying will overwhelm over factors and do not try to"time the market". If they cannot find individual stocks that are attractive, they might leave some monies in cash. This really reflects their ability to find attractive investment ideas rather than a call on the market. "Sector rotators" focus on the relative valuation of a stock compared to other stocks and the overall prospects for the stock market in general. They assess the relative valuation of individual stocks and move between stocks and industry groups when they are cheap by comparison using historical standards.

They also assess the the overall valuation of the market using aggregate data on earnings, price and other historical accounting measures and compare these to historical norms. Another valuation yardstick is a comparison to other financial assets, such as bonds and money market securities. Much emphasis is given to the relative levels of bond and money market yields and the market dividend yield. The stage of the economic cycle is important, as stock industry groups have differential performance over the course of a market and economic cycle. If their valuation measures suggest that the market is expensive, they sell stocks and raise cash to defend their portfolios from a potential market setback. The average investment manager combines stock picking and sector rotation, maintaining her portfolio reasonably similar to her index benchmark and other managers. This type of manager will make industry and security"bets" in their portfolio weightings, moving into defensive stocks and cash in overvalued markets and weighting stocks and industries that are relatively attractive.

FUNDAMENTAL VALUATION TECHNIQUES

Fundamental valuation of equity securities relies on financial analysis of historical financial data and an assessment of the business prospects of an issuer. The historical data demonstrates the "track record" of the company and its management. The assessment of the business prospects of an issuer involves a study of the conditions and environment under which a company operates. The financial analysis of the company examines trends in its profitably, efficiency in employing capital, financial capability and other factors that the analyst consideres important. These are assessed by calculating the applicable financial ratios and patterns of sales and profit growth. Important ratios would include: gross and net margin, sales and inventory turnover, financial and operating leverage, interest coverage, current and quick ratios. Valuation yardsticks would include price/earnings, book value per share, earnings yield, dividend yield and return on equity.

A basic assessment of a company's business prospects includes a review of all public information available on a company and third party research reports. A more "in depth" review would include interviews of senior management of the company, both telephone and in person, and even discussions of the company's prospects with suppliers, regulators and even competitors' personnel.

MARKET VALUE ADDED

Market Value Added is the difference between the current market value of a firm and the capital contributed by investors. If MVA is positive, the firm has added value. If it is negative, the firm has destroyed value. The amount of value added needs to be greater than the firm's investors could have achieved investing in the market portfolio, adjusted for the leverage of the firm relative to the market.

The formula for MVA is:

$$MVA = V - K$$

where:

- *MVA* is market value added
- *V* is the market value of the firm, including the value of the firm's equity and debt
- *K* is the capital invested in the firm

MVA is the present value of a series of EVA values. MVA is economically equivalent to the traditional NPV measure of worth for evaluating an after-tax cash flow profile of a project if the cost of capital is used for discounting.

2

Reading Financial Statements

INTRODUCTION

Reading financial statements may not be like leisurely reading a good novel, but when it comes to your own company, your investments, or potential investments, you have money at stake in being able to read and understand these statements. They just may contain more information than you thought. You can find out a lot about a company by reading between the lines and doing some analysis.

The balance sheet and income statement are fundamental to any business. They could be thought of as a"report card" on the performance of the business for the period. But what do they really tell you, other than the bottom line result? Once the financial statements have been prepared for your own business, how can you use them and learn from them to help you manage your business? Or, if you are considering making an investment in a company's stock, how can you use its financial statements to help you decide whether it might be a good investment? One of the tools you can use is ratio analysis.

RATIO ANALYSIS AS AN EVALUATION TOOL

Obviously there are many different aspects and factors involved in evaluating a business, including management capability, innovations in products and technology, shifts in market demands, and general economic conditions, among others. But one of the advantages of using financial statements is that they provide you with objective, concrete data with which to perform analysis. Ratio analysis by itself is just one tool you can use in evaluating your own business, or a potential investment opportunity. For example, comparisons of balance sheets and income statements from one period to another can be very effective in detecting changes, trends and shifts. Calculating ratios based on the current period balance sheet and income statement can be very useful, and when combined with a comparative analysis from period to period, it becomes a very dynamic way of gauging performance. How you use the insights you gain from your analytical work will of course depend on your purpose in reading the financial statements. If you are looking at a company in which you already have an investment, or in which you are thinking about investing, you may use the results of your analysis to either buy or sell, or to increase or decrease your holdings of that stock. If you are looking at your own company, you can use your analysis to see where your business is strong, and where it could use some adjustments or improvements. This will help you make financial decisions about your business operations.

TYPES OF RATIOS

Some of the different types of ratios that can be calculated from data in the financial statements and used to evaluate a business include:

- Liquidity ratios
- Solvency ratios
- Activity ratios
- Profitability ratios

LIQUIDITY RATIOS

Iquidity ratios measure a business's ability to cover its obligations, without having to borrow or invest more money in the business. The idea is that there should be sufficient cash and assets that can be readily converted into cash to cover liabilities as they come due.

One of the most common liquidity ratios is:

Current Ratio = Current Assets/Current Liabilities

Current assets basically include cash, short-term investments and marketable securities, accounts receivable, inventory, and prepaid expenses. Current liabilities include accounts payable to vendors and employees, and installments on notes or loans that are due within one year. This ratio could also be seen as a measure of working capital – the difference between current assets and current liabilities. A company with a lot of working capital will be in a better position to expand and improve its operations. On the contrary, a company with negative working capital does not have sufficient resources to meet its current obligations, and therefore is not in a position to take advantage of opportunities for growth.

Another stringent test of liquidity is the:

Acid-test Ratio = Current Assets minus Inventories /Current Liabilities

Inventory is a current asset that may or may not be quickly converted into cash. This depends on the rate at which inventory is being turned over. By excluding inventory, the acid-test ratio only considers that part of current assets that can be readily converted into cash. This ratio, also called the Quick Ratio, tells how much of the business's short-term debt can be met by using the company's liquid assets at short notice. A ratio that shows how many times inventory is turned over, or sold during the period is:

Inventory Turnover Ratio = Cost of Goods Sold /Average Inventory

A high turnover ratio is a sign that products are being produced and sold quickly during the period. A ratio of 1.0, for example, would mean that at any given time you have enough inventory on hand to cover sales for the entire period. The higher this ratio, the more quickly inventory is being turned over and producing assets that are more liquid — accounts receivable and then cash.

If you want an even clearer idea of exactly how much ready cash is on hand to cover current liabilities, you can use the:

Cash ratio = Cash + Marketable securities /Current Liabilities

The cash ratio measures the extent to which a business could quickly cover short-term liabilities, and therefore is of particular interest to short-term creditors. A ratio of 1.0 would indicate that all current liabilities would be covered at any average point in time by cash and marketable securities that could be readily sold and converted to cash. A ratio of less than 1.0 would mean that other assets, such as accounts receivable or inventory, would have to be converted to cash to cover short-term obligations. A ratio of greater than 1.0 means that there is more than enough cash on hand.

SOLVENCY RATIOS

Solvency ratios are measures to assess a company's ability to meet its long-term obligations and thereby remain solvent and avoid bankruptcy.

Two general, overall solvency ratios include:

Solvency Ratio = Total Assets/Total Liabilities and

Solvency Ratio = Net Worth (Total Capital or Equity) /Total Liabilities

These ratios basically tell whether a company owns more than it owes. The higher the ratio, the more solvent the company. Another ratio that can tell how much a company relies on debt to finance its assets is:

Debt Ratio = Total Debt/Total Assets

Traditionally, both short-term and long-term debts and assets are used in determining this ratio. In general, the lower a company's reliance on debt to finance its assets, the less risky the company.

The debt to equity ratio is a measure of a company's leverage – how much financing it has in the form of debt as compared with how much it has invested in the business.

Debt-equity Ratio = Total Liabilities/Total Owners' Equity, or

Debt-equity Ratio = Long-Term Liabilities /Total Owners' Equity

In assessing solvency, it is also important to take into consideration the breakdown of a company's liabilities. Not all liabilities are debt in the form of bank loans or notes payable, for example. There are also accounts payable to vendors, salaries and wages payable, taxes payable, and accrued liabilities, among others. One of the measures of what debt constitutes in terms of total liabilities is:

Indebtedness Ratio = Total Debts/Total Liabilities

In general, a company that is heavy on debt may be better leveraged, but is also less solvent. The debt repayment terms are another consideration. Short-term debt, payable within one year, may pose a greater burden on cash flow and eventual solvency than long-term debt, which is due beyond one year. A ratio used to quantify this is:

Short-term Debt Ratio or Quality of Debt = Short-term Debt/Total Debt

A lower value for this ratio would indicate less concern for installments coming due within a year. There are other ratios intended to assess a company's capacity to cover its debt repayments and financing costs. One of these ratios measures how interest expense is being covered by the net income the company is generating:

Interest expense coverage = Net income before interest and taxes/Interest expense

This ratio is also called Number of Times Interest Earned, and represents how many times the net income generated by the company, without considering interest and taxes, covers the total interest charge. The higher the ratio the more solvent the company. Another similar ratio often used to measure a company's capacity to cover its fixed charges is: Ratio of Earnings to Fixed Charges = Earnings before income tax and fixed charges/Interest expense (including capitalized interest) and amortization of bond discount and issue costs Capitalized interest is the amount of interest on a loan to finance a project or acquisition of fixed assets, that has been capitalized and included as part of the cost of the project or asset on the balance sheet. You will probably need to see the notes to the financial statements to find this figure.

ACTIVITY RATIOS

Many useful gauges of operations can be calculated from data reported in the financial statements. For example, you can determine the average number of days it takes to collect on customer accounts, the average number of days to pay vendors, and how much of the operation is effectively being financed with payment terms extended by vendors.

Accounts Receivable Turnover = Total Credit Sales/Average Accounts Receivable

This tells you the average duration of accounts receivable for credit sales to customers. This in turn can be expressed in terms of the collection period, as follows: Average Collection Period = Days in Year/Accounts Receivable Turnover or

Days to Collect = Trade Accounts Receivable /Credit Sales × 365

A similar calculation can be made on the liabilities side, with accounts payable to vendors:

Days to Pay = Trade Accounts Payable/Purchases × 365

To determine how much of a company's accounts receivable and inventory are effectively being financed by the credit extended to the company by its vendors: Financing of Trade Accounts Receivable in terms of Trade Accounts Payable = Trade Accounts Payable/Trade Accounts Receivable:

Financing of Inventory in terms of Trade Accounts Payable = Trade Accounts Payable/Inventory. Effectively managing the credit extended by vendors can help a company's cash flow and therefore its liquidity and solvency. From data reported on the income statement, various relationships can be calculated between different expenses and revenues, or a certain type of expense as a percentage of total expenses.

Labour Cost Percentage = Payroll and Related Expenses/Total Revenue or Total Expenses

Interest Expense Percentage = Interest Expense/Total Revenue or Total Expenses

These types of ratios or percentages can be calculated for any item on the income statement. Which accounts are more important will depend on the nature of the business. For example, some operations are more labour intensive and some are more capital intensive. In a labour intensive operation, the percentage that employee-related expenses, including wages, salaries and benefits, represent in terms of total operating expense is relevant. In a capital intensive operation, repairs and maintenance may take on more importance.

PROFITABILITY RATIOS

One of the most common profitability ratios is the profit margin. This can be expressed as the gross profit margin or net profit margin, and it can be expressed by company, by sector, by product, or by individual unit. The information reported on the income statement will enable you to determine the overall profit margin. If additional breakdowns are provided, more detailed margins can be calculated.

Gross Profit Margin = Gross Income/Total Revenue

Net Profit Margin = Net Income/Total Revenue

Other commonly used ratios are returns, expressed as return on investment or equity, return on assets, and return on capital employed. These ratios measure a company's ability to use its capital, or its assets, to generate additional value.

- Return on Investment (ROI) or Return on Owners' Equity = Net Income/Average Owners' Equity

- Return on Assets (ROA) = Net Income/Average Total Assets
- Return on Capital Employed (ROCE) = Net Income Before Interest and Tax/Capital Employed (Total Assets minus Current Liabilities)
- When evaluating investment opportunities, profits are often measured per share:
- Earnings per Share = Net Profit After Tax and Dividends/Ordinary Shareholders' Equity

Another commonly used ratio to show the yield on an investment is:

Dividend Yield Ratio = Dividends per Share
/Market Value per Share

And, to measure how the price of an investment correlates with the earnings on that investment, you can use the:

Price to Earnings Ratio = Market Value per Share
/After-Tax Earnings per Share

NOW WE CAN SAY

The bottom line on the income statement is not the only important figure on the financial statements, and may not even be the most important. There is another whole dimension of valuable information that can be obtained from the data reported in the financial statements. Ratio analysis is one of many tools that can be used to evaluate a company's performance, its current status, and its evolution over time. And if you are the owner of the business, this type of analysis can help you make the right decisions to improve your operations and make your business stronger and more successful.

3

Analysis and Interpretation of Financial Statements

ANALYSIS OF FINANCIAL STATEMENT

Financial statement analysis is defined as the process of identifying financial strengths and weaknesses of the firm by properly establishing relationship between the items of the balance sheet and the profit and loss account. There are various methods or techniques that are used in analyzing financial statements, such as comparative statements, schedule of changes in working capital, common size percentages, funds analysis, trend analysis, and ratios analysis.

Financial statements are prepared to meet external reporting obligations and also for decision making purposes. They play a dominant role in setting the framework of managerial decisions. But the information provided in the financial statements is not an end in itself as no meaningful conclusions can be drawn from these statements alone. However, the information provided in the financial statements is of immense use in making decisions through analysis and interpretation of financial statements.

TOOLS AND TECHNIQUES OF FINANCIAL STATEMENT ANALYSIS

Following are the most important tools and techniques of financial statement analysis:

- Horizontal and Vertical Analysis
- Ratios Analysis

HORIZONTAL ANALYSIS

In business, horizontal analysis refers to a type of fundamental analysis in which a financial analyst uses certain financial data to assess a company's performance over time. The analyst compares the same items or ratios for a particular company over a period of time in order to assess the company's growth during that time. Horizontal analysis can also be performed on multiple companies in the same industry, to assess a company's performance relative to its competitors. The data used in horizontal analysis is found in a company's financial statements, which include the balance sheet, income statement, and statement of cash flows. It can be line items, such as expense items, or it can be a ratio. A ratio is determined by comparing two or more items, for example, dividing expenses by net sales to determine the operating ratio. Horizontal analysis can be performed on a quarterly or on an annual basis. Performance can be compared to the previous period or, in the case of quarterly analysis, to the same quarter in a previous year. If an analyst compares the same information from one quarter to the next, it is referred to as quarter-to-quarter, as in, 'quarter-to-quarter sales increased 10 per cent.' If the comparison is to the same quarter in the prior year, it is referred to as quarter-over-quarter, as in, 'quarter-over-quarter earnings were up 3 per cent.' In seasonal industries, such as retail, the quarter-over-quarter comparison is usually more valuable as it reflects the change compared to the same quarter a year ago.

The value of horizontal analysis lies in its usefulness in comparing the results of one company over time to determine whether its financial situation is improving. It is also useful for comparing the results of multiple companies in the same industry to determine which company has the best performance over time. It is most useful when comparing companies in the same industry, because metrics such as gross margin can vary widely from one industry to another. In contrast to horizontal analysis, vertical analysis refers to the representation of assets, liabilities and equities as a percentage of the whole. These three major balance sheet categories are added up, and each one is expressed as the per cent of the total it represents. Vertical analysis can be useful in comparing companies of different sizes, as it makes it easy to see which company has a greater percentage of liabilities as opposed to equity, or which company has more assets, relative to liabilities and equity.

VERTICAL ANALYSIS

Vertical analysis is an integral part while carrying out the overall financial analysis of any firm. The process of restating and summarizing data by establishing ratios and trends is known as financial analysis. The analysis is carried out on a company's financial as well as income statement. The main objective behind carrying out a financial analysis of a company is to know its current financial position and its returns compared to risks. Financial analysis also helps in future forecasting. Financial analysis has three sud-divisions – vertical analysis, horizontal analysis and financial ratios. A detailed explanation on vertical analysis is provided below. Vertical analysis is a technique of financial statement analysis wherein every entry under all three major accounting categories – equities, assets and liabilities, in a balance sheet are presented as a part of the total account. Using vertical analysis, it is easier to compare balance sheets of small as well as large business organizations. Another benefit of doing a vertical analysis of financial statements is that it helps to bring to notice any changes in a business within a year. For example, if SOS Corp. has three assets – machinery (US $6 million), inventory (US $10 million) and cash and equivalents (US $4 million). After carrying out a vertical analysis of these assets, the asset column would appear like:

Machinery:30%
Inventory: 50%
Cash and equivalents: 20%

Difference between Horizontal and Vertical Analysis

In vertical analysis, every amount in the financial or income statement is expressed as a percentage of another amount. Thus, in the assets column, after vertical analysis is done, each value is shown as a percentage of the total value of all assets combined.

These proportional values, when represented, are known as a common-size balance sheet. Similarly, for income statement, values derived are a percentage of total sales. The restated values form the common-size income statement. Companies find this useful for comparing their financial and income statements with other companies or the industry average. In horizontal analysis, values on the balance sheet over past years are compared with each other. For example, stock balance represented on the balance sheet for December 31 2009, 2008, 2007 and 2006, will be a percentage of the stock amount as on 31 December 2006. Amounts are expressed in percentages and not dollars, indicating an increase or decrease in value from the base year. All items on the balance sheet and income statement are compared in this manner. This analysis is also known as trend analysis, and helps a company to notice change in a particular item over the years as compared to changes in other items.

How to do a Vertical Analysis?

Particulars	Amount	Percentage
Land	$10,000	20%
Building and Equipment	$15,000	30%
Accounts Receivable	$5,000	10%
Prepaid Expenses	$12,500	25%
Cash	$7,500	15%
Total Assets	$50,000	100%
Paid-in Capital	$25,000	50%
Retained Earnings	$10,000	20%
Bonds Payable(6%)	$7,500	15%
Notes Payable	$2,500	5%
Accounts Payable	$5,000	10%
Total Liabilities	$50,000	100%

The example is an hypothetical balance sheet of a company. To do a vertical analysis of the balance sheet, the total of assets is calculated and given a value of 100%. All other values on the asset side are divided by the total amount and then then expressed as a percentage of total assets. Similarly, for all liabilities, the total is calculated first and then every individual item is divided by this amount to arrive at the corresponding percentage value. A good way to recheck the calculations is by adding up all percentage values (except the total), which should come up to 100.

Particulars	Amount	Percentage
Total Sales	$50,000	100%
(-) Cost of Goods Sold	$20,000	40%
Gross Profit	$30,000	60%
(-) Operating Expenses	$12,500	25%
Net Operating Income	$17,500	35%
(-) Interest and Tax	$7,500	15%
Net Income	$10,000	20%

To do vertical analysis of income statements, the total sales figure is given the value of 100%. All other items are will therefore be calculated by dividing them with the sales figure to get the percentage value. The total of all figures excluding sales will not be 100 as certain values are subtracted from the total.

FINANCIAL RATIO ANALYSIS

Financial ratio analysis is the calculation and comparison of ratios which are derived from the information in a company's financial statements. The level and historical trends of these ratios can be used to make inferences about a company's financial condition, its operations and attractiveness as an investment. Financial ratios are calculated from one or more pieces of information from a company's financial statements. For example, the "gross margin" is the gross profit from operations divided by the total sales or revenues of a company, expressed in percentage terms. In isolation, a financial ratio is a useless piece of information. In context, however, a financial ratio can give a financial analyst an excellent picture of a company's situation and the trends that are developing. A ratio gains utility by comparison to other data and standards. Taking our example, a gross profit margin for a company of 25% is meaningless by itself. If we know that this company's competitors have profit margins of 10%, we know that it is more profitable than its industry peers which is quite favourable. If we also know that the historical trend is upwards, for example has been increasing steadily for the last few years, this would also be a favourable sign that management is implementing effective business policies and strategies.

Financial ratio analysis groups the ratios into categories which tell us about different facets of a company's finances and operations. An overview of some of the categories of ratios is given below.

- Leverage Ratios which show the extent that debt is used in a company's capital structure.

- Liquidity Ratios which give a picture of a company's short term financial situation or solvency.
- Operational Ratios which use turnover measures to show how efficient a company is in its operations and use of assets.
- Profitability Ratios which use margin analysis and show the return on sales and capital employed.
- Solvency Ratios which give a picture of a company's ability to generate cashflow and pay it financial obligations.

It is imperative to note the importance of the proper context for ratio analysis. Like computer programming, financial ratio is governed by the GIGO law of *"Garbage In...Garbage Out!"* A cross industry comparison of the leverage of stable utility companies and cyclical mining companies would be worse than useless.

Examining a cyclical company's profitability ratios over less than a full commodity or business cycle would fail to give an accurate long-term measure of profitability. Using historical data independent of fundamental changes in a company's situation or prospects would predict very little about future trends. For example, the historical ratios of a company that has undergone a merger or had a substantive change in its technology or market position would tell very little about the prospects for this company. Credit analysts, those interpreting the financial ratios from the prospects of a lender, focus on the "downside" risk since they gain none of the upside from an improvement in operations. They pay great attention to liquidity and leverage ratios to ascertain a company's financial risk. Equity analysts look more to the operational and profitability ratios, to determine the future profits that will accrue to the shareholder. Although financial ratio analysis is well-developed and the actual ratios are well-known, practicing financial analysts often develop their own measures for particular industries and even individual companies. Analysts will often differ drastically in their conclusions from the same ratio analysis.

Profitability Ratios

These ratios tell us whether a business is making profits - and if so whether at an acceptable rate.

The key ratios are:

Ratio	Calculation	Comments
Gross Profit Margin	[Gross Profit / Revenue] x 100 (expressed as a percentage	This ratio tells us something about the business's ability consistently to control its production costs or to manage the margins its makes on products its buys and sells. Whilst sales value and volumes may move up and down significantly, the gross profit margin is usually quite stable (in percentage terms). However, a small increase (or decrease) in profit margin, however caused can produce a substantial change in overall profits.
Operating Profit Margin	[Operating Profit / Revenue] x 100 (expressed as a percentage)	Assuming a constant gross profit margin, the operating profit margin tells us something about a company's ability to control its other operating costs or overheads.
Return on capital employed ("ROCE")	Net profit before tax, interest and dividends ("EBIT") / total assets (or total assets less current liabilities	ROCE is sometimes referred to as the "primary ratio"; it tells us what returns management has made on the resources made available to them before making any distribution of those returns.

Efficiency ratios

These ratios give us an insight into how efficiently the business is employing those resources invested in fixed assets and working capital.

Ratio	Calculation	Comments
Sales /Capital Employed	Sales / Capital employed	A measure of total asset utilisation. Helps to answer the question - what sales are being generated by each pound's worth of assets invested in the business. Note, when combined with the return on sales it generates the primary ratio - ROCE.
Sales or Profit / Fixed Assets	Sales or profit / Fixed Assets	This ratio is about fixed asset capacity. A reducing sales or profit being generated from each pound invested in fixed assets may indicate overcapacity or poorer-performing equipment.
Stock Turnover	Cost of Sales / Average Stock Value	Stock turnover helps answer questions such as "have we got too much money tied up in inventory"?. An increasing stock turnover figure or one which is much larger than the "average" for an industry, may indicate poor stock management.
Credit Given / "Debtor Days"	(Trade debtors (average, if possible) / (Sales)) x 365	The "debtor days" ratio indicates whether debtors are being allowed excessive credit. A high figure (more than the industry average) may suggest general problems with debt collection or the financial position of major customers.
Credit taken / "Creditor Days"	((Trade creditors + accruals) / (cost Of sales + Other purchases)) x 365	A similar calculation to that for debtors, giving an insight into whether a business i taking full advantage of trade credit available to it.

Liquidity Ratios

Liquidity ratios indicate how capable a business is of meeting its short-term obligations as they fall due:

Ratio	Calculation	Comments
Current Ratio	Current Assets / Current Liabilities	A simple measure that estimates whether the business can pay debts due within one year from assets that it expects to turn into cash within that year. A ratio of less than one is often a cause for concern, particularly if it persists for any length of time.
Quick Ratio (or "Acid Test"	Cash and near cash (short-term investments + trade debtors)	Not all assets can be turned into cash quickly or easily. Some - notably raw materials and other stocks - must first be turned into final product, then sold and the cash collected from debtors. The Quick Ratio therefore adjusts the Current Ratio to eliminate all assets that are not already in cash (or "near-cash") form. Once again, a ratio of less than one would start to send out danger signals.

Stability Ratios

These ratios concentrate on the long-term health of a business - particularly the effect of the capital/finance structure on the business:

Ratio	Calculation	Comments
Gearing	Borrowing (all long-term debts + normal overdraft) / Net Assets (or Shareholders' Funds)	Gearing (otherwise known as "leverage") measures the proportion of assets invested in a business that are financed by borrowing. In theory, the higher the level of borrowing (gearing) the higher are the risks to a business, since the payment of interest and repayment of debts are not "optional" in the same way as dividends. However, gearing can be a financially sound part of a business's capital structure particularly if the business has strong, predictable cash flows.
Interest cover	Operating profit before interest / Interest	This measures the ability of the business to "service" its debt. Are profits sufficient to be able to pay interest and other finance costs?

Investor Ratios

There are several ratios commonly used by investors to assess the performance of a business as an investment:

Ratio	Calculation	Comments
Earnings per share ("EPS")	Earnings (profits) attributable to rdinary shareholders / Weighted average ordinary shares in issue during the year	A requirement of the London Stock Exchange - an important ratio. EPS measures the overall profit generated for each share in existence over a particular period.
Price-Earnings Ratio ("P/E Ratio")	Market price of share / Earnings per Share	At any time, the P/E ratio is an indication of how highly the market "rates" or "values" a business. A P/E ratio is best viewed in the context of a sector or market average to get a feel for relative value and stock market pricing.
Dividend Yield	(Latest dividend per ordinary share / current market price of share) x 100	This is known as the "payout ratio". It provides a guide as to the ability of a business to maintain a dividend payment. It also measures the proportion of earnings that are being retained by the business rather than distributed as dividends.

ADVANTAGE AND DISADVANTAGES OF FINANCIAL STATEMENT ANALYSIS

There are three main financial statements investors analyse. They are the balance sheet, income statement and the cash flow statement. The balance sheet is a snapshot in time. It shows all the assets owned and liabilities owed for a company. It also shows the amount of equity or ownership that is paid for by investors. The income statement looks at the entire year. It starts with revenues and then deducts expenses for net income. The cash flow statement shows where the cash is really coming by breaking down cash flow into cash from operations, investing and financing. There are advantages and disadvantages to analyzing financial statements for investment decisions.

FULL DISCLOSURE

Full disclosure is one of the main advantages of, and one of the main purposes for, financial statements. The Securities and Exchange Commission made the 10K report a requirement for all public companies. This 10K includes full disclosure of all financial statements as well as notes explaining all assumptions contained with the notes.

INTRINSIC VALUE VS. MARKET VALUE

While financial statements are good for the data needed to conduct a thorough ratio analysis, they are based on the accrual system of accounting, which is not market based. This is both an advantage and a disadvantage. It's good to have a basis for comparing book value to market value.

All it helps to pinpoint bargains in the market. However, value discrepancies can also work to the disadvantage of financial statement analysis. It can make it difficult to know the real value of assets, which translates into unreliable ratios.

TRANSPARENCY

Unfortunately, since financial statements are easy for everyone to understand, it's also very easy for people to hide information. For instance, an analyst has to look at the cash flow statement to know if cash flow is coming from operations or additional financing activities. There are also certain conventions like depreciation and inventory accounting that can increase or decrease net income, depending on the convention used.

INTERPRETATION OF FINANCIAL STATEMENTS

The Interpretation of Financial Statements is a wonderful reference guide for those who want to understand published financial statements and reports. Although some of the information is slightly out of date, you can be sure this book will still be useful in twenty years.

- Offers an explanation of the most common terms found on financial statements
- Gives ratios and formulas for investors to calculate
- Includes many examples

CONS

- Some of the information is dated due to changes in accounting rules
- The reader should have a working knowledge of stocks

DESCRIPTION

- Small, easy to carry edition with classic typeface.
- Makes an excellent business gift for clients and colleagues.
- Published by Harper Collins.

4

Profit Planning and Break-even Analysis

PROFIT PLANNING

Profit planning is simply the development of your operating plan for the coming period. Your plan is summarized in the form of an income statement that serves as your sales and profit objective and your budget for cost.

USE OF PROFIT PLANNING

The profit plan is used in the following ways:

- Evaluating operations. Each time you prepare an income statement, actual sales and costs are compared with those you projected in your original profit plan. This permits detection of areas of unsatisfactory performance so that corrective action can be taken.
- Determining the need for additional resources such as facilities or personnel. For example, the profit plan may show that a sharp increase in expected sales will overload the company's billing personnel. A decision can then be made to add additional invoicing personnel, to retain an EDP service, or to pursue some other alternative.
- Planning purchasing requirements. The volume of expected sales may be more than the business' usual suppliers can handle or expected sales may be sufficient to permit taking advantage of quantity discounts. In either case, advance knowledge of purchasing requirements will permit taking advantage of cost savings and ensure that purchased goods are readily available when needed.
- Anticipating any additional financing needs. With planning, the search for needed funds can begin as early as possible. In this way, financial crises are avoided and financing can be arranged on more favourable terms.

ADVANTAGES OF PROFIT PLANNING

Profit planning offers many advantages to your business. The modest investment in time required to develop and implement the plan will pay liberal dividends later. Among the benefits that your business can enjoy from profit planning are the following:

- *Performance evaluation*: The profit plan provides a continuing standard against which sales performance and cost control can quickly be evaluated.
- *Awareness of responsibilities*: With the profit plan, personnel are readily aware of their responsibilities for meeting sales objectives, controlling costs, and the like.
- *Cost consciousness*: Since cost excesses can quickly be identified and planned, expenditures can be compared with budgets even before they are incurred, cost consciousness is increased, reducing unnecessary costs and overspending.
- *Disciplined approach to problem-solving*: The profit plan permits early detection of potential problems so that their nature and extent are known. With this information, alternate corrective actions can be more easily and accurately evaluated.
- *Thinking about the future*: Too often, small businesses neglect to plan ahead: thinking about where they are today, where they will be next year, or the year after. As a result, opportunities are overlooked and crises occur that could have been avoided. Development of the profit plan requires thinking about the future so that many problems can be avoided before they arise.
- *Financial planning*: The profit plan serves as a basis for financial planning. With the information developed from the profit plan, you can anticipate the need for increased investment in receivables, inventory, or facilities as well as any need for additional capital.
- *Confidence of lenders and investors*. A realistic profit plan, supported by a description of specific steps proposed to achieve sales and profit objectives, will inspire the confidence of potential lenders and investors. This confidence will not only influence their judgment of you as a business manager, but also the prospects of your business' success and its worthiness for a loan or an investment.

LIMITATIONS OF PROFIT PLANNING

Profit plans are based upon estimates. Inevitably, many conditions you expected when the plan was prepared will change.

Crystal balls are often cloudy. The further down the road one attempts to forecast, the cloudier they become. In a year, any number of factors can change, many of them beyond the con-trol of the company. Customers' economic fortunes may decline, suppliers' prices may increase, or suppliers' inability to deliver may disrupt your plan.

The profit plan requires the support of all responsible par-ties. Sales quotas must be agreed upon with those responsible for meeting them.

Expense budgets must be agreed upon with the people who must live with them. Without mutual agreement on objectives and budgets, they will quickly be ignored and serve no useful purpose. Finally, profit plans must be changed from time to time to meet changing conditions. There is no point in trying to operate a business according to a plan that is no longer realistic because conditions have changed.

FORECASTING SALES AND GROSS PROFIT

Development of your profit plan should usually begin with a forecast of your expected sales and gross profit for the coming year.

The sales and gross profit must be considered together since they are so closely interrelated. Gross profit percentages are determined by pricing policy, which also affects expected sales volume. A decision to increase the expected gross profit percentage will usually tend to decrease expected sales, while reducing the expected gross profit per-centage should increase sales.

A second major reason for beginning the profit plan with a sales forecast is that the volume of expected sales often determines a number of other factors such as the following:

- Expected changes in variable expenses, those expenses that tend to change in direct proportion to changes in sales. These could include expenses such as sales commissions or delivery costs.
- The impact of the added sales volume on the various fixed costs of operating your business. These costs, by definition, do not tend to vary in direct proportion to changes in sales volume. However, substantial increases in sales over an extended period can force an increase in many fixed expenses. For example, a sales increase realised through the addition of many new accounts could affect bookkeeping and credit costs.
- The ability of present resources such as storage space, display area, delivery capability, or supervisory personnel to accommodate the added volume.
- The need for funds to invest in increased inventory or accounts receivable to accommodate sales increases.
- Cash generated from operations to meet current operating needs as well as expansion requirements, debt repayments, and owners' compensation.

REALISM

A realistic sales forecast must rely on careful analysis of market potential and the ability of your business to capture its share of this potential. The forecast should not be based upon "what you would like to do" or "what you hope to do." It must be "what you can do" and "what you will do." Any forecast of a sales increase must be supported by realistic expectations for stronger market demand and specific marketing steps that will be taken to capture a share of this market.

The key to successful forecasting is realism. You only fool yourself if you reject reality in forecasting. Such fore-casts serve neither as a realistic planning basis nor as a reliable means of performance evaluation. Your forecast can be the basis for important decisions such as decisions to add personnel, lease additional facilities, or increase promotional costs. If these decisions are based upon unrealistic sales expectations, any money expended on them will be wasted. Forecasts are often presented to lenders or potential investors to guide them in their decisions. If they lack confidence in your forecast, they will certainly be reluctant to commit their funds to your business.

Every forecast should be supported by carefully considered, specific action plans. It is inadequate to forecast a sales increase of 20% or 30% without plans for specific actions to achieve the increase. These actions could include the intro-duction of new products, opening of new branches, market expansion, commitments from new customers, increased require-ments from existing customers, additional salesmen, or an intensified promotional effort to attract new customers.

ANALYSING CURRENT SALES AND GROSS PROFIT

Your sales and gross profit forecast begins with analysis of current performance. Sales are usually divided into various categories. Each category is examined individually to deter-mine expected sales for the coming year.

SELECTING SALES CATEGORIES

The selection of categories will depend upon the nature of your business. For example, a food broker selling to a large number of relatively small accounts might be interested pri-marily in analysing sales by product. The owner of a single retail store might choose to analyse sales by selling department, while the owner of a retail chain would probably be interested in analysing sales by outlet. An insurance broker with several agents might categorize sales by agent. An individual wholesaler might consider sales by sales territory.

FACTORS AFFECTING SALES

After categories have been selected and current sales divided among them, the various factors which can affect sales in each category must be considered. These factors could be either internal or external. Internal factors are those that you can influence. External factors are those that affect the market served by your business, but are generally beyond your control.

INTERNAL FACTORS

The following are typical internal factors that could influence your sales forecast:

- Promotional plans
- Expansion plans
- Capacity restrictions
- New product introductions
- Product cancellations
- Sales force changes
- Pricing policy
- Profit expectations
- Market expansion to new customers or territories

EXTERNAL FACTORS

Among the external factors that must be considered are the following:

- Business trends
- Government policies
- Inflation
- Changes in population characteristics
- Economic fortunes of customers
- Changes in buying habits
- Competitive pressures

ANALYSING GROSS PROFIT PERCENTAGES

It is often useful to begin a sales forecast with an examina-tion of your current gross profit percentage (mark-up percentage or gross profit percentage). The gross profit percentage is usually the best indicator of pricing policy which can have significant impact on sales volume.

To some extent, the gross profit percentage will also reflect the buying economies of your business. However, the range over which costs of purchased goods will vary is not ordinarily as wide as the possible range of prices you may seek for your products.

THREE BASES OF COMPARISON

Examination of current gross profit percentages can indicate the need for pricing policy revisions to meet competition or closer attention to purchasing costs in order to provide extra gross profit without increasing prices.

The evaluation of gross profit percentages requires comparison of current performance with three bases:

- Objectives originally set for the current year, if available
- Other businesses in the same industry
- Results of prior years

Comparison with objectives permits you to determine how well you have done compared with your original expectations. Assuming that these objectives were realistic, this is often the best single performance indicator. Deviations from objectives can quickly be identified and explored in detail to determine the cause of the deviation. Comparison with industry averages permits identification of areas where the experience of similar businesses indicates room for improvement in your own. Unfortunately, businesses are often too quick to dismiss the applicability of industry averages to their own operation, claiming that"Our circumstances are different." Such an attitude is self-defeating. It prevents you from taking advantage of the experience of others to improve your own sales and profit.

A far more productive attitude is to say,"If everybody else can realise a gross profit of x per cent, then we should be able to." Until specific circumstances are identified that make it impossible for your business to be consistent with industry averages, every attempt should be made to bring performance in line with the experience of others. Comparison of current operations with performance in prior periods permits detection of trends so that progress, or the lack of it, can be identified. It also permits evaluation in light of those specific considerations that may be unique to your business. For example, if your gross profit as a percentage of sales is low compared with the industry, analysis of your historic performance may reveal the cause of this apparent deficiency such as reliance upon a major customer where severe competition restricts the available gross profit percentage.

EVALUATING GROSS PROFIT PERCENTAGES

Refer to the table below, which is an analysis of gross profit percentages realised by My Appliances in the year 2002.

Percentages are shown for cost of sales, gross profit, total expenses, and profit before taxes as follows:

- 2002 actual
- 2001 actual
- 2001 actual
  - Industry average
  - 2002 objective

CONFLICTS

Sometimes financial analysis can lead to conflicting conclusions derived from identical facts. Comparing My Appliances' 20.0% gross profit with the 18.2% industry average could raise questions.

If My Appliances were more com-petitive in its pricing, could it capture a larger market share? A reasonable answer to this question would depend upon thorough knowledge of their operations and the experience of their sales personnel in dealing with specific customers. Perhaps their pricing is fully competitive in their area or local retailers are willing to pay slightly more because of the superior services they offer. If this is the case, price cutting might only trim profit margins with no realistic hope of additional sales volume to offset the effects of the price reduction.

On the other hand, if their gross profit percentage is below that of the industry, a number of other questions would be raised, such as the following:

- Are they purchasing at prices that are too high to provide an adequate gross profit?
- Is their pricing structure so low that adequate gross profit margins cannot be attained?
- Are salesmen too quick to cut prices?
- Is their marketing effort too heavily concentrated in those product lines that offer a relatively low gross profit percentage?
- Is their marketing effort directed towards those high-volume accounts that are so highly competitive that gross profit must be trimmed to an unrealistically low level?

SUBDIVIDING SALES CATEGORIES

My APPLIANCES, Pty Ltd. Customer Sales Analysis - Giant Discount

				2002 Actual	**2003 Forecast**	
Product line	**Sales**	**Gross profit**	**%**	**Sales**	**Gross profit**	**%**
Television	$160,000	$16,000	10.0	$184,800	$18,500	10.0%
Automotive radios	20,000	6,000	30.0	--	--	--
Table radios	30,000	6,000	20.0	34,700	6,900	20.0
Stereo	40,000	7,000	18.0	46,200	8,300	18.0
Small appliances	50,000	10,000	20.0	57,800	11,600	20.0
Total	$300,000	$45,000	15.0%	$323,500	$45,300	14.0

It is often useful to subdivide sales into more detailed classifications in order to develop a more precise forecast such as potential sales to a single customer. As an example, refer to the table below, My Appliances' sales summary by product line to Giant Discount, its major customer in XXX2. Sales, gross profit, and the gross profit percentage are shown by product line so that each line may be considered separately to determine a realistic forecast for 2003. Development of the 2003 forecast will assume that Giant Dis-count's various stores are located in areas that are represen-tative of the general economy and therefore will reflect the industry's expected sales growth of 10%; the price increase of 5% will have no significant effect on Giant Discount's sales; and competition among appliance wholesalers for Giant Dis-count's business will prevent My Appliances from increas-ing its gross profit percentage in any product line. The first product line on the table, television sales, could then be forecast as follows:

2002 Sales	$160,000
+ 5% Price Increase	8,000
= Subtotal	$168,000
+ 10% Demand Increase	16,800
= Total	$184,800

Assuming that the gross profit percentage of 10.0% on television sales is maintained in 2003, the forecast for gross profit can then be calculated as follows:

$184,800 × 0.100 = $18,480, rounded to $18,500

Giant Discount plans to discontinue its sales of automotive radios in 2003. Therefore, sales, gross profit, and the gross profit percentage for all are shown as zero on the table. Sales, gross profit, and gross profit percentages have all been determined for the remaining product lines and shown on the 2003 forecast on the table. You will note that the gross profit as a percentage of total sales in the 2003 forecast, 14.0%, is well below the 2002 experience of 15.0% even though the gross profit on each product line remains the same. This is due to the elimination of the highly profitable automotive radio line which produced a 30% gross profit but is being discontinued from Giant Discount's stores. In fact, the net effect of this discontinuation is that My Appliances will realise addi-tional gross profit of less than $1,000 on sales to Giant Discount despite a sales increase of almost $24,000. This important fact probably would not have been revealed if sales to Giant Discount had not been subdivided into individual product lines for analysis.

This negligible increase in gross profit will probably be more than offset by normal cost increases in various expense accounts required to handle Giant Discount's business in 2003, At this point, the owners of My Appliances would be well advised to take a hard look at their pricing strategy to see if more favourable prices can be realised in any product line without any significant sales loss so that the gross profit earned from this, its largest account, can be improved.

DEVELOPING EXPENSE BUDGETS

After a realistic forecast has been developed for sales and gross profit, expenses for the coming year must be estimated in order to establish expense budgets and to determine ex-pected operating profit.

COMPARISONS

As with the forecast of sales and gross profit, expense estimating begins with a review of the current year's per-formance based upon comparison with the following indicators:

- Performance in prior periods
- Industry averages
- Objectives established for the current year

For purposes of comparison, it is often useful to express each expense as a percentage of total sales.

COMPARING VARIABLE EXPENSES

The use of percentages as a basis of comparison and forecast-ing is particularly applicable when analysing variable expenses. Variable expenses are those that tend to change as a result of changes in sales volume.

For example, if salesmen's commissions are based upon a percentage of sales, the total dollar amount of commissions earned would increase as sales increase. If sales in a month were 20% higher than expected, commissions paid would also increase 20% as a direct result of the higher sales volume.

COMPARING FIXED EXPENSES

On the other hand, fixed expenses are not directly affected by short-term variations in sales volume. Therefore, a 20% increase in the dollar amount of any fixed expense such as salaries or rent would normally be considered unacceptable even if sales for the period increased by 20%. When com-paring fixed expense levels with objectives or from one period to another, it is more realistic to make comparisons in absolute dollars rather than in percentages.

A business has sales and rent expense in January, February, and March as follows:

Month	Rent Expense $	Sales	% Sales
January	$100,000	1,000	1.00
February	80,000	1,000	1.25
March	125,000	1,000	0.80

As a percentage of sales, rent expense was high in February and low in March. However, this does not indicate that con-trol of this expense was more or less effective in either month. It simply reflects the changes in sales volume. In all three cases, the actual rent expense was 1,000.

LONG-RANGE CONSIDERATIONS

Despite the shortcomings of using percentages to evaluate fixed expense control within the business from month to month, they can be useful when making long-term comparisons or com-parisons with industry averages. These averages normally express expenses as percentages of sales, regardless of whether they are fixed or variable. For example, assume that a business found that its rent expense as a percentage of sales was 2% compared with an industry average of 1%. This differential would have to be offset by better than average performance in gross profit or other expense classifications if the business expects to realise net profit equal to its industry average. Perhaps the reason for the high percentage is due to an exorbitant rental expense, or it may be caused by inadequate sales. In either case, certain questions must be answered.

These could include the following:

- Are we renting more space than we need?
- Is our space too expensive for our requirements?
- Could a less elaborate facility be located that would be adequate for our needs?
- Would a less costly location be sufficient?
- Is our space utilization inefficient?
- Will expected sales increases be handled without renting additional space? Will this bring our rent expense per-centage in line with the industry?
- Can the terms of our lease be re-negotiated?

Similarly, when comparing long-term performance with prior periods, the use of fixed expense percentages can be helpful. For example, if you found that warehouse salaries jumped from 2% of sales to 4%, a number of important questions would be raised.

These could include the following:

- Are we now using too many warehouse personnel?
- Are warehouse personnel less efficient?
- Has ineffectiveness crept into the warehouse layout or operating procedure?
- Are warehouse workers overpaid?
- Is warehouse supervision inadequate?

IDENTIFYING EXCESSIVE EXPENSES

At My Appliances, no objectives were available for 2002 performance. Therefore, excessive expenses can be identified only by comparison with 2001 results, and, in some cases, with industry averages.

INDUSTRY AVERAGE COMPARISONS

Comparisons with industry averages are not available in all of My Appliances' expense accounts. However, this can be determined by examining those accounts on the company's income statement that can be combined for comparison with industry averages. For example, the industry averages show that office salaries for the industry were 4.9% of sales. Examining the operating expense accounts at My Appliances, the accounts that would appear to fall into this classification are the following:

- Salary: Office Manager 1.4%

- Salaries: Clerical 1.0%
- *Salaries*: Warehouse 1.8%

The total of these expenses, 4.2% of sales, compares favourably with the industry average of 4.9%.

COMPARISON WITH PREVIOUS PERIODS

The information permits comparison of all expenses in 2002 with 2001 results. The only variable expense at My Appliances in 2002 is salesmen's commissions. These represented 2.0% of sales in both 2001 and 2002. Therefore, they would not appear to be excessive. In the fixed expense accounts, sharp increases could be noted in the following accounts and would warrant review and pos-sible corrective action.

Account	2002	2001
Salary - Owner	$24,000	$20,000
Salaries - Warehouse	22,000	18,000
Salaries - Clerical	12,000	10,000
Employee Benefits	8,000	6,000
Utilities	4,000	3,000
Telephone	4,000	2,000
Supplies	2,000	1,000
Travel and Entertainment	13,000	10,000

Comparing My Appliances' 2002 fixed expenses with its experience in 2001, significant increases are noted in almost every account. Some of these increases should be regarded with more concern than others and therefore given prompt attention. Reasons for the increases and possible corrective action must be determined.

Some increases were probably unavoidable, having been dictated by contract, legal requirements, or price increases beyond the company's control. Others could probably be reduced with closer control. For example, travel and entertainment expense jumped from $10,000 to $13,000, an increase of $3,000. This sharp increase should indicate that a closer look at all travel and entertainment expenditures is in order to determine whether or not all were necessary.

Could some have been avoided by restricting salesmen's expense accounts? Could more economical means of travel have been used? Could the company eliminate unnecessary trips that resulted in costs far beyond any real value to the business? Supplies expense doubled from $1,000 to $2,000 although the volume of business increased by only about 10%. This sales increase would not seem to indicate a need for such a sharp increase in supplies usage.

Such an expense could be con-trolled by closer attention to purchasing procedures and supplies issued to employees, use of less expensive supplies where possible, and so on.

DETERMINING EXPENSE BUDGETS

Budgets for each expense must be established, considering both external and internal factors, as in sales forecasting.

From the standpoint of expense budgeting, the following would be considered internal factors:

- Corrective actions planned to bring excessive expenses in line.
- Policy changes such as new commission plans.
- Commitments such as equipment purchases, leases on new facilities, or professional service contracts.
- Planned salary increases.
- Planned changes in benefit programmes.
- Additional personnel.
- Promotional plans.
- External factors could include the following:
- Inflation and its effect on price increases from suppliers.
- Tax rate increases including payroll taxes, local property taxes, inventory taxes, and so on.
- Utility rate increases.

Additionally, the interrelated effects of expense increases must be considered. For example, payroll increases will increase payroll taxes and, possibly, employee benefits. Rent on larger facilities can also involve additional utilities expense.

INITIAL FORECAST

- The table below shows My Appliances' initial forecast for 2003 operating expenses.
- The owner's salary will be increased from $24,000 to $26,000.
- The office manager's salary will be increased from $17,000 to $18,000.
- Salesmen's salaries will remain unchanged.
- The expected sales increase will cause salesmen's commissions, 2% of sales, to increase from $24,000 to $28,000.
- Warehouse salaries will be increased about 5% from $22,000 to $23,000.
- Clerical salaries will be increased about 17% from $12,000 to $14,000.
- Payroll taxes, approximately 8% of total compensation, will increase to $10,000 as a result of the compensation increases
- Employee benefits expense is expected to increase from the present $8,000 to $9,000. This increase is dictated by increased premium costs for employees' health insurance.
- Rent expense will increase from $9,000 to $10,000 due to a tax escalator clause in the lease agreement and a proposed municipal tax increase.

- Utilities expense is expected to remain unchanged at $4,000.
- Telephone expense is expected to be reduced from $4,000 to $3,000 because of tighter controls introduced by management in response to the sharp increase in 2002.
- New controls on supplies should hold this expense at $2,000 despite price increases.
- To increase sales, the advertising and promotion budget will be increased from $13,000 to $15,000, a 20% increase.
- Through tighter control, the owner expects to restrict travel and entertainment expense to the 2002 level of $13,000 despite the general increase in travel-related costs.
- Freight expense will increase from $16,000 to $18,000 reflecting the increased sales volume and higher freight tariffs.
- Professional fees are expected to remain at $5,000.
- Depreciation expense will increase from $6,000 to $8,000 due to the addition of new receiving equipment being purchased at a cost of $10,000 and depreciated over 5 years.
- Total operating expenses will increase from $200,000 to $218,000. Profit before interest and taxes will be $62,000, an increase from $40,000 in 2002

Once an initial plan has been established, it is often useful to review it in order to identify areas of further improvement.

BREAK-EVEN ANALYSIS

Break-even analysis is a technique widely used by production management and management accountants. It is based on categorising production costs between those which are "variable" (costs that change when the production output changes) and those that are "fixed" (costs not directly related to the volume of production). Total variable and fixed costs are compared with sales revenue in order to determine the level of sales volume, sales value or production at which the business makes neither a profit nor a loss (the "break-even point").

THE BREAK-EVEN CHART

In its simplest form, the break-even chart is a graphical representation of costs at various levels of activity shown on the same chart as the variation of income (or sales, revenue) with the same variation in activity. The point at which neither profit nor loss is made is known as the "break-even point" and is represented on the chart below by the intersection of the two lines:

In the diagram, the line OA represents the variation of income at varying levels of production activity ("output"). OB represents the total fixed costs in the business. As output increases, variable costs are incurred, meaning that total costs (fixed + variable) also increase.

At low levels of output, Costs are greater than Income. At the point of intersection, P, costs are exactly equal to income, and hence neither profit nor loss is made.

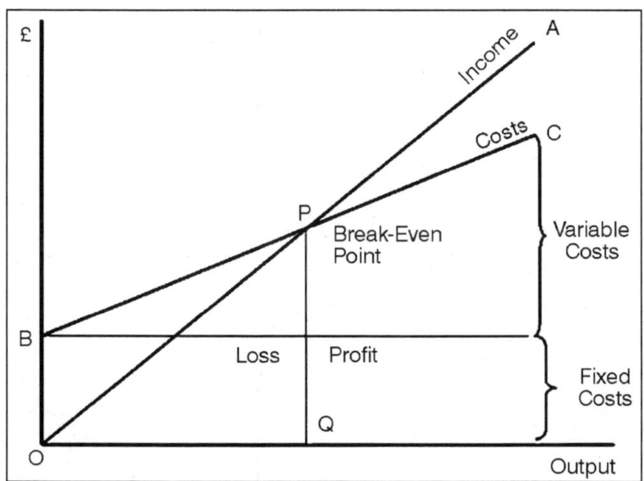

FIXED COSTS

Fixed costs are those business costs that are not directly related to the level of production or output. In other words, even if the business has a zero output or high output, the level of fixed costs will remain broadly the same. In the long term fixed costs can alter - perhaps as a result of investment in production capacity (e.g. adding a new factory unit) or through the growth in overheads required to support a larger, more complex business.

Examples of fixed costs:

- Rent and rates
- Depreciation
- Research and development
- Marketing costs (non- revenue related)
- Administration costs

VARIABLE COSTS

Variable costs are those costs which vary directly with the level of output. They represent payment output-related inputs such as raw materials, direct labour, fuel and revenue-related costs such as commission. A distinction is often made between "Direct" variable costs and "Indirect" variable costs. Direct variable costs are those which can be directly attributable to the production of a particular product or service and allocated to a particular cost centre. Raw materials and the wages those working on the production line are good examples. Indirect variable costs cannot be directly attributable to production but they do vary with output. These include depreciation (where it is calculated related to output - e.g. machine hours), maintenance and certain labour costs.

SEMI-VARIABLE COSTS

Whilst the distinction between fixed and variable costs is a convenient way of categorising business costs, in reality there are some costs which are fixed in nature but which increase when output reaches certain levels. These are largely related to the overall "scale" and/or complexity of the business. For example, when a business has relatively low levels of output or sales, it may not require costs associated with functions such as human resource management or a fully-resourced finance department. However, as the scale of the business grows (e.g. output, number people employed, number and complexity of transactions) then more resources are required. If production rises suddenly then some short-term increase in warehousing and/or transport may be required. In these circumstances, we say that part of the cost is variable and part fixed.

5

Budgets and Financial Statements

CONCEPT

DEFINITION

Budgets are statements of estimated resources set apart for execution of planned works or activities over a specified period of time. A budget is the blue print of the outcome of the organization's operations in a financial year. Budget indicates the quantitative parameters of an organization's performance. Terry has defined budgetary control "as a process of finding out what is being done and comparing the result with corresponding budget data to verify accomplishments, or to remedy differences."

A Comprehensive budget reflects the national sources of income and heads of expenditure and also the surplus or deficit in a period under consideration. Dimock says "A budget is a financial plan summarizing the financial experience of the past, stating the current plan and projecting it over a specified period of time in future." Thus a budget is the keystone of financial administration and the various operations in the field of public finance are correlated through the instrument of budget. A budget is a financial report of statement and proposals which are periodically placed before the legislature for its approval and sanction. It is the report of the entire financial operations of the government and gives us a glimpse of future fiscal policy. Willoughby states "The real significance of the budget lies in providing for an orderly administration of the financial affairs of a government."

BUDGET SYSTEM IN INDIA

Budget in India is called 'Annual Financial Statement.' This statement is prepared separately for railways and other than railways or what is called a general budget. The states have their own budgets but the Parliament prepares budget for the country as a whole.

Another significant feature of the budget in India is its division into two categories, namely 'Voteable Budget' and 'Non-voteable Budget.' The non-voteable budget includes the salaries and allowances of such high dignitaries as the President of India, Chairman and Members of U.P.S.C., Chief Justice of India and such other dignitaries.

FORMULATION OF BUDGET

Heads of the offices are required to prepare preliminary estimates giving the developmental plans of their departments and approximate income and expenditure under each head. In case a department is interested in including a new item, it will have to give a detailed explanatory not for the purpose. The budget proposals thus prepared are scrutinized by the controlling officers, and finally passed on to the finance ministry. The Finance Ministry is empowered to cut down any proposal forwarded by any department.

The main idea of loading the Ministry of Finance with such responsibility is that it is not a spending ministry. Being overall in charge of all the proposals made by different departments, it has a very comprehensive picture of the situation and the finance limitations. In case a department feels that its proposals have unreasonably been turned down, the matter may be referred to the cabinet which is the final authority.

FORMAT OF THE BUDGET

All the budget estimates are prepared under three heads:

- *Part* I: Indicates establishment charges.
- *Part* II (a): Deals with such items of expenditure in which there is considerable fluctuation.
- *Part* II (b): Deals with such expenditure which is more or less not fluctuating in nature.
- *Part* III: Deals with the new items of expenditure on which the sanction of government is yet to be taken.

In India budget is prepared for the financial year which commences on 1st April and ends on 31st March of the succeeding year. A final shape is given only when the representative of departments, Accountant General and Ministry of Finance have come to the same conclusion.

BUDGETING AND BUDGETARY CONTROL

INTRODUCTION

Budgets can be prepared for and used by anyone and anything. That is, we can prepare and use personal budgets and organisations, ministries and non profit making organisations can all use them.

Budgets, by definition, have to be prepared in advance; and for this reason, they are often referred to in terms of their being part of a feedforward system. Feedback is a term frequently heard both in accounting and ordinary use. Feedforward, on the other hand tends to be less frequently heard, yet this word incorporates the most important aspect of budgeting: looking at situations in advance, thinking about the impact and implications of things in advance, attempting to take control of situations in advance.

BUDGETS

A budget is a plan expressed in quantitative and money terms. Budgets need to be prepared and approved in advance of the period in which they are to be used. Budgets can include some or all of income, expenditure, and the capital to be employed.

Moreover, a budget can be drawn up for an entire organization, any segment of the organization such as a department or sales territory or division, or for a significant activity such as the production and sale of a specific product.

We should also add that a budget can include non monetary as well as monetary information in it.

BUDGETARY CONTROL

Budgets are simply exercises in calculation unless they are used. When we use a budget, we do so as part of a system of budgetary control. That is, we have some basic ideas of what we want to do, we prepare budgets to help us achieve those ideas; and then once we have done whatever it is that we wanted to do, we check to see if we kept to our budget.

Budgetary control relates to the establishment of budgets relating the responsibilities of budget holders the needs of a policy. Budgetary control also relates to the continuous comparison of actual with budgeted results: it does this to try to ensure that the objectives of that policy are achieved; or to provide a basis for the change of those objectives.

In summary, a budget is a statement setting out the monetary, numerical or non quantitative aspects of an organisation's plans for the coming week or month or year. Budgetary control is the analysis of what happened when those plans came to be put into practice, and what the organisation did or did not do to correct for any variations from these plans.

THE BENEFITS OF BUDGETING

Many of us prepare budgets on a personal level: how much is my income for the month?; how much am I going to spend?; and, most importantly, is there anything left over? It seems true, however, that many businessmen do not prepare budgets for their businesses. Thus, even though managers prepare budgets for their relatively simple lives, when it comes to the much more complex situation of their business, they prefer to let cash inflows and outflows look after themselves. The purpose of this part of the chapter is to demonstrate that budgets are useful, informative and communicative. We will see that a budget is a necessity not a luxury.

We will also see some of the problems underlying organisations: the nature of the organisation and the interactions of the people working in them.

By considering these problems, we will be considering ways in which your budgeting system, or the organisation itself, can be changed, if necessary, to overcome them.

APPLICABILITY OF BUDGETING AND BUDGETARY CONTROL

Budgeting can be applied to virtually every situation. It does not matter whether we work in the Public or Private Sector of the Economy. We may work for a profit making business or a non profit making business. Your company may be engaged in trading, manufacturing, or providing a service. In all of these situations, budgeting and budgetary control is of use to you. As we will see, there are many issues underlying the use of a budgeting system that need careful consideration. For example, we will see that budgeting systems cannot just be imposed on an organisation nor do they run themselves. Managers at all levels often resent budgets and budget targets for a variety of reasons.

THE BUDGETING PROCESS

It would be easy to dismiss the budgeting process as beginning when the first budget is prepared, and as being complete when the master budget is finalised. In reality, the budgeting process begins for many organisations a long time before the budget period begins; and the process ends once the budget period has ended. This means the budgeting process is a very lengthy process: typically, for a large organisation, the pre budgeting phase can begin up to a year before the budget period starts.

Jones and Pendlebury (1984), pp62-63, give us some insight into the beginning of the budgeting cycle when they present a "Timetable for preparation of detailed revenue budget and capital programme" for a Local Authority. They show that the process starts in June in the year preceding the budget period with the draft budget manual being sent to Finance Officers, who will discuss this draft with their departmental staff (with a view to adoption or amendment). The budgetary planning phase is completed in March (ready for an April start) when the printed budget book is published and the approved estimates are put into the financial control system. (Colville (1989) presents a similar view, but this time of the budgeting for a Police Authority in the UK).

THE BUDGET PERIOD

The budget period is the period for which a set of budgets is prepared: typically the budget period is of one year's duration, and will be designed to coincide with an organisation's financial, or fiscal, year. There is no reason why a budget period has to be one year, but typically it is.

On the other hand, if we are dealing with a project, then the budget will clearly be linked to that project. A three month project will have a budget covering the whole project and will thus be a three months budget. Most organisations will divide their budget period into calendar months (or periods); whereas others have thirteen period years (all of an equal four week period). In certain situations, the budget period will be analysed according some particular feature of the work in that situation: for example, stockbrokers have their year divided into "accounts" of two and three weeks' duration. These divisions of a budget period are control periods.

BUDGET CENTRES

In a similar way to the way in which the financial year is divided, the organisation will be divided up into budget centres. A budget centre is one part of an organisation for which budgets are prepared. That is, a budget centre, like a cost or profit centre, is a section of an organisation (division, department, building, individual) for which a separate budget is prepared.

Whilst there is a lot of organisational work that is put into budgeting and budgetary control, this page is concerned mainly with an outline and understanding of the preparation aspects of budgets. A later page may deal with the organisational and strategic aspects of budgetary control.

INTERRELATIONSHIPS OF BUDGETS

One of the key reasons why management accountants and other planners are using spreadsheets more and more for budgeting purposes is because of the many inter relationships that exist in budgeting and budgetary control. If we are preparing budgets for our organisation we will quickly find that the sales budget has strong links with the stock budget and it has strong links with the cash budget.

When, then, the sales budget is changed, the stock and cash budgets will also have to change. Similarly, if the stock levels are changed, as a result of a revision of managerial policy during the budgeting process, say, then that could impact on both the sales and cash budgets.

The more complex the organisation and the more complex the processes within that organisation, the greater the number and variety of interrelationships that any budget for that organisation is bound to contain. The following diagram takes a general view of some of the interrelationships found in organisation. The diagram is relatively complex but we will find that a study of it helps us to understand the examples that follow.

Not all organisations have all of these interrelationships; and, as we saw above, some organisations prepare budgets only for part of the organisation so some aspects of the above diagram will apply to them and others will not.

Whenever you come across a budgeting and budgetary control situation, try to fit that situation to this diagram: make and not any changes you feel are necessary to the diagram following on from what you have found.

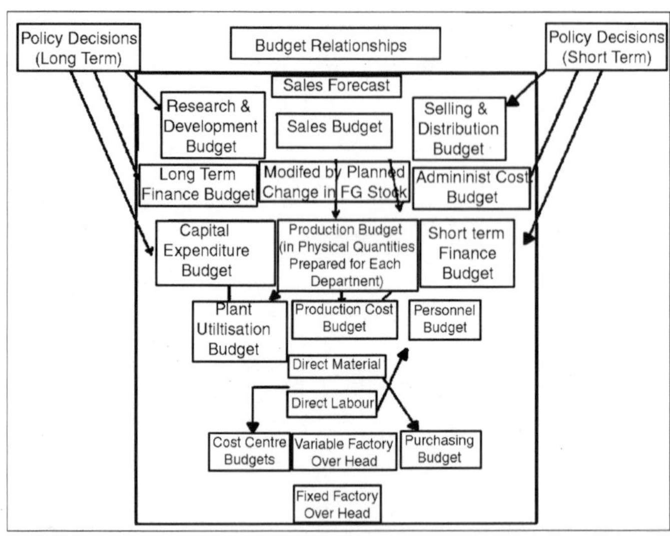

We can see that this diagram begins with the sales forecast and then the sales budget. This is not an accident; and it doesn't always have to be this way. The reason that sales are the starting point of the diagram is because the organisation on which the diagram is based must believe that sales are its limiting factor.

LIMITING FACTOR

In the example that follows, we will find: "As far as sales are concerned, they are fixed anyway: everything else depends on them." In the examples we are working through this will be true: everything the Andy's wholesaling organisation was does centres around its sales levels: both purchases and stock levels depended upon the level of sales for any given month. In this situation, Sales is considered to be the limiting factor (which is also known as the principal budget factor, and the key factor). The limiting factor is anything that limits the activity of an entity. Examples of limiting factors are shortages of supply of a resource and a restriction on sales at a particular price. That is, the limiting factor is the one factor that dominates all other factors: the limiting factor can be any factor that is important to the carrying out of the organisation's activities can be the limiting factor.

EXAMPLES OF THE LIMITING FACTOR

Each of the following can be, depending on the circumstances of the case, the limiting factor:

- Cash
- Raw materials
- Skilled labour
- Land
- Equipment

CRUCIAL ELEMENT CONCERNING

The most important point about the limiting factor, then, is that this must be the budget that is prepared before all others. There is no point in preparing every budget except the raw materials budget only to find that the assumptions built into all other budgets means that the amount of raw materials needed just cannot be acquired. Similarly, if cash is the limiting factor, preparing any budgets that take no account of the cash position may lead to a lot of unnecessary work having to be carried out. The following section uses an example to demonstrate the full impact of the inter relationships of budgets: it does so in a wholesaling environment.

WORKED EXAMPLE

Andy is a wholesaler of cricketing equipment: he trades in cricket bats, pads, gloves, sweaters and so on. Andy's territory covers much of the South and East of England and his business is sufficiently large that he needs to consider each product line as its own revenue centre. To this end, he prepares detailed budgets line by line. Consider the following details for his purchases and sales of cricket bats.

Andy's assessment of the coming season is that the weather will be hot and dry, and the demand for cricket bats will be high from June and for the rest of the season (until early September). After September, Andy will concentrate on his overseas business (selling to agents in India, Australia, New Zealand and South Africa).

Andy's 1994

	J	J	A	S	O	N	D
Sales (units)	950	950	750	600	600	500	600

Stocks at the end of any month is to be set at the level of 100 bats plus 20% of the number of bats scheduled to be sold in the following month.

REQUIRED

For the seven month period June to December 1994, prepare the stock and purchases budget and the sales budget: the selling price per bat is œ20 and the purchase price per bat is œ15. The first part of the solution to this example is the purchases budget, expressed in terms of units. The format is that we start the schedule with the opening stock, add purchases and subtract the closing stock to leave us with the sales amounts.

Purchases Budget (Units). Cricket bats 1994

	J	J	A	S	O	N	D
Balance b/d	290	290	250	220	220	200	220
Purchases	950	910	720	600	580	520	640
	1,240	1,200	970	820	800	720	860

Balance c/d	290	250	220	220	200	220	260
Sales	950	950	750	600	600	500	600

Once we have the units situation sorted out, it is a straight forward matter to multiply the relevant parts of the stock and purchases budget by the relevant cost and sales values, so that we obtain the stock, purchases and sales budgets expressed in terms of monetary amounts.

Stock Budget (£). Cricket bats

	J	J	A	S	O	N	D
Opening stock	4,350	4,350	3,750	3,300	3,300	3,000	3,300
Closing stock	4,350	3,750	3,300	3,300	3,000	3,300	3,900

Purchases budget (£). Cricket bats

	J	J	A	S	O	N	D
Purchases	14,250	13,650	10,800	9,000	8,700	7,800	9,600

Sales budget (£). Cricket bats

	J	J	A	S	O	N	D
Sales	19,000	19,000	15,000	12,000	12,000	10,000	12,000

INTERRELATIONSHIP ASPECTS

The interrelationship aspects of this example have probably not bothered us so far: the nature of interrela-tionships is that they often pass by unnoticed! In order to arrive at the purchases in units, we have had to determine the opening and closing stock amounts, and we were given the sales units. Thus, if we have calculated the stock budgets incorrectly, the purchase amounts will be wrong, and the purchases budget will be misleading. Similarly, an error in the sales budget guarantees an error in the purchase and stock budgets.

We can assess the extent of the interrelationships between the various budgets we are preparing by, for example, changing one of the variables involved in this example. Assume the stock levels are to be set at 50 bats plus 20% of the sales units for the following month: what effect does that have on the purchases, opening and closing stock budgets?

Stock and Purchase REVISED budget (Units). Cricket bats 1994

	J	**J**	**A**	**S**	**O**	**N**	**D**
Balance b/d	240	240	200	170	170	150	170
Purchases	950	910	720	600	580	520	640
	1190	1150	920	770	750	670	810
Balance c/d	240	200	170	170	150	170	210
Sales	950	950	750	600	600	500	600

Stock REVISED Budget (£). Cricket bats

	J	**J**	**A**	**S**	**O**	**N**	**D**
Openingstock	3,600	3,600	3,000	2,550	2,550	2,250	2,550

	J	J	A	S	O	N	D
Closingstock	3,600	3,000	2,550	2,550	2,250	2,550	3,150

Purchases REVISED budget (£). Cricket bats

	J	J	A	S	O	N	D
Purchases	14,250	13,650	10,800	9,000	8,700	7,800	9,600

The workings for these revised schedules are identical to the workings for the original budgets. The effects of what we have done are that the opening and closing stock units and values have changed, but the effect on purchases and sales has been nil. As far as sales are concerned, they are fixed anyway: everything else depends on them. Purchases can change with stock levels, but since the change to stock levels is constant between opening and closing stock, there is no overall change to purchases.

This page has introduced the basic ideas and theory underlying budgeting and budgetary control. We have explored the ideas underlying budgets: what they are and what they contain, whether that be monetary, qualitative or non quantitative aspects. We have also seen that budgeting needs to be used as part of a budgetary control system, otherwise budgets are merely arithmetical exercises that mean little. We have also seen the basic elements of the budgeting process, the budget period and budget centres. Finally, this page has also shown the interrelationships that exist between the various parts of a budget and the nature and meaning of the limiting factor.

A budget is a plan expressed in quantitative, usually monetary term, covering a specific period of time, usually one year. In other words a budget is a systematic plan for the utilization of manpower and material resources.

In a business organization, a budget represents an estimate of future costs and revenues. Budgets may be divided into two basic classes: Capital Budgets and Operating Budgets. Capital budgets are directed towards proposed expenditures for new projects and often require special financing. The operating budgets are directed towards achieving short-term operational goals of the organization, for instance, production or profit goals in a business firm. Operating budgets may be sub-divided into various departmental of functional budgets.

CHARACTERISTICS OF A BUDGET

- It is prepared in advance and is derived from the long-term strategy of the organization.
- It relates to future period for which objectives or goals have already been laid down.
- It is expressed in quantitative form, physical or monetary units, or both.

Different types of budgets are prepared for different purposed e.g. Sales Budget, Production Budget, Administrative Expense Budget, Raw-material

Budget etc. All these sectional budgets are afterwards integrated into a master budget, which represents an overall plan of the organization.

TYPES OF BUDGETS

A budget is a detailed plan of operations that is predetermined for a particular period. Budgets are quantitative or financial statements prepared for the purpose of attaining a particular objective.

BUDGETING PROCESS

Budgeting is the formal procedure of preparing budgets. It involves the following basic steps:

- Identifying expenses
- Determining different sources of income
- Preparing the budget
- Establishing the budget period
- Laying down the budget procedure
- Allocating income for expenses
- Monitoring the efficiency of the budget
- Re-assessing the budget

NATIONAL BUDGET

National budgets are legal documents, which are provided by legislatures before being passed by the executive head of the nation, such as the president, prime minister or other chief official of a nation.

The budgeting process of a nation involves:

Classifying expenses: The expenses allocated in a government budget include consumption and investment expenditure on infrastructure development and research and development. It also includes transfer payments, such as social security and unemployment benefits.

Revenue determination: The primary source of revenue generation for a government budget is taxes. *Preparing budgets*: A government budget may be for a quarter, a year, five years or ten years. The period of the budget and the procedure of revenue allocation are exclusively mentioned by the government. Examples of specific country budgeting processes, such as those in US, Canada, UK, Germany, Australia, New Zealand, Japan, India and Brazil, are detailed at the end of this article.

COMPANY BUDGET

A company budget is prepared by the owner and shareholders of the company. It may also be prepared with the inputs of other stakeholders, such as employees and creditors.

The budgeting process of a company involves:

- *Categorizing Expenses*: Business expenses include capital expenditure on acquisition and modification of assets and revenue expenditure on routine activities such as payment of electricity and rent.

- *Revenue calculation*: Sources of business revenue include capital, borrowed funds and sale of goods.
- *Budget preparation*: This is generally prepared for a financial year. The purpose of the budget is to allocate funds for various business activities, such as production and distribution.

PERSONAL BUDGET

A personal budget is prepared by individuals and families to allocate income for various expenses, savings, investments and other financial obligations, such as debts. A personal budget is prepared by:

Organizing expenses: Personal expenses include expenditure on present consumption or future savings and investments. This includes incorporation of travel and leisure expenses and savings for the education fund of children.Revenue summation: An individual earns an income from a number of sources, including salary, social security, worker's compensation and rent collection.

Budget preparation: This is generally prepared on a weekly or monthly basis. The idea of a personal budget is to allocate income for various expenses, while setting aside a portion for savings.

The budgeting process of governments, companies and individuals involves re-evaluation and revision of the budget. The budget is periodically monitored with respect to established targets and results obtained. Shortcomings in the outcome are evaluated and necessary modifications are made in the future budget to avoid unnecessary expenses.

COUNTRY BUDGETS

US Budget

United States government budget is a federal document submitted by U.S. president to Congress not earlier than first Monday of January and not later than February's first Monday. US budget is for following fiscal year beginning 1st October.

Budget resolutions are developed separately by Senate and House budget committees, which provide spending limits for different subcommittees of Senate and House Appropriations Committees. Subsequently, these Appropriations Committees approve appropriation bills allocating funds for different federal programs.

After being approved by Congress these appropriation bills are sent to President for his signature into a law. President might also veto that bill, which once again is placed before Congress who in turn can pass it into a law by passing it by two-thirds majority in each chamber. U.S. President may also request Congress to pass supplementary or emergency appropriation bills. Budget data and analysis are provided by Congressional Budget Office, U.S. Treasury Department, Government Accountability Office, and Office of Management and Budget.

CANADA BUDGET

Canadian federal budget is presented annually and released in February or March for forthcoming fiscal year from 1st April to 31st March. This budget announced by Minister of Finance in House of Commons is put to vote. It is important that budget receives votes of members of House of Commons.

This being a confidence measure, counter-voting can result in collapse of ruling government. Provincial budgets, dependent onmoney received from federal government, are released after acceptance of federal budget.

UK BUDGET

UK budgeting procedure deals with receipts of Her Majesty's Customs and Revenue and expenditure of public sector departments. Annual budget in UK is from 6th April of one financial year to 5th April of next financial year.

GERMANY BUDGET

Budget of Germany is passed by Bundestag for a period of one or two years. Expenses and revenues are calculated for each single ministry and other administrative units for fiscal period extend from 1st January to 31st December. This budget is enacted before commencement of a fiscal year.

AUSTRALIA BUDGET

Federal budget in Australia is initiated in November with Accrual Information Management System meeting their Prime Minister, Federal Treasurer, Minister for Administration and Finance. This Senior Ministers' Review determines budget submissions of different portfolios to Cabinet. Thereafter in March, an Expenditure Review Committee meets to consider all budgetary submissions.

Commonwealth Treasurer on second Tuesday of May or 'budget night' presents budget at Parliament House. Australian budget is effective for fiscal period 1st July of a fiscal to 30th June next year.

NEW ZEALAND BUDGET

Budget in New Zealand is presented by their finance minister in New Zealand House of Representatives. Budget process in New Zealand is divided into a number of phases: i) Strategic Phase wherein all targets for revenues, expenditures, public debt and fiscal surplus are set; ii) Initiatives Phase where budget submissions are reviewed; iii) Parliamentary Phase entails garnering parliamentary support for this budget package; and iv) Implementation Phase in which subsequent amendments might be considered.

New Zealand's budget policy statement must be tabled in Parliament not later than 31st March for forthcoming fiscal year beginning 1st April and ending on 31st March.

JAPAN BUDGET

Fiscal year in Japan is from 1st April to 31st March during when their annual budget remains effective.

Budgetary process in Japan begins with budgetary requests of ministries to Ministry of Finance (MOF) by August end. These requisitions are subject to an upward expenditure ceiling fixed by their Cabinet. Thereafter, examinations of these proposals are done by Budget Bureau of Finance Ministry.

Additional data or supporting material may be requested by this Budget Bureau from individual ministries. After this process is over by early December, MOF releases 'budget formulation guidelines' based on which a 'draft budget' is prepared. This 'draft budget' after being finalized by MOF is sent to various ministries and agencies before getting it authorized by cabinet. Cabinet approves this 'draft budget' by end December.

In final stages, this 'draft budget' is presented to 'Diet' towards second half of January. After being deliberated upon by Budget Committee of House of Representatives this 'draft budget' is put to voting. Subsequently it is sent to House of Councilors where a similar procedure is followed. After being passed by House of Councilors, this 'budget' becomes effective from 1st April.

INDIA BUDGET

Budget in India for fiscal year 1st April to 31st March is presented by Finance Minister to Parliament on 28th February or 29th February in case of a leap year.

Preparation of Indian budget is an exhaustive process which involves preparation of 'annual financial statements', 'demand for grants', 'appropriation bill', 'finance bill', 'memorandum explaining provisions in finance bill', 'macro-economic framework for relevant financial year', 'fiscal policy statement for concerned financial year', 'medium term fiscal policy statement', 'expenditure budget volumes', 'receipts budget', and 'highlights of budget'.

Budget bill is passed in both Houses of Parliament, that is Lok Sabha and Rajya Sabha before being finally presented.

BRAZIL BUDGET

Brazilian federal budget is presented by their President to National Congress of Brazil in September for fiscal period 1st January to 31st December.

STATIC AND FLEXIBLE BUDGETING

WHAT IS A STATIC BUDGET

A static budget is a budget that does not change as volume changes. If a company's annual master budget is a static budget, the budget for sales commissions expense will be one amount such as $200,000 for the year. In other words, in a static budget the budgeted amount for sales commissions expense will remain at $200,000 even if the actual sales during the year are $3 million, $4 million or $5 million.

In contrast to a company's static master budget, the company's sales department might have a flexible budget. In the flexible budget, the sales commissions expense budget might be expressed as 5% of sales. In that instance, the department's budget for sales commissions expense will be $200,000 when actual sales are $4 million, but it will decrease to $150,000 when actual sales are $3 million, and the budget will increase to $300,000 when actual sales are $6 million, and so on.

FLEXIBLE BUDGET

A flexible budget is a budget that adjusts or flexes for changes in the volume of activity. The flexible budget is more sophisticated and useful than a static budget, which remains at one amount regardless of the volume of activity.

Assume that a manufacturer determines that its cost of electricity and supplies for the factory are approximately $10 per machine hour (MH). It also knows that the factory supervision, depreciation, and other fixed costs are approximately $40,000 per month. Typically, the production equipment operates between 4,000 and 7,000 hours per month. Based on this information, the flexible budget for each month would be $40,000 + $10 per MH.

Now let's illustrate the flexible budget by using some data. If the production equipment is required to operate for 5,000 hours during January, the flexible budget for January will be $90,000 ($40,000 fixed + $10 x 5,000 MH). If the equipment is required to operate in February for 6,300 hours, then the flexible budget for February will be $103,000 ($40,000 fixed + $10 x 6,300 MH). If March requires only 4,100 machine hours, the flexible budget for March will be $81,000 ($40,000 fixed + $10 x 4,100 MH).

If the plant manager is required to use more machine hours, it is logical to increase the plant manager's budget for the additional cost of electricity and supplies. The manager's budget should also decrease when the need to operate the equipment is reduced. In short, the flexible budget provides a better opportunity for planning and controlling than does a static budget.

A budget is a plan for the future. Hence, budgets are planning tools, and they are usually prepared prior to the start of the period being budgeted. However, the comparison of the budget to actual results provides valuable information about performance. Therefore, budgets are both planning tools and performance evaluation tools.

Usually, the single most important input in the budget is some measure of anticipated output. For a factory, this measure of output is the number of units of each product produced. For a retailer, it might be the number of units of each product sold. For a hospital, it is the number of patient days (the number of patient admissions multiplied by the average length of stay).

The static budget is the budget that is based on this projected level of output, prior to the start of the period. In other words, the static budget is the "original" budget. The static budget variance is the difference between any line-item in this original budget and the corresponding line-item from the statement of actual results. Often, the line-item of most interest is the "bottom line": total cost of production for the factory and other cost centers; net income for profit centers.

The flexible budget is a performance evaluation tool. It cannot be prepared before the end of the period. A flexible budget adjusts the static budget for the actual level of output. The flexible budget asks the question: *"If I had known at the beginning of the period what my output volume (units produced or units sold) would be, what would my budget have looked like?"* The motivation for the flexible budget is to compare apples to apples.

If the factory actually produced 10,000 units, then management should compare actual factory costs for 10,000 units to what the factory should have spent to make 10,000 units, not to what the factory should have spent to make 9,000 units or 11,000 units or any other production level.

The flexible budget variance is the difference between any line-item in the flexible budget and the corresponding line-item from the statement of actual results.

The following steps are used to prepare a flexible budget:

- Determine the budgeted variable cost per unit of output. Also determine the budgeted sales price per unit of output, if the entity to which the budget applies generates revenue (e.g., the retailer or the hospital).
- Determine the budgeted level of fixed costs.
- Determine the actual volume of output achieved (e.g., units produced for a factory, units sold for a retailer, patient days for a hospital).
- Build the flexible budget based on the budgeted cost information from steps 1 and 2, and the actual volume of output from step 3.

Flexible budgets are prepared at the end of the period, when actual output is known. However, the same steps described above for creating the flexible budget can be used prior to the start of the period to anticipate costs and revenues for any projected level of output, where the projected level of output is incorporated at step 3.

If these steps are applied to various anticipated levels of output, the analysis is called pro forma analysis. Pro forma analysis is useful for planning purposes. For example, if next year's sales are double this year's sales, what will be the company's cash, materials, and labour requirements in order to meet production needs?

Pro Forma Analysis at Guess Who Jeans

Following are pro forma monthly income statements for Guess Who Jeans, a small, start-up fashion jeans manufacturer. The pro forma analysis was prepared at the beginning of the month and considered three alternative sales levels. The company has no variable marketing costs.

Table. Guess who Jeans Pro Forma Analysis For The Upcoming Month

Income Statement line-item	Budgeted amount per unit	Pro Forma Analysis for Alternative Output Levels		
		10,000 units	20,000 units	30,000 units
Revenue	$40	$400,000	$800,000	$1,200,000
Variable costs:				
Materials	15	150,000	300,000	450,000
Labor	10	100,000	200,000	300,000
Overhead	5	50,000	100,000	150,000
Total	30	300,000	600,000	900,000
Contribution margin	$10	100,000	200,000	300,000
Fixed costs:				
Manufacturing Overhead		100,000	100,000	100,000
Marketing costs		50,000	50,000	50,000
Total fixed costs		150,000	150,000	150,000
Operating income		($50,000)	$50,000	$150,000

Since by definition, fixed costs are not expected to change as volume of output changes within the relevant range, fixed costs remain the same at all three projected levels of output. Revenue and variable costs vary with output in a linear fashion. Hence, when output increases 100% from 10,000 units to 20,000 units, revenue, each line-item for variable costs, and contribution margin all increase 100%.

Static Budget Variance at Guess Who Jeans

Guess Who management decides that 10,000 units is the most likely output volume, and sets the static budget based on this sales and production level.

After the end of the month, company personnel prepare the following table, showing the static budget, actual results, and the static budget variance.

Table:Guess Who Jeans Static Budget Variance For The Month Just Ended

Income Statement line-item	Budgeted amount per unit	Static Budget (A) 10,000 units	Actual Results (B) 16,000 units	Static Budget Variance (A) – (B)
Revenue	$40	$400,000	$670,000	$270,000
Variable costs.				
Materials	15	150,000	230,000	(80,000)
Labor	10	100,000	167,000	(67,000)
Overhead	5	50,000	84,000	(34,000)
Total	30	300,000	481,000	(181,000)
Contribution margin	$10	100,000	189,000	89,000
Fixed costs.				
Manufacturing Overhead		100,000	105,000	(5,000)
Marketing costs		50,000	49,000	1,000
Total fixed costs		150,000	154,000	(4,000)
Operating income		($50,000)	$35,000	$85,000

In the variance column, positive numbers are favorable variances (good news), and negative numbers are unfavorable (bad news). The static budget variance shows a large favorable variance for revenue, and large unfavorable variances for variable costs. These large variances are due primarily to the fact that the static budget was built on an output level of 10,000 units, while the company actually made and sold 16,000 units. The revenue variance might also be due to an average unit sales price that differed from budget. The variable cost variances might also be due to input prices that differed from budget (e.g., the price of fabric), or input quantities that differed from the per-unit budgeted amounts (e.g., yards of fabric per pair of pants).

There are also small variances for fixed costs. These costs should not vary with the level of output (at least within the relevant range). However, many factors can cause actual fixed costs to differ from budgeted fixed costs that are unrelated to output volume. For example, property tax rates and the fixed salaries of front office personnel can change, and depreciation expense can change if unexpected capital acquisitions or dispositions occur.

FLEXIBLE BUDGET VARIANCE AT GUESS WHO JEANS

In order to better understand the causes of the large revenue and variable cost variances in the static budget variance column, Guess Who personnel prepare the following flexible budget. From this table, Guess Who management sees that even after adjusting for sales volume, revenue was higher than would have been expected.

The favorable $30,000 variance must be due entirely to an average sales price that was higher than planned (almost $42 per pair compared to the original budget of $40 per pair). Materials costs were lower than would have been expected for a sales volume of 16,000 units. This favorable variance could be due to lower fabric prices, or to more efficient utilization of fabric (less waste than expected), or a combination of these two factors. Labour and overhead were higher than expected, even after adjusting for the sales volume of 16,000 units.

Table. Guess Who Jeans Flexible Budget Variance For The Month Just Ended

Income Statement line-item	**Budgeted amount per unit**	**Flexible Budget (A) 16,000 units**	**Actual Results (B) 16,000 units**	**Flexible Budget Variance (A) – (B)**
Revenue	$40	$640,000	$670,000	$30,000
Variable costs:				
Materials				
Labor	15	240,000	230,000	10,000
Overhead	10	160,000	167,000	(7,000)
Total	5	80,000	84,000	(4,000)
	30	480,000	481,000	(1,000)
Contribution margin				
	$10	160,000	189,000	29,000
Fixed costs:				
Manufacturing Overhead				
Marketing costs		100,000	105,000	(5,000)
Total fixed costs		50,000	49,000	1,000.
		150,000	154,000	(4,000)
Operating income				
		$10,000	$35,000	$25,000

Once again, positive variances are favorable (good news), and negative variances are unfavorable (bad news). This unfavorable flexible budget variance implies that either wage rates were higher than planned, or labour was not as efficient as planned, or both.

Similarly, the components of variable overhead were either more expensive than budgeted, or were used more intensively than budgeted. For example, electric rates might have been higher than planned, or more electricity was used than planned per unit of output.

The fixed cost variances are identical in this table to the previous table. In other words, the flexible budget and flexible budget variance provide no additional information about fixed costs beyond what can be learned from the static budget variance.

PREPARATION OF CASH BUDGET

OVERVIEW

Just as you would not purchase new furniture for your home without enough cash, or at least a solid plan to cover a personal loan from your bank, your business needs the same careful handling of its expenditures.

All businesses, no matter what type or size, need to properly develop a plan for their expected cash intake and spending. This plan is commonly known as a cash budget, and it can be prepared quarterly or annually.

PURPOSES OF CASH BUDGETING

Properly preparing your cash budget will show how cash flows in and out of your business. Also, it may then be used in planning your short-term credit needs.

In today's financial world, you are required by most financial institutions to prepare cash budgets before making capital expenditures for new assets as well as for expenditures associated with any planned expansion.

The cash budget determines your future ability to pay debts as well as expenses. For example, preliminary budget estimates may reveal that your disbursements are lumped together and that, with more careful planning, you can spread your payments to creditors more evenly throughout the entire year. As a result, less bank credit will be needed and interest costs will be lower.

Banks and other credit-granting institutions are more inclined to grant you loans under favorable terms if your loan request is supported by a methodical cash plan. Similarly, businesses that operate on a casual day-to-day basis are more likely to borrow funds at inopportune times and in excessive amounts. Without planning, there is no certainty that you will be able to repay your loans on schedule.

However, once you've carefully mapped out a cash budget, you will be able to compare it to the actual cash inflows and outflows of your business. You will find that this comparison will go a long way in assisting you during future cash budget preparation. Also, a monthly cash budget helps pinpoint estimated cash balances at the end of each month which may foresee short-term cash shortfalls.

CONSISTENT BUDGETS

Cash budgeting is a continuous process that can be checked for consistency and accuracy by comparing budgeted amounts with amounts that can be expected from using typical ratios or financial statement relationships.

For example, your treasurer will estimate the payments made to your suppliers of merchandise or materials, the payments to employees for wages and salaries, and the other payments that you are obligated to make.

These payments can be scheduled by dates so that all discounts will be taken, and so that no obligation will be overlooked when it comes due. Cash collections from customers can also be estimated and scheduled by dates along with other expected cash receipts. With careful cash planning, you should be able to maintain a sufficient cash balance for your needs and not put yourself in the position of holding excessive balances of nonproductive cash.

In the normal course of operations in a merchandising business, for example, merchandise is purchased and sold to customers who eventually pay for the merchandise sold to them. Usually there is a time lag in business operations. It may be necessary to pay the suppliers for merchandise before the merchandise is sold to the customers.

Before and during a busy selling season the demand for cash may be higher than the inflow of cash from operations. In this case it may be necessary to arrange short-term loans. When the selling season is over, cash collections from customers will be relatively large and the loans can be paid off.

EXAMPLE OF A CASH BUDGET

The following is an example of a cash budget for the 90 days provided below for the XYZ Company.

Table. Cash Budget For 90 Days

Beginning cash balance	$ 320,000
Add:	
Estimated collections on accounts receivable	750,000
Estimated cash sales	250,000
	$1,320,000
Deduct:	
Estimated payments on accounts payable	$ 800,000
Estimated cash expenses	150,000
Contractual payments on long-term debt	150,000
Quarterly dividend	50,000
	$1,150,000
Estimated ending cash balance	$ 170,000

ANALYSIS OF EXAMPLE CASH BUDGET

Analysis of the financial statements of the XYZ Company shows that the accounts receivable remain at about $500,000 throughout the year; that is, there is no seasonal fluctuation in sales. The account's receivable turns over six times a year, or once every 60 days. The inventory throughout the year remains at about $800,000 and turns over every 90 days. The accounts payable remains at about $400,000 and turns over eight times a year, about once every 45 days.

With an accounts receivable collection period of 60 days and an average balance outstanding of $500,000, it appears that $750,000 is the amount that should be collected on the receivables in 90 days. Cash sales should amount to about $250,000 if the inventory of $800,000 valued at cost turns over once in 90 days and if the average markup is about $200,000. Therefore, if an inventory of $1,000,000 at retail turns over once every 90 days and $750,000 flows through accounts receivable, then approximately $250,000 must be sold on a cash basis. Cash payments for expenses are estimated to be $150,000 in the next 90 days. This figure can be roughly checked by referring to the expenses on the income statement. A rough measure of the cash expenses can usually be obtained by using the operating expenses less any non-cash expenses such as depreciation. For example, if there is no seasonal factor, the total amount divided by four should be an approximate check on the amount budgeted for the next 90 days.

CHECKING REASONABLENESS OF BUDGET

If it appears that the budgeted amounts will differ substantially from ratios and relationships taken from past statements, then further attention should be given to the budget. For instance, some factors may have been overlooked in budgeting, or past statement relationships may no longer be applicable, due to unrecognized changes.

SALES AND POTENTIAL CASH SOURCES

Normally, sales activity is expected to produce the bulk of the cash receipts. If sales are made on a credit basis, accounts receivable will eventually be translated into cash as the customers pay their accounts. The time required to collect outstanding accounts will have to be estimated, and provisions must be made for discounts, returns, allowances granted, and uncollectable accounts. In addition to sales, there are many other potential cash sources. These sources must be examined for possible additions to cash when setting up a total cash receipts budget for the year.

Dividends and interest may be collected on investments or cash may be received from an incidental operation (i.e., rent or sale of scrap material). Ordinarily, cash will be realized from the sale of investments in stocks and bonds and from the sale of machinery or other assets not incurred in the normal course of trade.

As a result of cash flow, stock may be issued or debt may be incurred with cash flowing. The various cost budgets, plans for capital acquisitions, commitments for the discharge of debt, and plans for dividend payments are brought together in a cash disbursements budget. If possible, payments will be scheduled at convenient times, when cash balances are expected to be sufficiently high.

Frequently, the demand for cash is not spread evenly throughout the year. Several large payments may become due in one particular month. If cash receipts in that month are not expected to be sufficient, the company will either plan to hold back cash for these payments or will borrow. It is unlikely that disbursements will be made in every instance when costs are incurred or when materials and services are used. Advertising, insurance and rent, for example, are often paid in advance with the cost being absorbed against future operations. A debt of cash disbursements is made by scheduling payments required for materials, labour, other operating costs, dividends, debt service, and so forth.

Budgeted cash receipts and disbursements are brought together to form a total cash budget. From this summary of estimated cash flow, it is possible to anticipate future cash balances. In some months, receipts may not be large enough to cover disbursements. If this happens, the cash balance will have to be reduced. If the outflow of cash is too great, plans will have to be made to borrow funds. In other months, when receipts are greater than disbursements, loans can be repaid and cash balances can be built up.

RESERVE

Financial plans are drawn up so that a minimum balance of cash will be available at all times. The amount to be held will depend on estimated future cash flows and the financial policy adopted. In general, the cash balance should be large enough to enable the company to meet its payrolls and pay its operating costs for the next month, with some allowance made for contingencies and miscalculations in planning.

By holding adequate cash balances, management can cope with small adversities and will not be forced to borrow under unfavorable conditions. If trouble strikes, there will be a reserve to draw upon. While the reserve is being used, management can make alternate plans and can secure additional cash from other sources to meet future needs. Opinions differ as to what amount of cash should be held in reserve.

Some companies maintain fairly substantial cash balances as well as a secondary reserve that consists of investments that can easily be converted into cash. Other companies prefer to operate with small cash reserves and when cash is needed depend on a line of credit which is established at a bank. Cash up to a certain limit may be borrowed when needed and arrangements are made for eventual repayment.

PREPARING A CASH BUDGET

At its most basic level, a budget is a plan for owners and managers to achieve their goals for the company during a specific time period. Learn the fundamental concepts of cash budgets and to evaluate your budget on a month-to-month basis.

- Time Period
- Desired Cash Position
- Estimated Sales and Expenses
- Blank Worksheet

What to Expect

This Business Builder will introduce you to the fundamental concepts of cash budgets and outline the steps necessary for preparing a cash budget for your business. It will also show you how to evaluate your budget on a month-to-month basis. This Business Builder assumes that an income statement and a balance sheet have been prepared for your business. Information from these financial statements are an integral part of creating a budget. Without this information, this Business Builder may not be as helpful as it could be.

IDEA

At its most basic level, a budget is a plan. It is a plan for owners and managers to achieve their goals for the company during a specific time period.

The preparation of a cash budget is an important management task. While some small businesses may be able to survive for a time without budgeting, savvy business owners will realise its importance. A cash budget can protect a company from being unprepared for seasonal fluctuations in cash flow or prepare a company to take advantage of unexpected quantity discounts from suppliers. While there are other types of budgets that can be prepared, such as projected or pro forma financial statements, a cash budget is a management plan for the most important factor of a company's viability its cash position. A company's cash position determines how suppliers will be paid, how a banker will respond to a loan request, how fast a company can grow, as well as directly influencing dividends, increases to owner's equity, and profitability.

Many Small Businesses Find It Helpful To Prepare Monthly Cash Budgets And To Analyse Any Variances Between The Bud geted And Actual Amounts On A Monthly Basis. This enables small business owners and managers to stay on top of any unexpected cash uses.

Watch out for: The creation of a cash budget requires you to make estimates (or best guesses) about many different aspects of your company and the environment in which it operates. Future sales will be contingent on many things, not the least of which is competition, the local economic climate and your own internal operations and capacity. In addition, after sales are estimated, potential costs must also be derived. The important thing to keep in mind while arriving at these figures is that past experience is important, but so is intuition. The estimates you will need to develop must be based in reality and yet contain a dose of creativity and, if warranted, optimism.

There are budgets, other than the cash budget, that are important for your company. However, the cash budget is a good first step if you are new to budgeting. Acash Budget Cannot Be Created In A Vacuum. Before and during the budgeting process, business owners must consult with line managers, suppliers, and key personnel to make the best guess possible about the relationship between the goals for the period and their effect on cash receipts and cash expenditures.

Why Prepare a Cash Budget

A cash budget is important for a variety of reasons. For one, it allows you to make management decisions regarding your cash position (or cash reserve). Without the type of monitoring imposed by the budgeting process, you may be unaware of the cycle of cash through your business. At the end of a year or a business cycle, a series of monthly cash budgets will show you just how much cash is coming into your company and the way it is being used. Seasonal fluctuations will be made clear.

A cash budget also allows you to evaluate and plan for your capital needs. The cash budget will help you assess whether there are periods during your operations cycle when you might need short-term borrowing. It will also help you assess any long-term borrowing needs. Basically, a cash budget is a planning tool for management decisions.

How To Create A Cash Budget

There are three main components necessary for creating a cash budget. *They are*:

- Time period
- Desired cash position
- Estimated sales and expenses

Time Period

The first decision to make when preparing a cash budget is to decide the period of time for which your budget will apply. That is, are you preparing a budget for the next three months, six months, twelve months or some other period? In this Business Builder, we will be preparing a 3-month budget. However, the instructions given are applicable to any time period you might select.

Cash Position

The amount of cash you wish to keep on hand will depend on the nature of your business, the predictability of accounts receivable and the probability of fast-happening opportunities (or unfortunate occurrences) that may require you to have a significant reserve of cash.

You may want to consider your cash reserve in terms of a certain number of days' sales. Your budgeting process will help you to determine if, at the end of the period, you have an adequate cash reserve.

Estimated Sales And Expenses

The fundamental concept of a cash budget is estimating all future cash receipts and cash expenditures that will take place during the time period. The most important estimate you will make, however, is an estimate of sales. Once this is decided, the rest of the cash budget can fall into place.

If an increase in sales of, for example, 10 per cent, is desired and expected, various other accounts must be adjusted in your budget. Raw materials, inventory and the costs of goods sold must be revised to reflect the increase in sales. In addition, you must ask yourself if any additions need to be made to selling or general and administrative expenses, or can the increased sales be handled by current excess capacity? Also, how will the increase in sales affect payroll and overtime expenditures?

Instead of increasing every expense item by 10 per cent, serious consideration needs to be given to certain economies of scale that might develop. In other words, perhaps, a supplier offers a discount if you increase the quantities in which you buy a certain item or, perhaps, the increase in sales can be easily accommodated by the current sales force, all of these types of considerations must be taken into account before you start budgeting.

Each type of expense (as shown on your income statement) must be evaluated for its potential to increase or decrease. Your estimates should be based on our experience running your business and on your goals for your business over the time frame for which the budget is being created. At a minimum, the following categories of expected cash receipts and expected cash payments should be considered:

- Cash balance
  - *Expected cash receipts*:
  - Cash sales
  - Collections of accounts receivable
  - Other income
- Expected cash expenses:
  - Raw material (inventory)
  - Payroll
- *Other direct expenses*:
  - Advertising
  - Selling expenses
  - Administrative expense
  - Plant and equipment expenditures
  - Other payments

Following is a Description of Each Line Item

Cash balance: The cash balance is your cash on hand. This includes what is in your checking accounts, savings accounts, petty cash and any other cash accounts that you might have.

- *Cash sales:* After arriving at a base figure of cash sales, it must be adjusted for any trade or other discounts and for possible returns. As stated previously, the base level of sales (and of accounts receivable) will be determined by the company's projections, goals and past experience.

- *Collections of accounts receivable*: After a base level of accounts receivable is established (based on sales projections), it must be adjusted to reflect the amount that will actually be paid during the time period. Typical adjustments for a small business might be to assume that 90 per cent of accounts receivable will be collected in the quarter in which the sales occur, 9 per cent will be collected in the following quarter, and 1 per cent will remain uncollectible. Of course, past experience will be the most reliable indicator for making these adjustments.

Other income: Your cash position may be affected positively by income other than that received from sales. Perhaps there are investments, dividends, or an expected borrowing that will be introducing cash to the company during the time period. These types of cash sources are referred to as "other income."

Expected Cash Expenses

- Raw Materials (inventory).
- For small business retailers and manufacturers, the largest cash expense is usually the amount spent for inventory or raw materials. Again, past experience will be your best indicator of future cash outlays. But don't forget to factor in any necessary increases to keep up with projected sales. You may also want to consult with your suppliers as to whether any pricing changes are expected.
- Payroll.
- Salaries are commonly the second largest expense item during an accounting period. Don't forget to include estimates for all appropriate local, state, and federal taxes.
- Other Direct Expe nses.
- Use this line item for any additional expense that does not fit conveniently under the other headings. If you are making payments on a loan, include it here.
- Advertising.
- The role of advertising varies by type of business. If you are projecting an increase in sales, is there an accompanying marketing or advertising campaign? These costs must be budgeted. Include any expenses for print (brochures, mailers, and newspaper ads), radio, or other advertising services.
- Selling Expenses.
- Typical selling expenses include salaries and commissions for sales personnel and sales office expenses. However, this line item can also include any traveling or other sales-related expense not covered elsewhere.
- Administrative Expenses.
- General office expenses are included here. This will include your

utilities, telephone, copying and day-to-day office expenses. Unless big changes are underway, past experience will guide you in evaluating future administrative expenses.

- Plant And Equipment.
- Cash payments for equipment loans, mortgages, repairs, or other upkeep should be included here. Past experience will, again, be your guide.
- Other Payments.
- If there are any cash payments you expect to make that are not covered in the above listing, include them here. (If they are repeatable, you may consider adding a separate line item.) However, typically, interest payments and taxes fall here.

Table. Small Business Cash Budget

Item	Jan	Feb	March
Beginning cash balance	15,000	-13,500	20,000
Expected Cash Receipts:			
Cash Sales	20,000	25,000	30,000
Collection of accounts receivable	45,000	55,000	70,000
Other income	0	0	5,000
Total cash collected	80,000	66,500	125,000
Expected cash payments:			
Raw materials (or inventory)	50,000	11,000	5,000
Payroll	10,400	10,400	10,400
Other direct expenses	2,000	2,000	2,000
Advertising	10,000	0	0
Selling expense	6,000	8,000	6,000
Administrative expense	4,500	4,500	4,500
Plant and equipment expenditures	10,000	10,000	10,000
Other payments	600	600	600
Total cash expenses	93,500	46,500	38,500
Cash surplus (or deficit)	-13,500	20,000	86,500

Step 1: Create A Cash Budget For Your Company For A Three Month Period.

Analyse A Cash Budget

The preparation of a cash budget is only the first step toward good financial management. The next step is to analyse to see how close the company is performing to expectations. Have any unexpected cash outflows occurred? If so, is the company's financial position seriously affected?

A simple method for monitoring the cash budget is to prepare a budget-versus-actual report of actual and budgeted expenses every month. This type of report consists of three columns. The first column shows the budgeted amounts, the second column shows actual company performance, and the third column shows the difference in terms of a per cent.

Below is a sample month-end budget report for the fictional Turtle Company.

Item	**Budget**	**Actual**	**Variance**
Cash balance	5,000	5,000	0%
Cash Receipts:			
Cash sales	20,000	22,000	110%
Collection of accounts receivable	15,000	13,500	90%
Other income	0	0	
Total cash	40,000	40,500	101%
Cash payments:			
Raw materials (or inventory)	15,000	15,000	100%
Payroll	7,200	9,400	130%
Other direct expenses	500	500	100%
Advertising	500	1,000	200%
Selling expense	1,500	1,400	93%
Administrative expense	500	500	100%
Plant and equipment expenditures	5,000	7,500	150%
Other payments	0	0	
Total cash expenses	30,200	35,300	116%
Cash surplus (or deficit)	9,800	5,200	53%

As you can see, cash expenses for payroll, advertising and plant and equipment exceeded the budgeted amounts for the Turtle Company. But because the company analyses these figures monthly, changes can be made before the increased expenses become unmanageable. The use of an budget vs. actual report allows owners to pinpoint how actual cash inflows and outflows vary from expectations and to make adjustments.

Step 2: If The Data Is Available, Construct A Budgeted Versus Actual Report For Your Business.

This Business Builder focuses on the creation of a cash budget for your business. While there are several other types of budgets that can be prepared, small business owners should pay close attention to their cash position and create a cash budget for their company. Preparing a monthly budget vs. actual report will give small business owners the information they need to make important decisions about the cash position of their company.

CHECKLIST

- When preparing your cash budget, did you remember to make the ending cash balance the beginning cash balance for the next period?
- When estimating cash expenses, did you remember to factor any additional material, labour or other expenses for projected sales?

- Is your sales goal for the period realistic?
- Did you remember to adjust accounts receivable for possible uncollectible amounts?
- Do expenditures for payroll include taxes?

SALES BUDGET

THE SALES BUDGET

We need to forecast the volume of sales to understand the possible revenue that the business will generate. Sales are estimated in physical units of production and dollar values, as we saw earlier in the breakeven point section.

To enable us to forecast sales for the budget period we can use a number of methods and some are listed below:

Customer Surveys

Customer surveys include surveys of past customers as well as future customers and groups identified as being possible customers. These groups can provide information that will assist in predicting future trends in sales, such as whether sales demand will increase, decrease or remain stable.

Market Research

Market research can be carried out by organisations that specialise in this field and are skilled in market research techniques.

Market research will enable those preparing the budget to make decisions on possible changes in the market and to identify new markets to move their products and services into.

Statistical Analysis

Statistical analysis will enable those preparing the budget to predict possible future demand. Statistical analysis can be as simplistic as calculating averages based on past sales to identify trends that can be extrapolated into the future.

It can also include more complex regression analysis that takes into account changes in past sales and converts these into expectations on the basis of sales forecasting.

Example: To illustrate this point let us consider the example involving $20 million in annual sales. Let us assume that projections suggest that sales of 400,000 units at an average price of $100 can be confidently included in the budget.

Product Type	Units Produced	Revenue
X	160,000	6,000,000
Y	80,000	2,000,000

Z	60,000	8,000,000
ZX	20,000	4,000,000
Total	320,000	20,000,000

INSTRUCTIONS

Features

The sales budget is the first component of the master operating budget. This is because sales affect all other parts of the master budget.

It includes the total sales valued in quantity. It consists of three parts; break even, target and projected sales. The budget also includes sales by product, location, customer density and seasonal sales patterns. It provides a plan for both cash and credit sales. The basis of a sales budget is the sale price per unit of goods to be sold multiplied by the quantity of goods to be sold. A sales budget is planned around the competition, the material available, cost of distribution, government controls and the political climate.

Significance

A sales budget controls the finances allocated for achieving sales targets of a company. It is the standpoint for comparing the actual sales performance and the budgetary sales performance of a company. The budget guides the company with regard to how much money should be allocated to selling distribution and sometimes for advertising and marketing. A sales budget that sets realistic targets will help the company make a profit.

Effects

A good sales budget should serve as a guide to company with regard to its sales target. It should be flexible and resilient to the volatile changes in the market. The budget should not put too many restraints on the sales functions of the company. A sales budget is a financial plan for the sales of goods and services of a company. It is the basis on which all the financial decisions of a company with regard to sales are taken. The budget also controls the general sales prospects of a company. Online and off line marketing, marketing in the media and other advertising expenditures are planned around a sales budget.

Benefits

A sales budget helps a company achieve its sales targets. It helps prevent sales losses and provides a basis for sales evaluation. A sales budget helps to integrate all departments in a company because achieving a sales target is the secret of making profits. It helps each department to assess their performance and correct any mistakes in function. It helps a company distribute goods and services in a cost effective way. It also helps the company to keep its marketing expenditure within affordable limits.

Warning

A sales budget comes with inherent limitations and a good sales budget is made by overcoming these limitations. A sales budget cannot effectively forecast the future trends of events. It may not be easily accepted by all people in the organization. Preparing a sales budget takes up too much managerial time. Usually sales budgets shy away from expenditure that will give returns in the long run.

PRODUCTION BUDGET

Production requirements for a period are influenced by the desired level of ending inventory. Inventories should be carefully planned. Excessive inventories tie up funds and create storage problems. Insufficient inventories can lead to lost sales or crash production efforts in the following period.

EXPLANATION OF PRODUCTION BUDGET

At Hampton Freeze, management believes that an ending inventory equal to 20% of the next quarter's sales strikes the appropriate balance.

Example contains the productionbudget for Hampton Freeze. The first row in the production budget contains the budgeted sales, which have been taken directly from the sales budget. The total needs for the first quarter are determined by adding together the budgeted sales of 10,000 cases for the quarter and the desired ending inventory of 6,000 cases. The ending inventory is intended to provide some cushion in case problems develop in production or sales increase unexpectedly.

Since the budgeted sales for the second quarter are 30,000 cases and management would like the ending inventory in each quarter to 20% of the following quarter's sales, the desired ending inventory is 6,000 cases (20% of 30,000 cases). Consequently, the total needs for the first quarter are 16,000 cases. However, since the company already has 2,000 cases in beginninginventory, only 14,000 cases need to be produced in first quarter.

Pay particular attention to the year column to the right of the production budget in the example. In some cases (e.g., budgeted sales, total needs, and required production), the amount listed for the year is the sum of the quarterly amounts for the item. In other cases (e.g., desired inventory of finished goods and beginning inventory of finished goods), the amount listed for the year is not simply the sum of the quarterly amounts.

From the standpoint of the entire year, the beginning inventory of finished goods is the same as the beginning inventory of finished goods for the first quarter—it is not the sum of the beginning inventories of the finished goods for all quarters. Similarly, from the standpoint of the entire year, the ending inventory of finished goods is the same as the ending inventory of finished goods for the fourth quarter—it is not the sum of the endinginventories of finished goods for all four quarters.

MATERIAL BUDGET

The material budget as function of pseudo-rapidity η was calculated by tracing 10000 geantinos through the pixel detectors. The vertex of geantinos was fixed in the interaction point. The beryllium vacuum pipe was not accounted, while the all other elements including the air up to the radius of 29.5 cm and Z=110 cm were accounted.

The production budget is the starting point for determining the estimated quantities of direct materials to be purchased. Multiplying these quantities by the expected unit purchase price determines the total cost of direct materials to be purchased.

In Colt Manufacturing, Inc. production operations leather and lining are required for the production of wallets and handbags. The quantity of direct materials expected to be used for each unit of product is as follows:

Wallets:	Handbags:
Leather: 0.30 square yard per unit	Leather: 1.25 square yards per unit
Lining: 0.10 square yard per unit	Lining: 0.50 square yard per unit

Based on this data and the production budget, the *direct materials purchases budget* is prepared. As shown in the table below, for Colt Manufacturing, Inc., to produce 520,000 wallets, 156,000 square yards (520,000 units X 0.30 square yard per unit) of leather are needed. Likewise, to produce 292,000 handbags, 365,000 square yards (292,000 units X 1.25 square yards per unit) of leather are needed. We can calculate the needs for lining in a similar manner. Then adding the desired ending inventory for each material and deducting the estimated beggining inventory determines the amount of each material to be purchased. Multiplying these amounts by the estimated cost per square yard yields us the total materials purchase cost.

Table. Colt Manufacturing

	Direct Materials		
	Leather	Lining	Total
Square Yards needed for production (*)			
Wallets (Note A)	156,000	52,000	
Handbags (Note B)	365,000	146,000	
Plus desired inventory, December 31, 2008	20,000	12,000	
Total	541,000	210,000	
Less estimated inventory, January 1, 2008	18,000	15,000	
Total square yards to be			

purchased	523,000	195,000	
Unit price (per square yard)	X $4.50	X $1.20	
Total Direct Materials Purchases	$2,353,500	$234,000	$2,587,500

ADVANTAGES OF BUDGETS

A budget helps us in the following ways:

- It brings about efficiency and improvement in the working of the organization.
- It is a way of communicating the plans to various units of the organization. By establishing the divisional, departmental, sectional budgets, exact responsibilities are assigned. It thus minimizes the possibilities of buck passing if the budget figures are not met.
- It is a way or motivating managers to achieve the goals set for the units.
- It serves as a benchmark for controlling on-going operations.
- It helps in developing a team spirit where participation in budgeting is encouraged.
- It helps in reducing wastage and losses by revealing them in time for corrective action.
- It serves as a basis for evaluating the performance of managers.
- It serves as a means of educating the managers.

BUDGETARY CONTROL

No system of planning can be successful without having an effective and efficient system of control. Budgeting is closely connected with control. The exercise of control in the organization with the help of budgets is known as budgetary control.

The process of budgetary control includes:

- Preparation of various budgets.
- Continuous comparison of actual performance with budgetary performance.
- Revision of budgets in the light of changed circumstances.

A system of budgetary control should not become rigid. There should be enough scope of flexibility to provide for individual initiative and drive.

Budgetary control is an important device for making the organization. More efficient on all fronts. It is an important tool for controlling costs and achieving the overall objectives.

BUDGETARY CONTROL SYSTEM

Having understood the meaning and significance of budgetary control in an organization, it will be useful for you to know how a budgetary control system can be installed in the organization. This requires, first of all, finding answers to the following questions in the context of an organization:

- What is likely to happen?
- What can the objectives to be achieved?
- What are the constraints and to what extent their effects can be minimized?

Having found answers to the above questions, the following steps may be taken for installing an effective system of budgetary control in an organization.

Organization for Budgeting: The setting up of a definite plan of organization is the first step towards installing budgetary control system in an organization a budget manual should be prepared giving details of the powers, duties, responsibilities and areas of operation of each executive in the organization.

- *Budget Manual*: "A document which setout, inter alias, the responsibilities of the persons engaged in, the routine of, and the forms and records required for, budgetary control."
- Web for obtaining the necessary approval of budgets, the authority of granting approval should be stated in explicit terms. Whether one, two or more signatures are to be required on each document should also be clearly stated.
- Timetable for all stages of budgeting.
- Reports, statements, forms and other records to be maintained.
- The accounts classification to be employed. It is necessary that the framework within which the costs, revenues and other financial amount are classified must be identical both in accounts and the budget department.

There are many advantages attached to the use of budget manual. It is a formal record defining the functions and responsibilities of each executive. The methods and procedures of budgetary control are standardized. There is synchronization of the efforts of all which result in maximization of the profits of the organization. The responsibility for preparation and implementation of the budgets may be fixed as under.

Budget Controller

Although the chief executive is finally responsible for the budget programme, it is better if a large part of the supervisory responsibility is delegated to an official designated as Budget Controller or Budget Director. Such a person should have knowledge of the technical details of the business and should report directly to the president or the Chief Executive of the organization.

Fixation of the budget period

Budget period mean the period for which a budget is prepared and employed. The budget period depends upon the nature of the business and the control techniques. For example, a seasonal industry will budget for each season while an industry requiring long periods to complete work will budget for four, five or even larger number of year. However, it is necessary of control purposes to prepare budgets both for long as well as short periods.

BUDGET PROCEDURES

Having established the budget organization and fixed the budget period, the actual work or budgetary control can be taken upon the following pattern:

STEPS IN BUDGETARY CONTROL

- Organization for budgeting
- Budget manual + Theory

"A document which sets out, inter alias, the responsibilities of the persons engaged in, the routine of and forms and records required for budgetary control." The budget manual is a written document or booklet that specifies the objectives of budgeting organization and procedures. Following are some of the important matters covered in a budget manual:

- A statement regarding the objectives of the organization and how they can be achieved through budgetary control.
- A statement regarding the functions and responsibilities of each Executive by designation both regarding preparation and execution of budgets.
- Procedures to be followed for obtaining the necessary approval of budgets.
- The authority of granting approval should be stated in explicit terms.
- Whether one, two or more signatures are to be required on each document
- Should also be clearly stated.
- Timetable for all stages of budgeting.
- Reports, statements, forms and other records to be maintained.
- The accounts classification to be employed. It is necessary that the framework within which the

  costs, revenues and other financial amount are classified must be identical both in accounts and the budget departments.

There are many advantages attached to the use of budget manual. It is a formal record defining the functions and responsibilities of each executive. The methods and procedures of budgetary control are standardized. There is synchro-nization of the efforts of all which result in maximization of the profits of the organization.

Making a forecast

Consideration of alternative combination of forecasts: Alternative combinations of forecasts are considered with a view to contain the most efficient overall plan so as to maximize profits. When the optimum -profit combination of forecasts is selected, the forecasts should be regarded as being finalized.

Sales Budget

Past sales figures and trend. The record of previous experience forms the most reliable guide as to future sales as the past performance is related to actual business conditions. However the other factors such as seasonal fluctuations, growth of market, trade cycles etc., should not be lost sight of salesmen's estimates. Salesmen are in a position to estimate the potential demand of the customers more accurately because they come in direct contact with the customers. However, proper discount should be made for over-optimistic or too conservative estimates of the salesmen depending upon their temperament.

Plant Capacity

It should be the endeavor of the business to ensure proper utilization of plant facilities and that the sale budget provides an economic and balanced production on the factory.

General trade prospects

The general trade prospects considerable affect the sales. Valuable information can be gathered in this connection from trade papers and magazines.

Orders on hand

In case of industries where production is quite a lengthy process, orders on hand also have a considerable influence in the amount of sales.

Seasonal fluctuations

Past experience will be the best guide in this respect. However, efforts should be made to minimize the effects of seasonal fluctuations by giving special concessions or off-season discounts thus increasing the volume of sales.

Potential market

Market research should be carried out for ascertaining the potential market, for the company's products. Such an estimate on the basis of expected population growth, purchasing power of consumers and buying habits of the people.

Availability of material and supply

Adequate supply of raw materials and other supplies must be ensured before drafting the sales programme.

Financial aspect

Expansion of sales usually require increase in capital outlay also, therefore, sales budget must be kept within the bounds of financial capacity.

OTHER FACTORS

- The nature and degree of competition within the industry;
- Cost of distributing goods;
- Governments controls, rules and regulations related to the industry;
- Political situation - national and international as it may have an influence upon the market.

The sales manager, after taking into consideration all these factors, will prepare the sales budget in terms if quantities and money, distinguishing between products, periods and areas of sale.

Production budget

Inventory policies. Inventory standards should be predetermined as that neither there is a shortage nor over-stocking of goods. Sales requirements. The quantity of goods to be sold would decide to a great extent how much is to be produced. Therefore, this budget depends upon the sales budget. Production stability.

For reduction of costs, stability in employment and better utilization of plant facilities, the production should be evenly distributed throughout the year. In case of seasonal industries, since it is not possible to have stable levels of production or inventory, an effort should be made to have the optimum balance between the two. Plant capacity. How much can be produced depends upon the available plant capacity. There must be sufficent capacity to procede the annual requirements and also to meet seasonal high demands.

- Availability of material and labour. Adequate and timely supply of raw material and labour should have an important effect on the planning of production.
- Time taken in production process. The production should commence well in time deeping in view how much time it would take in the factory to translate the raw materials into finished goods.

Capital Expenditure Budget

The budget provides a guidance as to the amount of capital that may be Needed for procurement of capital assets during the budget period. The budget is prepared after taking into account the available productive capacitates, probable reallocation of existing assets and possible improvement in production techniques. If necessary separte budgets may be prepared for edach item o assets, such a building budget, a plnat and equipment budget etc.

Cash budget

The cash budget can be prepared by any of the following methods:

- Receipts and payments method
- The adjusted profit and loss method

- The balance sheet method.
- *Receipts and payments method*: In case of this method the cash receipts from various sources and the cash payments to various agencies are estimated. In the opening balance of cash, estimated cash receipts are added and From the total, the total of estimated cash payments are deduted to find out the closing balance.
- *The adjusted profit and loss method*: In case of this method the cash budget is prepared on the basis of opening cash and bank balances, projected profit and loss account and the balances of the various assests and liabilities.
- *The balance sheet methos*: With the helop of budget balances at the end except cash and bank balances, a budgeted balance sheet can be prepared and the balancing figure would be the estimated closing cash/bank balance.

Thus under this method, closing balances other than cash/bank will have to be found out first to be put in the budgeted balance sheet. This can be done by adjusting the anticipated.

Research and Development Budget

Research and development costs are to be incurred so that the products or the methods of the concern do not become out of date. The research and development budget is a forecast of all such expenses.

Classification Of Budgets

Budgets can be classified into different categories on the basis of time, function or flexibility. The different budgets covered under each category are

Rolling Budget

Some organizations follow the practice of preparing a rolling or Progressive budget. In such organizations, a budget for a year in advance will always be there. Immediately after a month, or a quarter, passes, as the case may be, a new budget is prepared for a twelve months.

The figures for the month/quarter which has rolled down are dropped and the figures for the next month/quarter are added. For example, if a budget has been prepared for the year 19*7, after the expire of the first quarter ending 31st march 19*7, a new budget for the full year ending 31st march, 19*8 will be prepared by dropping.

The extent of influence of this factor must first be assessed in order to ensure that the budget targets are met. It would be desirable to prepare first the budget relating to this particular factor, and then prepare the other budgets.

We are giving below an illustrative list of key factors in certain industries. Industry Motor car Aluminum Petroleum refinery Electro-optics Hydel power generation

Key Factor

Sales demand Power Supply of crude oil Skilled technicians Monsoon The key factors should be correctly identified and examined. The key Factors need not be of a permanent nature. In the long run, the management may overcome the key factors by introducing new products, by changing material mix or by working overtime or extra shifts etc.

Making a Forecast

A forecast is an estimated of the future financial conditions or Operating results. Any estimation is based on consideration of probabilites. An estimate differs from a budget in that the latter embodies an operating plan of an organization.

A budget envisages a commitment to certain objectives or targets which The management seeks to attain on the basis of the forecasts prepared. A forecast on the other hand is an estimate based on probabilities of an event. A forecast may be prepared in financial or physical terms for sales,roduction cost, or other resources required for business. Instead of just one forecast a number of alternative forecasts may be considered with a view to obtaining the most realistic overall plan.

Consideration of alternative combination of forecasts. Alternative combinations of forecasts are considered with a view to contain the most efficient overall plan so as to maximize profits. When the optimum-profit combination of forecasts is selected, the forecasts should be regarded as being finalized.

Preparing Budgets

After the forecasts have been finalised the prepareation of budgets follows. The budget activity starts with the preparation of the sales budget. Then production budget is prepared on the basis of sales budget and the production capacity available. Financial budget (i.e., cash or working capital budget) will be prepared on the basis of sales forecasts and the production budget. All tehse budgets are combined and coordinated into a master budget. The budget may be revised in the course of the financial period if it Becomes necessary to do so in view of the unexpected developments which have already taken place or are likely to take place.

Choice between fixed and flexible budgets A budget may be fixed or flexible. A fixed budget is base on a fixed Volume of activity. It may lose it s effectiveness in planning and controlling if the actual capacity utilisation is different from what was planned for any particular unit of time e.g., a month or a quarter. The flexible budget is more useful for changing levels of activity as it considers fixed and vaiable costs separately fixed costs as you are aware, remain unchanged over a certain range of output. Such costs change when there is a change in capacity level.

The vaiable costs change in direct proportion to output. If flexible budgeting approach is adopted, the budget controller can analyses the variance between actual costs and budgeted costs depending upon the actual level of activity attained during a period of time. This will be explained in detail a little later.

Choice Between Fixed and Flexible Budgets

A budget may be fixed flexible. A fixed budget is base on a fixed volume of activity. It may lose its effectiveness in planning and controlling if the actual capacity utilisation is different from what was planned for any particular unit of time e.g., a month or a quarter. The lfexible budget is more useful for changing levels of activity as it considers fixed and vaiable costs separatley fixed costs as you are aware, remain unchanged over a certain range of output. Such costs change when there is a change in capacity leve.

The variable costs change in direct proportion to output. If flexible budgeting approach is adopted, the budget controllet can analyses the variance between actual costs and budgeted costs depending upon theactual level of activity attained during a period fo time. This will be explained in detail a little later.

Sale Budget

Sales budget generally forms the fundamental basis on which all other Budgets are built. The budget is based on projected sales to be achieved in a budget period. The sales manager is directly responsible for the preparation and execution of this budget. Usually takes into consideration the following organizational and environmental factors while preparing the sales budget:

- Organizational Factors
- Past sales (figure and trends)
- Salesmen's estimates
- Plant capacity
- Order on hand
- Proposed expansion or discontinuation of products
- Availability of material of supplies
- Financial aspect
- Cost of distribution of goods
- Environmental factors
- General trade prospects
- Seasonal fluctuations
- Potential market
- Degree of competition
- Government controls, rules and regulations relating to the industry
- Political situation and its impact on market

It is desirable to break up the entire sales budget on the basis of Different products, time periods and sales areas or territories.

Description

- *Past sales figures and trend*: The record of previous experience forms the most reliable guide as to future sales as the past performances related to actual business conditions. However, the other factors such as seasonal fluctuations, growth of market, trade cycles etc., should not be lost sight of.
- *Salesmen's estimates*: Salesmen are in a position to estimate the potential demand of the customers more accurately because they come in direct contact with the customers. However, proper discount should be make for over-optimistic or to conservative estimates of the salesmen depending upon their temperament.
- *Plant capacity*: It should be the endeavor of the business to ensure proper utilization of the plant facilitates and that the seal budget provides an economic and balanced production on the factory.
- *General trade prospects*: The general trade prospects considerably affect the sales. Valuable information can be gathered in this connection from trade papers and magazines.
- *Orders on hand*: In case of industries where production is quite a lengthy process, orders on hand also have a considerable influence in the amount of sales.
- Proposed expansion of discontinuance of products. It is affects sales and therefore, it should also be considered.
- *Potential market*: Market research should be carried out for ascertaining the potential market for the company's products. Such an estimate is made on the basis of expected population growth, purchasing power of consumers and buying habits of the people.
- *Availability of material and supply*: Adequate supply of raw materials and other supplies must be ensured before drafting the sales programme.
- *Financial aspects*: Expansion of sales usually require increase in capital outlay also, therefore, sales budget must be kept within the bounds of financial capacity.
- *Other factors*:
  - The nature and degree of competition within the industry;
  - Cost of distributing goods;
  - Governments controls, rules and regulations related to the industry;
  - *Political situation:* national and international as it may have an influence upon the market.

Production Budget

This budget provides an estimate of the total volume of production Distributed product-wise with scheduling of operations by days, weeks and months, and a forecast of the inventory of finished products. Generally, the production budget is based on the sales budget. The responsibility for the overall production budget ties with works manager and that of with departmental works managers.

Production budget may be expressed in physical or financial terms or both in relation to production.

The production budgets attempt to answer questions like:

- What is to be produced?
- When it is to be produced ?
- How is to be produced?
- Where it is to be produced? The production budget envisages the production programme for achieving the sales target. It serves as a basis for preparation of related cost budgets, e.g., materials cost budget, labour cost budget, etc. it also facilities the preparation of a cash budget. The production budget is prepared after taking into consideration several factors like - Inventory policies, sales requirements, production stability, plant capacity, availability of materials and labour, time taken in production process etc.
- *Inventory policies*: Inventory standards should be predetermined as that neither there is a shortage nor over-stocking of goods.
- *Sales requirements*: The quantity of goods to be sold would be decide to a great extent how much is to be produced. Therefore, this budget depends upon the sales budget.
- *Production stability*: For reduction of costs, stability in employment and better utilization of plant facilities, the production should be evenly distributed throughout the year. In case of seasonal industries, since it is not possible to have stable levels of production or inventory, an effort should be made to have the optimum balance between the two.
- *Plant capacity*: How much can be produced depends upon the available plant capacity. There must be sufficient capacity to proceed the annual requirements and also to meet seasonal high demands.
- *Availability of materials and labour*: Adequate and timely supply of raw materials and labour force should have an imporant effect on the plannning of production.
- *Time taken in production process*: The production should commence well in time keeping in view how much time it would take in the factor to translate the raw materials into finished goods.

Production Costs Budgets

Basically, there are three elements of costs, namely direct material, Direct labour and overheads. Separate budgets for each of there elements have to be prepared.

The direct materials budget has tow components:

- Materials Requirement budget,
- Materials procurement or purchase budget.

The former deals with the total quantity of materials required during the budget period, while the latter deals with the materials to be acquired from the market during the budget period. Materials to be acquired are estimated after taking into account the closing and the opening inventories and the materials from which orders have already been place.

Overhead Budget

The overheads may relate to factory, general administration, selling and distribution function. Separate budgets may, therefore, be prepared for factory overheads, administrative overheads and selling and distribution overheads.

Manufacturing Overheads Budget

Factory or manufacturing overheads includes the cost of indirect material, indirect labour and indirect expenses. Manufacturing overheads may be classified into

- Fixed overheads i.e., which tend to remain constant irrespective of change in the volume of output,
- Variable overheads i.e., which tend to vary with the output,
- Semi-variable overheads, i.e., which are partly variable and partly fixed. The manufacturing overhead budget will provide an estimate of these Overheads to be incurred during the budget period.

Fixed manufacturing overhead can be estimated on the basis of past Information and knowledge of any changes which may occur during the ensuring budget period. Variable overheads are estimated after considering the scheduled production and operating conditions in the budget period.

Administrative Overheads Budget

This budget covers the administrative expenses including the salaries Of administrative expenses including the salaries of administrative the managerial staff. A careful analysis of the needs of all administrative departments of the enterprise is necessary. The minimum requirement for the efficient operation of each administrative department of the budget period. The budget of all administrative departments.

Selling and Distributing Overhead Budget

This budget includes all the expenses relating to selling, advertising, delivery of goods to customers etc. It is better if such costs are analysed according to products, types of customers, territories and the sales departments. The responsibility of the preparation of this budget rests with the executives of the sales expected and an effort should be made to control the costs of distribution. The preparation of the budget would depend on analysis of the market situation by the management, advertising policies, research programmes, and the fixed and variable elements.

Cash Budget

The cash budget is a summary of the firm's expected cash inflows and Outflows over a particular period of time. In other words, cash budget involves a projection of future cash receipts and cash disbursements over various time intervals.

A cash budget helps the management in: Determining the future cash needs of the firm. Planning for financing of those needs. Exercising control over cash and liquidity of the firm.

The overall cash budget can be prepared by any of the following methods:

- Receipts and payments method
- The adjusted profit and loss method
- The balance sheet method

Receipts and payments method: In case of this method the cash receipts From various sources and the cash payments to various agencies are estimated. In the opening balance of cash estimated cash receipts are added and from the total, the total of estimated cash payments are deducted to find out the closing balance. *The adjusted profit and loss method:* In case of this method the cash Budget is prepared on the basis of opening cash and bank balances, projected profit and loss account and the balances of the various assets and liabilities.

The balance sheet method: With the help of budgeted balances at the End except cash and bank balances, a budgeted balance sheet can be prepared and the balancing figure would be the estimated closing cash/bank balance.

Thus, under this method, closing balances other than cash/bank will have to be found out first to be put in the budgeted balance sheet. This can be done by adjusting the anticipated transactions of the year in the opening balances.

Budgetary Control Methods

- *Budget*:
  - A formal statement of the financial resources set aside for carrying out specific activities in a given period of time.
  - It helps to co-ordinate the activities of the organisation.

An example would be an advertising budget or sales force budget.

- *Budgetary control*:
  - A control technique whereby actual results are compared with budgets.
  - Any differences (variances) are made the responsibility of key individuals who can either exercise control action or revise the original budgets.

Budgetary control and responsibility centres:

These enable managers to monitor organisational functions. A responsibility centre can be defined as any functional unit headed by a manager who is responsible for the activities of that unit.

There are four types of responsibility centres:

- *Revenue centres*: Organisational units in which outputs are measured in monetary terms but are not directly compared to input costs.
- *Expense centres*: Units where inputs are measured in monetary terms but outputs are not.
- *Profit centres*: Where performance is measured by the difference between revenues (outputs) and expenditure (inputs). Inter-departmental sales are often made using "transfer prices".
- *Investment centres*: Where outputs are compared with the assets employed in producing them, i.e. ROI.

Advantages of budgeting and budgetary control

There are a number of advantages to budgeting and budgetary control:

- Compels management to think about the future, which is probably the most important feature of a budgetary planning and control system. Forces management to look ahead, to set out detailed plans for achieving the targets for each department, operation and (ideally) each manager, to anticipate and give the organisation purpose and direction.
- Promotes coordination and communication.
- Clearly defines areas of responsibility. Requires managers of budget centres to be made responsible for the achievement of budget targets for the operations under their personal control.
- Provides a basis for performance appraisal (variance analysis). A budget is basically a yardstick against which actual performance is measured and assessed. Control is provided by comparisons of actual results against budget plan. Departures from budget can then be investigated and the reasons for the differences can be divided into controllable and non-controllable factors.
- Enables remedial action to be taken as variances emerge.
- Motivates employees by participating in the setting of budgets.
- Improves the allocation of scarce resources.
- Economises management time by using the management by exception principle.

Problems in Budgeting

Whilst budgets may be an essential part of any marketing activity they do have a number of disadvantages, particularly in perception terms.

- Budgets can be seen as pressure devices imposed by management, thus resulting in:

  - Bad labour relations
  - Inaccurate record-keeping.
- Departmental conflict arises due to:
  - Disputes over resource allocation
  - Departments blaming each other if targets are not attained.
- It is difficult to reconcile personal/individual and corporate goals.
- Waste may arise as managers adopt the view, "we had better spend it or we will lose it". This is often coupled with "empire building" in order to enhance the prestige of a department.
- Responsibility versus controlling, i.e. some costs are under the influence of more than one person, e.g. power costs.
- Managers may overestimate costs so that they will not be blamed in the future should they overspend.

Characteristics of a Budget

A good budget is characterised by the following:

- *Participation*: Involve as many people as possible in drawing up a budget.
- *Comprehensiveness*: Embrace the whole organisation.
- *Standards*: Base it on established standards of performance.
- *Flexibility*: Allow for changing circumstances.
- *Feedback*: Constantly monitor performance.
- Analysis of costs and revenues: this can be done on the basis of product lines, departments or cost centres.

Budget Organisation and Administration

In organising and administering a budget system the following characteristics may apply:

- *Budget centres:* Units responsible for the preparation of budgets. A budget centre may encompass several cost centres.
- *Budget committee:* This may consist of senior members of the organisation, e.g. departmental heads and executives (with the managing director as chairman). Every part of the organisation should be represented on the committee, so there should be a representative from sales, production, marketing and so on. Functions of the budget committee include:
  - Coordination of the preparation of budgets, including the issue of a manual
  - Issuing of timetables for preparation of budgets
  - Provision of information to assist budget preparations
  - Comparison of actual results with budget and investigation of variances.
- *Budget Officer: Controls the budget administration The job involves*:

  - liaising between the budget committee and managers responsible for budget preparation
  - Dealing with budgetary control problems
  - Ensuring that deadlines are met
  - Educating people about budgetary control.
- *Budget manual:*
  This document:
  - Charts the organisation
  - Details the budget procedures
  - Contains account codes for items of expenditure and revenue
  - Timetables the process
  - Clearly defines the responsibility of persons involved in the budgeting system.

Budget Preparation

Firstly, determine the principal budget factor. This is also known as the key budget factor or limiting budget factor and is the factor which will limit the activities of an undertaking. This limits output, e.g. sales, material or labour.

- Sales budget: this involves a realistic sales forecast. This is prepared in units of each product and also in sales value.
  Methods of sales forecasting include:
  - Sales force opinions
  - Market research
  - Statistical methods (correlation analysis and examination of trends)
  - Mathematical models.

  In using these techniques consider:
  - Company's pricing policy
  - General economic and political conditions
  - Changes in the population
  - Competition
  - Consumers' income and tastes
  - Advertising and other sales promotion techniques
  - After sales service
  - Credit terms offered.
- Production budget: expressed in quantitative terms only and is geared to the sales budget. The production manager's duties include.
  - Analysis of plant utilisation
  - Work-in-progress budgets.

  If requirements exceed capacity he may:
  - Subcontract
  - Plan for overtime

  - Introduce shift work
  - Hire or buy additional machinery
  - The materials purchases budget's both quantitative and financial.
- Raw materials and purchasing budget:
  - The materials usage budget is in quantities.
  - The materials purchases budget is both quantitative and financial.
  - Production requirements
  - Planning stock levels
  - Storage space
  - Trends of material prices.
- *Labour budget: is both quantitative and financial. This is influenced by:*
  - Production requirements
  - Man-hours available
  - Grades of labour required
  - Wage rates (union agreements)
  - The need for incentives.
- Cash budget: a cash plan for a defined period of time. It summarises monthly receipts and payments. Hence, it highlights monthly surpluses and deficits of actual cash. Its main uses are:
  - To maintain control over a firm's cash requirements, e.g. stock and debtors
  - To enable a firm to take precautionary measures and arrange in advance for investment and loan facilities whenever cash surpluses or deficits arises
  - To show the feasibility of management's plans in cash terms
  - To illustrate the financial impact of changes in management policy, e.g. change of credit terms offered to customers.

Receipts of cash may come from one of the following:

- Cash sales
- Payments by debtors
- The sale of fixed assets
- The issue of new shares
- The receipt of interest and dividends from investments.

Payments of cash may be for one or more of the following:

- Purchase of stocks
- Payments of wages or other expenses
- Purchase of capital items
- Payment of interest, dividends or taxation.

6

Control and Profitability

All executives and managers account for cost. In various ways, all business professionals manage cost, and most managers engage in capital investment decisions, forecasting, pricing, and product or service management. All these business activities are deeply embedded in the work of cost accounting. Cost-related tasks consume a significant amount of management time at all levels of the organization. A business professional must understand the organization's cost accounting practices to competently manage a specified area and understand how personal accountabilities are calculated and tracked.

An accounting instructor with considerable experience in the field always gave her MBA students the same advice, "Learn the language of accounting. It's the language of business, and if you don't learn it, some little bean counter wearing a green eyeshade will blow your grand marketing or operations idea right out of the water!" Bellwether organizations that employ advanced management systems still run their accounting systems—"keep their books"—just as to basic cost accounting principles. Importantly, conventional practices shape advanced techniques; therefore, more mature methods cannot be fully understood without reference to their predecessors. As a baseline, an organization's executives must establish management/cost accounting practice foundations that serve decision making and operations, first, and financial accounting, second, before moving to advanced systems. To accomplish this, executives need the ability to distinguish system alternatives.

THE PROFIT IMPERATIVE: DEFINING THE OBJECTIVES OF COST MANAGEMENT

Profitability, variously interpreted as net income, equity value, and return on investment is a results-focused indicator watched more carefully than any other performance measurement category. But if these measurements depict results, what measurements show the dimensions of performance for the processes that lead to those results? At the core, profit has only two components: revenue and cost. To understand how a cost management system works.

COST

An outflow of a resource, whether in cash, as a payable, a rendered service, or as a trade or barter, that is consciously made with expectation of benefit to the organization: goods, property, or services acquired.

COST ACCOUNTING

The accounting profession is divided into two major branches:

1. Financial and
2. Management accounting.

The later is synonymous with cost accounting. The term "management" refers to the comparatively internal focus of the cost accounting field as compared with the external focus of financial accounting. The word "traditional," when used to describe cost accounting methods, refers to the standard practices that are taught in basic management accounting courses and practiced in most North American firms. The standard practices include cost systems and procedures, methods of determining costs, points of cost accountability, forecasts, cost comparisons, and budgets. The purpose of cost accounting is to assist in the wise and prudent stewardship of overall organizational resources.

COST AND EXPENSE DISTINCTIONS

Both costs and expenses are expenditures. The word "expenditures" will be used to identify an organization's total outflow of assets in all forms. In the standard income statement of a for-profit firm, costs typically refer to the categories of material, labour, and overhead appearing above the income statement's gross margin line. An example of the income statement components for a manufacturing firm.

Expenditures typically called operating expenses are displayed below the gross margin line. On the income statement, the material, labour, and overhead items are called cost of goods sold. Operating expenses consist of monetary or asset outlays for general, administrative, selling, marketing, and other functions deemed to be indirectly related to production. Operating expenses are commonly abbreviated as SG&A for sales, general and administrative.

COST MANAGEMENT

The use of cost accounting systems and methods to guide current and future operations towards specified objectives; the analysis and interpretation of cost data is critical to the decision-making process.

COST MANAGEMENT SYSTEM

An expenditure information architecture that tracks, monitors, reports, and provides decisionquality information and insights. A CMS is less constrained by exacting professional standards and reporting formats than financial accounting; therefore, a CMS can and should be customised to match an organization's internal environment and specific cost structures.

A CMS sets direction for resource consumption priorities and makes course corrections by emphasizing operations first and accounting practices second. A CMS specifically answers the demands of the profit imperative when it aligns employee spending behaviours with the organizational strategy. The purpose of the CMS is to understand the nature and behaviour of cost, and thereby manage valuable assets wisely through optimizing limited resources. The chief CMS responsibility is to promote improvement in cost structure.

The CMS should:

- Support understanding of the nature and behaviour of cost (and the humans doing the spending).
- Promote, track, and give feedback on value creation and continuous improvement.
- Assist management in wise use of resources.

COST TYPES

Management accountants created cost types in an attempt to understand the nature and behaviour of different resources. Cost types are designations given to categories of resource expenditures. They are based on assumptions about the ways that resources are consumed in relation to the activities to which they are applied. They are also based on the purposes for which the resources are used.

Some traditional cost types include:

- *Fixed*: Costs assumed not to vary with production/ service unit volume
- *Variable*: Costs assumed to vary with production/ service unit volume
- *Semi-fixed/variable, also called step-fixed/variable*: Costs that vary at incremental volume levels
- *Direct*: Costs that can be clearly linked, and therefore assigned to, specific product/service units
- *Indirect*: Costs that cannot easily be linked to specific product/service units, and therefore, must be allocated to production/services based on a selected cost driver

FINANCIAL ACCOUNTING

Financial accounting is the branch of the accounting field concerned with formal, aggregate reporting of transactions related to the income statement (revenue minus expense equals profit/loss), the balance sheet (assets, liabilities, and owners' equity) and other related statements (*e.g.*, working capital, cash flow). Standard report forms used across companies and an external, shareholder focus, characterize financial accounting. The primary statement in financial accounting is the balance sheet.

VALUE

When accountants talk about value they refer to "any preferred object or interest therein"; and accounting valuation is "a judgment expressing or implying preference, or relative approval or disapproval." Organizations exist to become the provider of preference by conveying value to customers, clients, and constituents. This is as true of a spiritual organization with a humanitarian mission as it is of a large corporation focused chiefly on shareholder wealth.

The path to value is different for each organization, and value has many definitions beyond those of the accountant. In the last half of the twentieth century, the focus on value became rooted in the idea of creating shareholder value.What do customers, shareholders and employees value? What do they really want? How can we differentiate ourselves from the competitor in terms of value? Should we be as concerned about internal constituents (*i.e.*, employees) as we are about customers and shareholders? How do all the converging interests of those with a stake in the organization's success or failure work together to create a mutually satisfying sense of value?

A Simplified Traditional Balance Sheet Format

The Balance Sheet Equation: Assets= Liabilities + Owners* Equities

	Also known as
ASSETS	
Current Assets	Short Term Assets
Cash	
Temporary Investments	Short-term invests
Account Receivable	Sales Reciveable, A/R
Inventories	Subcategories: Raw materials,
work in process, finished	goods
Prepaid Expences	
Maturing portion of	Current debt: payment
Long-term Lons	receiveable
Total current Assets	
Long-term Assets	
Building	
Land	
Machiniary and Equipment	Fixed Assets, property plant and Equipment (PP&E)
(Less depreciation on above categories)	
Lones and Mortgages	
Total Assets	
LIABILITIES	
Current Liabilities	
Account payable	A/P

Wages and Salaries	payroll, Benifits
Debt-Current Portion	Maturing Debt, Current Debt
Long-term Liabilities	
Loans	
Mortgages	
Total Liabilities	
	STOCKHOLDER EQUITY,
NET WORTH	
OWNERS'	Paid-in Capital Stock at per value, stated
EQUITIES	Additional paid value
-in capital	Capital surplus
Retained Earnings	Earned surplus, based on
income/loss	

None of these questions has an easy answer, but one fact is certain:

- The first and most common cause of enterprise failure is, simply, overspending— a basic failure to manage expenditures flowing out and revenues flowing in. The solution to overspending behaviours involves little more than the skill set required to balance a checkbook. Creating value for the complex organization requires clear cost management objectives embedded in a cost management system.

OBJECTIVES

Nearly all business professionals know the major components of a general ledger (G/L) system, or at least two of the important reports generated by it: the income statement and the balance sheet. Far fewer managers can describe a cost management system—and with good reason. An effective CMS is customised to match an organization's internal environment and specific cost structures. While an experienced financial professional, and many managers, can move from company to company and quickly understand the financial statements of each, even practiced accountants need considerably more time to understand the intricacies of different cost management systems from company to company. A CMS is less constrained by exacting professional standards and reporting formats than are financial systems, with a few exceptions like the regulated cost guidelines of government contractors. Importantly, the CMS sets direction for resource consumption priorities and makes course corrections by emphasizing operations first and accounting practices second. A CMS specifically answers the demands of the profit imperative by aligning employee spending behaviours with the organizational strategy.

FOUR-STAGE MODEL

A good context for understanding the CMS is to ask not what it is, but rather how it functions. This book acknowledges and borrows from the approach used by Robert S. Kaplan and Robin Cooper, in 1998, Cost and Effect. Their "four-stage model of cost system evolution" describes how a CMS typically evolves over the life cycle of a maturing organization.

Table. Four Stage Model of Cost System Development

Stage One	Stage Two
• Broken • Many error with large variences • Inadiquate external reporting • Inediquate product, service, and cunsumer cost information • Inadiquate Operational and strategic control	• Driven by financial reporting • Meet audit standareds • External reports tailored to financial reporting needs • Inaccurate and hidden product, service, and consumer costs • Strategic feedback limited and delayed
Stage Three	**Stage Four**
• Specialized • Shared databasesbut stand alone systems with informal linkages • Same as Stage Two • Product, service, nad customer costs • Strategic/operational control with several seperate performance mesurement systems system	• Integrated • Fully linked databases • Financial reporting systems create external reports • Product, service, and customer costs in seperate ABM systems integrated in ABM systems • Strategic/operational control within an integrated performence measurement

Stage III systems are specialized, in that the cost and financial accounting systems use the same databases; however, the two systems remain isolated and specialized in application. In this stage, activitybased costing (ABC) and performance measurement systems often emerge. Stage IV systems are integrated, and present a unified reporting format supportive of operational strategy. Financial and operations data, as well as budget and actual information, are all linked. Organizations today remain spread across the Four-Stage spectrum. A healthy number of companies have moved to Stage III; but, it remains rare to find a true Stage IV company, although many claim to be.

An enterprise resource planning (ERP) implementation does not guarantee a Stage IV environment. Every executive and manager first needs to determine which stage current accounting systems are in, and then progressively move through each stage to the integrated level, whether by using the Kaplan/Cooper model or some other proven, logical method. Kaplan and Cooper caution against the high failure rate of organizations that try to jump stages. Operations Focus Is Primary The primary focuses of an effective

CMS are operations and the support of management decision making. In addition to routine bookkeeping, the CMS objectives include, but are not limited, to ten characteristics.

A CMS that supports decision making must:

- Display past, present, and future expenditures.
- Mirror the organization's cost structure and behaviours to support ongoing improvement and control.
- Support realistic, reliable strategic planning and explicit management intention.
- Influence individual and team behaviours towards goal accomplishment.
- Monitor and control resource use against mission and strategic intentions.
- Provide warning when unhealthy financial thresholds are imminent.
- Facilitate the repositioning of resources.
- Hold specific individuals and groups accountable for standards of performance.
- Assist in analyzing key discrete points of profitability: customer, process, product, and region.
- Display a 360-degree unbiased view of the organization's cost structure, one that is understood and actually used in decisionmaking by all executives and managers.

Display Past, Present, and Future Expenditures

This characteristic means that historical, current, and prospective (*i.e.*, forecast, simulation) expenditure data are accessible, timely, and accurate. Accessibility is primarily judged on ease of use. In other words, can nonfinancial managers make use of the system's data and information? Accuracy is based on compliance with cost system design and with data-gathering integrity. Timeliness is based on proximity to real-time information. In the Kaplan/Cooper four-stage model, Stage I systems frequently fail all these criteria and almost never address future expenditures except in budgetary terms. Stage II systems are more reliable for past and present data but often fall short in accessibility and timeliness. Only in Stage III do CMS designs begin to fulfill all criteria. Obviously, if executives work with less than the full timeline (*i.e.*, past, present, and future), their focus will most often be on historical data, while current and future cost conditions elude them.

Mirror the Organization's Cost Structure and Behaviours to Support Ongoing Improvement and Control

This characteristic means that historical, current, and prospective (*i.e.*, forecast, simulation) expenditure data are accessible, timely, and accurate. Accessibility is primarily judged on ease of use. In other words, can nonfinancial managers make use of the system's data and information? Accuracy is based on compliance with cost system design and with data-gathering integrity. Timeliness is based on proximity to real-time information.

In the Kaplan/Cooper four-stage model, Stage I systems frequently fail all these criteria and almost never address future expenditures except in budgetary terms. Stage II systems are more reliable for past and present data but often fall short in accessibility and timeliness. Only in Stage III do CMS designs begin to fulfill all criteria. Obviously, if executives work with less than the full timeline (*i.e.*, past, present, and future), their focus will most often be on historical data, while current and future cost conditions elude them. In practice, profit generation has only two components: revenue/sales and expenditures (*i.e.*, costs, expenses). Therefore, when planning for profitability (or breakeven) CMS information that fairly and accurately represents expenditure information promotes realistic planning and achievement targets. Again, only Stage III and IV cost management systems possess these attributes.

Influence Individual and Team Behaviours Towards Goal Accomplishment

This attribute is among the most important for a CMS. If people do not find the cost system relevant to their daily activities and long-term responsibilities, they will not use it. Relevance includes accountability for predetermined performance standards, the prudent management of resources, and visibility of companywide cost structures and behaviours. A Stage III CMS provides opportunity for achieving this desired criterion; however, only Stage IV provides the level of integration needed to maximize this goal.

Monitor and Control Resource Use Against Mission and Strategic Intentions

This means that the cost management system assists in aligning and allocating resources where they will best serve management's strategic intentions. The managers of organizations in Stages I and II of the Kaplan/Cooper model overlook this characteristic when designing the CMS, if they give any thought to system design at all. When different managers perform budgeting and strategic planning processes at different times, the compartmentalization undermines strategic achievements that depend on appropriate resource alignment.

Imagine an executive team energized from a strategic planning retreat returning to day-to-day operations, issuing mandates, directives, and a trainload of new projects, all without addressing resource allocation, budgets, or realignment of people, time, and facilities. This is a strategic plan scenario doomed to frustration and failure.

Provide Warning When Unhealthy Financial Thresholds Are Imminent

A thoughtfully designed CMS provides an early-warning system that identifies and averts overspending. It may also signal the need for additional resources due to volume and/or environmental changes. Often, CMS Stages I and II provide reactive reporting long after a decision opportunity for changing an operational process issue has passed.

Imagine the frustration of a manufacturing manager who is held accountable for subpar performance in material and labour efficiencies, but who receives efficiency reports two to four weeks after the "damage" is done. Only Stage III and IV organizations rectify these demoralizing dynamics.

Facilitate the Repositioning of Resources

This CMS characteristic partners with number 6 by overseeing the movement and realignment of resources to adapt to strategic changes.

In many companies, once an annual budget is set, woe to the manager who overspends it. If the strategic plan and the budget live separate lives, how can managers be expected to satisfy both?

Hold Specific Individuals and Groups Accountable for Standards Of Performance

A recurring error in strategic planning is the failure to assign responsibility for action plans and performance targets.When set up properly, the CMS signals expectations for cost targets and identifies the individuals/ groups responsible for meeting those targets. The CMS links cost targets with appropriate nonfinancial measures that discourage managers from working on cost and financial performance in isolation from other important indicators.

Assist In Analyzing Discrete Points Of Profitability: Custmor, Process, Product, And Region

A financial accounting system provides an aggregate consolidated view of profitability. An effective CMS provides an analytical extension that searches for suspected areas of underperformance related to specific customers, product lines, market sectors, and other identifiable objects of analysis. Although a Stage II CMS may provide rudimentary historical data on these targets of analysis, only Stage III and IV systems provide decision-quality reporting through use of such techniques as activity-based costing.

Display A 360-Degree Unbiased View of the Organisation's Cost Structure

Display a 360-Degree Unbiased View of the Organization's Cost Structure that is understood and actually used in decision-making by all executives and managers. A CMS that provides open-book views of companywide cost structures used concurrently by all managers to advance the organizational community's well-being as a whole encourages management creativity in resource use, as well as optimal use of available capacity.

In most cases, only a Stage IV CMS can satisfy this attribute requirement. To be an effective management decision-making guide, the cost management system has to be much more than a set of bookkeeping procedures, and it must not be the sole source of information for decision making. Never use a cost management system in isolation for operational decision making. Just as financial accounting delivers an important but narrow stream of results information, cost accounting also displays a critical but incomplete viewpoint.

Nonfinancial, noncost information is part of any mature cost analysis. This is particularly true for making business development decisions. For example, a research and development (R&D) function usually shows continuous losses when subjected to a profit-and-loss, P&L (*i.e.*, income statement), approach. However, the R&D function value remains invisible until seen in the context of potential future revenue and cost streams.

CONTROL AND PROFITABILITY

Every business professional wants to manage well by making the right decisions. Good decisions lead to profit. Effective management and profitability rely mutually on systems that control employee behaviour. This is the time to distinguish cost accounting and cost management. Cost accounting can be thought of in terms of structured data elements; cost management can be thought of in terms of the information yielded by analyzing cost accounting data elements. As defined earlier, cost accounting includes cost systems and procedures, methods of determining costs, points of cost accountability, forecasts, cost comparisons (*e.g.*, standard cost systems), and budgets (operational, project, and capital).

Interestingly, in many companies, these and other functionalities exist but are not actively managed. Unless cost managers create meaning out of the cost accounting data and reports, a good portion of cost accounting effort is wasted, and critical information for decision making remains hidden. Significant resources can be applied to cost accounting work, but if executives view cost accounting simply as part of financial accounting, meaning and insight remain hidden within transaction data. Only cost management can extract and create insight and meaning from raw cost data.

The cost accounting obligation is simple in concept: Provide accurate cost information. Implementing a cost accounting system that is accessible, aimed at the right targets of analysis, and supportive of management decision making is a more sophisticated task. The cost management responsibility is equally clear: Promote improvement in cost structure. Making good on this prospect is even more challenging. Make no mistake, accounting is part of the organizational control system.

The primary purpose of the control system is to protect the organization's assets. The important place that the accounting system occupies in the overall control system becomes more intriguing upon consideration of some basic accounting terminology. One common accounting definition of assets is "costs that have not yet been used." The accounting term for this is unexpired costs.

These unexpired costs represent current or future value to the organization. Controller is the title of the head accountant in many organizations.

Finally, consider that the two conventional financial statements that reflect this control and safeguarding of assets are:

1. The balance sheet, and
2. The statement of cash flows.

All this clearly speaks to the control focus in accounting activities. The next most important function of the accounting system is to monitor profitability as recorded on the periodic income statement. Profitability results from effective control. All managers follow profit across the shortest available reporting interval; however, responsibility for calculating profitability lies with financial accountants, who in turn rely heavily on cost accountants.

THE SHIFTING FOCUS OF CONTROL IN ACCOUNTING SYSTEMS

Traditionally, those charged with the maintenance of financial and cost accounting systems do not care what is happening in an organization as long as it is accurately recorded as a transaction and made available for reporting on the income statement and balance sheet. The focus of the mechanics of financial and cost accounting systems is distinctly different from the perspectives and priorities of internal control and audit systems, not to mention the concerns of executives and managers. While all accounting systems have two primary concerns—control and profitability—managers and executives must be able to distinguish the specific aspects that financial and cost accounting systems each contribute to the understanding of control and profitability.

Financial and management/cost accounting systems see business control and profitability from significantly different perspectives. Historically, the financial accounting focus has determined the organization's overriding control and profitability perspective: return on investment, which inherently includes profitability. The investor and the market in general focus on short-term financial results. Stock price performance reinforces the primacy of the financial accounting perspective. In contrast, cost accounting systems historically see business control and profitability from the operational perspective.

Financial accounting sees the organization from an external perspective; managerial accounting sees the organization from an internal perspective. Managers and executives who hope to steer their organizations towards continuous improvement have learned not to wait for the financials.They control and manage organizational performance based on continuous improvement and sustainable profit goals.

This proactive approach is supported by cost and performance management methodology and technology innovations over the last 20 years that have helped elevate the status of internal operational information. More recently, theoretical research and actual practice have shown that operational and nonfinancial elements are equally important in creating success and strategic achievement. The financial accounting system provides the motivation; the managerial cost accounting system information provides the means to improve processes and achieve profitability.

WHERE FINANCIAL AND COST ACCOUNTING SYSTEMS CONNECT

A return to the Kaplan/Cooper four-stage model helps to narrow the range of the many possible permutations of cost accounting system design. Using the context of the developmental stage of the organization's current cost accounting system, executives and managers can deliberately shepherd their cost accounting systems towards more integrated levels. Importantly, all cost accounting systems must first meet the Stage II baseline before aspiring to more advanced levels.

When business processes and accounting methods are in harmony, the aligned flow of a traditional, Stage II system would look like this:

- Plan strategic objectives → then determine budget allocations → that create expenditures → that are assigned just as to plan and budget. → Later, actual expenditures are compared to budget targets to show deviations → that lead to management intervention, as appropriate.

The accounting system tracks this overall process from financial and cost perspectives. Now consider three primary connection points that tie the cost and financial systems together as they each monitor the flow of value through business processes: inventories, capital spending, and period expenses (*i.e.*, SG&A).

Consider how an accounting system might:

- Support understanding of the nature and behaviour of cost— cost accounting.
- Promote, track, and give feedback on value creation—financial accounting.
- Assist management in wise use of resources—both.

Inventories

The first connection point, inventories valuation, flows as follows:

- Material+ labour + overhead → becomes inventory recorded on the balance sheet → becomes product cost → becomes cost of goods sold (COGS) reported on the income statement.

Material, labour, and overhead are cost information items that flow through the accounting system from the inventory assets on the balance sheet to COGS on the income statement—from the cost accounting system to the financial accounting system.

Capital Budgets

The second connection point, capital spending, has a flow that looks like this:

- Capital budget process selects investments. → Purchase is made and recorded as an asset, usually long-term. → Depreciation expense is recognized over the estimated useful life of the asset (tax methods aside). → Depreciation expense is recognized on the income statement.

In theory, traditional capital budgeting processes attempt to select long-term investments that will support strategic achievement over time. In practice, the process is often a cold-war battle between divisions, departments, or functions, wherein each attempts to garner as much investment money as possible for a parochial area. Once a capital investment is made—whether wisely or not—the expense of that investment is conventionally recognized over time by accounting formulas that most often do not reflect the actual use of the investment (*e.g.*, machine, computer system).

Period Expenses

The third connection point, period expenses (i.e., SG&A), has a flow that looks like this:

- Administrative and selling costs are budgeted and then incurred → then assigned to the current time period → classified as SG&A → and reported on the income statement.

Many companies run into financial difficulties because they fail to manage expenditures "below the line," the SG&A expenses below the gross margin line on the income statement.

COST ACCOUNTING AND OPERATIONS

Now it is time to give due attention to support of operations as the primary responsibility of a cost accounting system. Consider the following questions, this time in light of cost accounting responsibilities to operations, compared to its obligations to financial reporting requirements.

How might the accounting system:

- Support understanding of the nature and behaviour of cost?
- Promote, track, and give feedback on value creation?
- Assist management in wise use of resources?

The answers lie in the design of the cost management system. Deliberate and careful design of a cost management system promotes organizational control, as well as workforce focus. The managerial cost accounting system mandates specific control processes by means of the design of its cost management system.

More and more organizations look to their CFOs, controllers, and accountants for vital decision-making information and participation in strategic and long-term planning.

In contrast, operations-oriented firms often see accounting systems as a necessary evil, required by government and creditor agencies, but for the most part simply a nuisance to internal managers. The difference in viewpoint largely depends on the accounting system design. CMS designs that remain in Stage I and II may quickly become irrelevant to management's decision-making responsibilities. The importance of CMS design extends throughout the entire organization. Dr. CJ McNair summarizes the situation eloquently. "What cost management chooses to make visible—the focus of its work—will inform and constrain the organizations of the future.

In choosing a future for cost management, the future of business will be shaped." Cost management system design is a conscientious and deliberate process that avoids irrelevant detail and integrates seamlessly with the financial system. CMS design requires rigorous, periodic review to ascertain its continuing relevance.

To reiterate:

- *Cost accounting exists for a conceptually simple purpose*: Provide accurate cost information.
- The purpose of cost management is equally clear: Promote improvement in cost structure.

This part will address the essential steps that executives and managers can take to achieve these elusive goals and thereby develop a CMS that is easy to use, aimed at the most important targets of analysis, and supportive of management decision making. In Cost and Effect, Kaplan and Cooper conclude their introductory chapter by describing the vision for such cost systems where,"cost and performance measurement systems are explicitly designed to produce the right information at the right time for essential managerial learning, decisions, and control."

HISTORICAL OBSTACLES

Any executive with even a few years of experience knows the sharp difference between an accounting function that is pro-operations and one that is pro-finance. Likewise, any experienced accountant can tell when other functions (*e.g.*, operations, marketing) see the finance function as a necessary burden and when the function is appreciated for the value it adds to the organization. As in most complex situations, the ideal practice is a blend of both perspectives. Until this becomes true in their own organizations, managers must come to understand and acknowledge the historical animosity and inherent conflicts between operations and accounting.

Passions would not run so high if the relationship between operations and accounting were not essential to business health. At the root of this friction is that, financial staff and operations people see their work from culturally different perspectives and business worldviews. These unspoken viewpoints generate misunderstandings and outright conflict. The different perspectives must be discovered, exposed, and reconciled before they can be blended. All too often, nothing happens. Both sides fear the loss of control, and each is reluctant to take on new roles.

Not long ago, a financial accounting professional might spend an entire career never setting foot on the factory floor or talking with a customer face-to-face. Huddled in back rooms with whirring pencils scratching numbers on green ledgers (and erasing them, too), accountants literally had no time for any activities other than tallying, ticking, and tying the numbers. Today, although computerized accounting systems have replaced the demanding drudgery of manual ledgers, some accountants still seldom set foot in the land of operations. Cost accountants who match this profile—then or now—cannot serve their organizations to the best of their abilities.

The connections and the conflicts within the accounting/operations dynamic are easiest to conceptualize in the manufacturing sector where the tangible nature of production makes conflict stand out.

Making the Numbers Count, Brian Maskell cites five key shortcomings with management accounting:

1. Lack of relevance,
2. Cost distortion,
3. Inflexibility,
4. Incompatibility with world-class approaches, and
5. Inappropriate links to financial accounts.

By inversely examining each of these shortcomings as attributes, the inherent connections between cost accounting and operations, whereby a CMS brings value to management, can be explored in terms of:

- Relevance,
- Cost visibility,
- Flexibility,
- Support for advanced approaches, and
- Appropriate links to financial accounts.

APPROPRIATE LINKS TO FINANCIAL ACCOUNTS

Financial statements address the information needs of a range of constituents and government regulators. Since financial statements target external users and are governed by external standards and formats, at best they provide internal managers with a highly aggregated and shallow "report card" of business performance. Consequently, while the CMS should provide external managers the necessary and sufficient information to meet financial reporting requirements, the system should do so with all due dispatch in terms of the needs of internal managers for information focus and efficiency. Inventory valuation, COGS, expense classification, and absorption are among the few important connection points at issue between the financial accounting system and the CMS.

SUPPORT FOR ADVANCED APPROACHES

Because traditional accounting systems position cost accounting in the status of servant to the general ledger/financial statement system, the poorly designed CMS may consequently attempt to make vassals out of the other business functions. Practice the reverse. The most mature cost accountants have been given permission to support their executives to design a budgeting and cost reporting system that rapidly supports decision making, encourages efficiency throughout the organization, and requires value-added information from functional managers. In this context, all standard financial accounting-related routines should be automated and transparent to nonfinancial staff.

Capital spending is another connection point between accounting and operations functions for CMS value creation. Typically, North American companies use discounted cash flow (DCF) or return-oninvestment (ROI) measurements to choose between capital spending alternatives. These financially focused frameworks are based on tenuous estimates and forecasts that frequently prove grossly inaccurate. Additionally, these traditional, exclusively financial analysis tools look for rapid returns on invested capital. This is not always congruent with operations management or long-term strategic plans.

FLEXIBILITY

Protocols often become highly standardized when financial accounting perspectives control the cost accounting system. In contrast, when the CMS serves operations first and financial accounting second, its system and report designs adapt to changing operational environments.

COST VISIBILITY

As service organizations become a larger business sector and the business landscape loses its stability in terms of organizational structure (due to mergers, acquisitions, and virtual offices), traditional cost types become increasingly irrelevant. Cost types do not facilitate cost visibility—a transparency of the nature and behaviour of costs and resource spending that sustains informed decision making. More advanced cost management systems such as activity-based costing and resource consumption accounting, clarify cost dynamics and enable wise choices grounded on business interrelationships that more closely reflect business performance.

RELEVANCE

Closing the circle, a CMS that serves operations, supports advanced cost management approaches, adapts flexibly, and clearly displays the nature and behaviour of cost, de facto, becomes relevant. In a relevant CMS, cost work investments are generally viewed as valueadded activities, and organizational management relies on them for essential decision-making information.

When a CMS exhibits these five attributes it becomes a valuable organizational asset. Inversely, for organizations missing some of these attributes, the executives and managers see one more reason for nonfinancial functions to pay less attention to CMS information.

CONTROL AND PERFORMANCE MANAGEMENT SYSTEMS

At this point, it is worth making a final connection point. Since cost is such an integral element of the "profit imperative" and profit performance is a universal organizational requirement, it is natural and inevitable that cost and performance systems become intimately associated. Organizations with CMS designs in Stages I and II use financialonly accounting systems. If it exists at all, nonfinancial performance measurement is typically fragmented and isolated within the functional domains of an organization. Everyone wants to "keep score," and without a formal measurement system, good managers will create their own scoreboard. For example, a competent production manager always has a control system in place based on the principles of quality, theory of constraints, or some homegrown paradigm.

Companies developing into a Stage III CMS almost always navigate the same important barrier: exclusive reliance on financial measures for management and accountability purposes. An intense struggle ensues between the financially based management system and the more mature emerging system that values nonfinancial measures as equally important. Consequently, this can result in two performance management systems within the same company—the original financial-based accountability framework and the more balanced performance information paradigm. The subsequent conflicts are all too familiar; but, eventually, they must be resolved so that the entire organization embraces a single performance measurement standard of accountability.

Once again, the primary responsibility of cost accounting activities is conceptually simple: Provide accurate cost information. The cost management responsibility is equally clear: Promote improvement in cost structure.

NO SEPARATION

Cost and organizational performance are inseparable. The link between cost and performance may seem obvious today, but not long ago financial results were the organizational report card of choice. From a capital market perspective, the financials still reign supreme.

That said, studies reveal the same market analysts paying more and more attention to nonfinancial measurements and intangible asset valuation, as well as to shortterm quarterly financial measures like earnings per share and price/earnings ratio. Other operational frameworks, like the Quality Movement, helped shift the emphasis to some degree. However, when, in the early 1990s, performance measurement and management systems began developing independently from financial systems, performance managers found a structured way to move beyond the information constraints of general ledger financial systems. Increasingly, powerful performance management methods and software applications support the development and reporting of nonfinancial information.

CONCLUSION

Cost management systems can be powerful allies in organizational success, but only when deliberately designed and consistently utilized.

Here are some key points in accomplishing this:

- A CMS should focus primarily on internal operations management.
- A cost management system serves its organization when it is relevant, makes costs visible, is flexible, is supportive of advanced approaches, and has appropriate links to financial accounts.
- An accounting system that meets financial reporting requirements is not necessarily adequate for management decision making.
- Cost accounting/management's first responsibility is to internal operations, and only secondarily to financial accounting.
- Finance and operations professionals must be vigilant in maintaining healthy relationships, where the contributions of each are recognized and appreciated.
- Strategy, accountability, and performance concerns are central ingredients for CMS design to drive performance that is aligned with strategic intention.
- The behavioral implications of a CMS design have to be carefully anticipated and managed.
- Traditional cost accounting systems do not always make good management systems. When a cost accounting system is constructed with a primary goal of servicing financial accounting systems, management decision-support information suffers.
- Unlike general ledger systems, a CMS is more flexible and must be customised for each organization.

7

Financial Statements with Inventory

MANAGEMENT INVENTORY

Inventory is a list for goods and materials, or those goods and materials themselves, held available in stock by a business. Inventory are held in order to manage and hide from the customer the fact that manufacture/supply delay is longer than delivery delay, and also to ease the effect of imperfections in the manufacturing process that lower production efficiencies if production capacity stands idle for lack of materials.

BUSINESS INVENTORY

The Reasons for Keeping Stock

There are three basic reasons for keeping an inventory:

1. *Time*: The time lags present in the supply chain, from supplier to user at every stage, requires that you maintain certain amount of inventory to use in this "lead time"
2. *Uncertainty*: Inventories are maintained as buffers to meet uncertainties in demand, supply and movements of goods.
3. *Economies of scale*: Ideal condition of "one unit at a time at a place where user needs it, when he needs it" principle tends to incur lots of costs in terms of logistics. So Bulk buying, movement and storing brings in economies of scale, thus inventory.

All these stock reasons can apply to any owner or product stage.

- Buffer stock is held in individual workstations against the possibility that the upstream workstation may be a little delayed in long setup or change-over time. This stock is then used while that change-over is happening. This stock can be eliminated by tools like SMED.

These classifications apply along the whole Supply chain not just within a facility or plant. Where these stocks contain the same or similar items it is often the work practice to hold all these stocks mixed together before or after the sub-process to which they relate. This 'reduces' costs. Because they are mixed-up together there is no visual reminder to operators of the adjacent sub-processes or line management of the stock which is due to a particular cause and should be a particular individual's responsibility with inevitable consequences. Some plants have centralized stock holding across sub-processes which makes the situation even more acute.

Special Terms used in Dealing with Inventory

- Stock Keeping Unit (SKU) is a unique combination of all the components that are assembled into the purchasable item. Therefore any change in the packaging or product is a new SKU. This level of detailed specification assists in managing inventory.
- Stockout means running out of the inventory of an SKU.
- "New old stock" (sometimes abbreviated NOS) is a term used in business to refer to merchandise being offered for sale which was manufactured long ago but that has never been used. Such merchandise may not be produced any more, and the new old stock may represent the only market source of a particular item at the present time.

Inventory Examples

While accountants often discuss inventory in terms of goods for sale, organizations - manufacturers, service-providers and not-for-profits - also have inventories (fixtures, furniture, supplies,) that they do not intend to sell. Manufacturers', distributors', and wholesalers' inventory tends to cluster in warehouses. Retailers' inventory may exist in a warehouse or in a shop or store accessible to customers. Inventories not intended for sale to customers or to clients may be held in any premises an organization uses. Stock ties up cash and if uncontrolled it will be impossible to know the actual level of stocks and therefore impossible to control them.

Whilst the reasons for holding stock are covered earlier, most manufacturing organizations usually divide their "goods for sale" inventory into:

- *Raw materials*: Materials and components scheduled for use in making a product.
- *Work in process, WIP*: Materials and components that have begun their transformation to finished goods.
- *Finished goods*: Goods ready for sale to customers.
- *Goods for resale*: Returned goods that are salable.
- Spare parts

MANUFACTURING

A canned food manufacturer's materials inventory includes the ingredients to form the foods to be canned, empty cans and their lids (or coils of steel or aluminum for constructing those components), labels, and anything else (solder, glue,) that will form part of a finished can. The firm's work in process includes those materials from the time of release to the work floor until they become complete and ready for sale to wholesale or retail customers.

This may be vats of prepared food, filled cans not yet labelled or sub-assemblies of food components. It may also include finished cans that are not yet packaged into cartons or pallets. It's finished good inventory consists of all the filled and labelled cans of food in its warehouse that it has manufactured and wishes to sell to food distributors (wholesalers), to grocery stores (retailers), and even perhaps to consumers through arrangements like factory stores and outlet centers.

LOGISTICS OR DISTRIBUTION

The logistics chain includes the owners (wholesalers and retailers), manufacturers' agents, and transportation channels that an item passes through between initial manufacture and final purchase by a consumer. At each stage, goods belong (as assets) to the seller until the buyer accepts them.

Distribution includes four components:

1. *Manufacturers' agents*: Distributors who hold and transport a consignment of finished goods for manufacturers without ever owning it. Accountants refer to manufacturers' agents' inventory as "matériel" in order to differentiate it from goods for sale.
2. *Transportation*: The movement of goods between owners, or between locations of a given owner. The seller owns goods in transit until the buyer accepts them. Sellers or buyers may transport goods but most transportation providers act as the agent of the owner of the goods.
3. *Wholesaling*: Distributors who buy goods from manufacturers and other suppliers (farmers, fishermen, etc.) for re-sale work in the wholesale industry. A wholesaler's inventory consists of all the products in its warehouse that it has purchased from manufacturers or other suppliers. A produce-wholesaler (or distributor) may buy from distributors in other parts of the world or from local farmers. Food distributors wish to sell their inventory to grocery stores, other distributors, or possibly to consumers.
4. *Retailing*: A retailer's inventory of goods for sale consists of all the products on its shelves that it has purchased from manufacturers or wholesalers. The store attempts to sell its inventory (soup, bolts, sweaters, or other goods) to consumers.

High Level Inventory Management

It seems that around about 1880 there was a change in manufacturing practise from companies with relatively homogeneous lines of products to vertically integrated companies with unprecedented diversity in processes and products. Those companies (especially in metalworking) attempted to achieve success through economies of scale - the gains of jointly producing two or more products in one facility. The managers now needed information on the effect of product mix decisions on overall profits and therefore needed accurate product cost information. A variety of attempts to achieve this were unsuccessful due to the huge overhead of the information processing of the time. However, the burgeoning need for financial reporting after 1900 created unavoidable pressure for financial accounting of stock and the management need to cost manage products became overshadowed.

In particular it was the need for audited accounts that sealed the fate of managerial cost accounting. The dominance of financial reporting accounting over management accounting remains to this day with few exceptions and the financial reporting definitions of 'cost' have distorted effective management 'cost' accounting since that time. This is particularly true of inventory.

Hence high level financial inventory has these two basic formulas which relate to the accounting period:

1. Cost of beginning inventory at the start of the period + inventory purchases within the period + cost of production within the period = cost of goods
2. Cost of goods – cost of ending inventory at the end of the period = cost of goods sold

The benefit of these formulae is that the first absorbs all overheads of production and raw material costs in to a value of inventory for reporting. The second formula then creates the new start point for the next period and gives a figure to be subtracted from sales price to determine some form of sales margin figure.

Manufacturing management is more interested in inventory turnover ratio or average days to sell inventory since it tells them something about relative inventory levels. Inventory turn over ratio (also known as inventory turns) = cost of goods sold/Average Inventory=Cost of Goods Sold/((Beginning Inventory + Ending Inventory)/2) and its inverse. Average Days to Sell Inventory=Number of Days a Year/Inventory Turn Over Ratio=365 days a year/Inventory Turn Over Ratio

This ratio estimates how many times the inventory turns over a year. This number tells us how much cash/goods are tied up waiting for the process and is a critical measure of process reliability and effectiveness.

So a factory with two inventory turns has six months stock on hand which generally not a good figure (depending upon industry) whereas a factory that moves from six turns to twelve turns has probably improved effectiveness by 100%.

This improvement will have some negative results in the financial reporting since the 'value' now stored in the factory as inventory is reduced. Whilst the simplicity of these accounting measures of inventory are very useful they are in the end fraught with the danger of their own assumptions. There are in fact so many things which can vary hidden under this appearance of simplicity that a variety of 'adjusting' assumptions may be used. These include:

ACCOUNTING PERSPECTIVES

THE BASIS OF INVENTORY ACCOUNTING

Inventory needs to be accounted where it is held across accounting period boundaries since generally expenses should be matched against the results of that expense within the same period. When processes were simple and short then inventories were small but with more complex processes then inventories became larger and significant valued items on the balance sheet. This need to value unsold and incomplete goods has driven much new behaviour into management practise. Perhaps most significant of these are the complexities of fixed cost recovery, transfer pricing, and the separation of direct from indirect costs.

This, supposedly, precluded "anticipating income" or "declaring dividends out of capital". It is one of the intangible benefits of Lean and the TPS that process times shorten and stock levels decline to the point where the importance of this activity is hugely reduced and therefore effort, especially managerial, to achieve it can be minimised.

ACCOUNTING FOR INVENTORY

Each country has its own rules about accounting for inventory that fit with their financial reporting rules. So for example, organizations in the U.S. define inventory to suit their needs within US Generally Accepted Accounting Practices (GAAP), the rules defined by the Financial Accounting Standards Board (FASB) (and others) and enforced by the U.S. Securities and Exchange Commission (SEC) and other federal and state agencies. Other countries often have similar arrangements but with their own GAAP and national agencies instead.

It is intentional that financial accounting uses standards that allow the public to compare firms' performance, cost accounting functions internally to an organization and potentially with much greater flexibility. A discussion of inventory from standard and Theory of Constraints-based (throughput) cost accounting perspective follows some examples and a discussion of inventory from a financial accounting perspective. The internal costing/ valuation of inventory can be complex.

Whereas in the past most enterprises ran simple one process factories, this is quite probably in the minority in the 21st century. Where 'one process' factories exist then there is a market for the goods created which establishes an independent market value for the good. Today with multi-stage process companies there is much inventory that would once have been finished goods which is now held as 'work-in-process' (WIP). This needs to be valued in the accounts but the valuation is a management decision since there is no market for the partially finished product. This somewhat arbitrary 'valuation' of WIP combined with the allocation of overheads to it has led to some unintended and undesirable results.

Financial Accounting

An organization's inventory can appear a mixed blessing, since it counts as an asset on the balance sheet, but it also ties up money that could serve for other purposes and requires additional expense for its protection. Inventory may also cause significant tax expenses, depending on particular countries' laws regarding depreciation of inventory, as in Thor Power Tool Company v. Commissioner. Inventory appears as a current asset on an organization's balance sheet because the organization can, in principle, turn it into cash by selling it. Some organizations hold larger inventories than their operations require in order to inflate their apparent asset value and their perceived profitability.

In addition to the money tied up by acquiring inventory, inventory also brings associated costs for warehouse space, for utilities, and for insurance to cover staff to handle and protect it, fire and other disasters, obsolescence, shrinkage (theft and errors), and others. Such holding costs can mount up: between a third and a half of its acquisition value per year. Businesses that stock too little inventory cannot take advantage of large orders from customers if they cannot deliver. The conflicting objectives of cost control and customer service often pit an organization's financial and operating managers against its sales and marketing departments. Sales people, in particular, often receive sales commission payments, so unavailable goods may reduce their potential personal income. This conflict can be minimised by reducing production time to being near or less than customer expected delivery time.

This effort, known as "Lean production" will significantly reduce working capital tied up in inventory and reduce manufacturing costs role of a cost accountant on the 21st-century in a manufacturing organization. By helping the organization to make better decisions, the accountants can help the public sector to change in a very positive way that delivers increased value for the taxpayer's investment. It can also help to incentivise progress and to ensure that reforms are sustainable and effective in the long term, by ensuring that success is appropriately recognized in both the formal and informal reward systems of the organization. To say that they have a key role to play is an understatement.

Finance is connected to most, if not all, of the key business processes within the organization. It should be steering the stewardship and accountability systems that ensure that the organization is conducting its business in an appropriate, ethical manner. It is critical that these foundations are firmly laid. So often they are the litmus test by which public confidence in the institution is either won or lost. Finance should also be providing the information, analysis and advice to enable the organizations' service managers to operate effectively.

This goes beyond the traditional preoccupation with budgets - how much have we spent so far, how much have we left to spend? It is about helping the organization to better understand its own performance. That means making the connections and understanding the relationships between given inputs - the resources brought to bear - and the outputs and outcomes that they achieve. It is also about understanding and actively managing risks within the organization and its activities.

FIFO VS. LIFO ACCOUNTING

When a dealer sells goods from inventory, the value of the inventory is reduced by the cost of goods sold (CoG sold). This is simple where the CoG has not varied across those held in stock; but where it has, then an agreed method must be derived to evaluate it.

For commodity items that one cannot track individually, accountants must choose a method that fits the nature of the sale. Two popular methods exist: FIFO and LIFO accounting (first in - first out, last in - first out). FIFO regards the first unit that arrived in inventory as the first one sold. LIFO considers the last unit arriving in inventory as the first one sold. Which method an accountant selects can have a significant effect on net income and book value and, in turn, on taxation.

Using LIFO accounting for inventory, a company generally reports lower net income and lower book value, due to the effects of inflation. This generally results in lower taxation. Due to LIFO's potential to skew inventory value, UK GAAP and IAS have effectively banned LIFO inventory accounting. In computer science, FIFO and LIFO correspond to the queue and stack data structures, respectively. In fact, the acronyms are commonly used to denote the corresponding data structures.

STANDARD COST ACCOUNTING

Standard cost accounting uses ratios called efficiencies that compare the labour and materials actually used to produce a good with those that the same goods would have required under "standard" conditions.

As long as similar actual and standard conditions obtain, few problems arise. Unfortunately, standard cost accounting methods developed about 100 years ago, when labour comprised the most important cost in manufactured goods. Standard methods continue to emphasize labour efficiency even though that resource now constitutes a (very) small part of cost in most cases. Standard cost accounting can hurt managers, workers, and firms in several ways. For example, a policy decision to increase inventory can harm a manufacturing managers' performance evaluation. Increasing inventory requires increased production, which means that processes must operate at higher rates. When (not if) something goes wrong, the process takes longer and uses more than the standard labour time.

The manager appears responsible for the excess, even though s/he has no control over the production requirement or the problem. In adverse economic times, firms use the same efficiencies to downsize, rightsize, or otherwise reduce their labour force. Workers laid off under those circumstances have even less control over excess inventory and cost efficiencies than their managers. Many financial and cost accountants have agreed for many years on the desirability of replacing standard cost accounting. They have not, however, found a successor.

THEORY OF CONSTRAINTS COST ACCOUNTING

Eliyahu M. Goldratt developed the Theory of Constraints in part to address the cost-accounting problems in what he calls the "cost world". He offers a substitute, called throughput accounting, that uses throughput (money for goods sold to customers) in place of output (goods produced that may sell or may boost inventory) and considers labour as a fixed rather than as a variable cost.

He defines inventory simply as everything the organization owns that it plans to sell, including buildings, machinery, and many other things in addition to the categories listed here. Throughput accounting recognizes only one class of variable costs: the operating expenses like materials and components that vary directly with the quantity produced. Finished goods inventories remain balance-sheet assets, but labour efficiency ratios no longer evaluate managers and workers.

Instead of an incentive to reduce labour cost, throughput accounting focuses attention on the relationships between throughput (revenue or income) on one hand and controllable operating expenses and changes in inventory on the other. Those relationships direct attention to the constraints or bottlenecks that prevent the system from producing more throughput, rather than to people - who have little or no control over their situations.

- *National Accounts:* Inventories also play an important role in national accounts and the analysis of the business cycle. Some short-term macroeconomic fluctuations are attributed to the inventory cycle.
- *Distressed Inventory:* Also known as distressed or expired stock, distressed inventory is inventory whose potential to be sold at a normal cost has or will soon pass. In certain industries it could also mean that the stock is or will soon be impossible to sell. Examples of distressed inventory include products that have reached its expiry date, or has reached a date in advance of expiry at which the planned market will no longer purchase it (*e.g.* 3 months left to expiry),

clothing that is defective or out of fashion, and old newspapers or magazines. It also includes computer or consumer-electronic equipment that is obsolescent or discontinued and whose manufacturer is unable to support it.

IMPACT ON FIRMS' PERFORMANCE

A firm is required to maintain a balance between liquidity and profitability while conducting its day to day operations. Liquidity is a precondition to ensure that firms are able to meet its short-term obligations and its continued flow can be guaranteed from a profitable venture. The importance of cash as an indicator of continuing financial health should not be surprising in view of its crucial role within the business. This requires that business must be run both efficiently and profitably.

In the process, an asset-liability mismatch may occur which may increase firm's profitability in the short run but at a risk of its insolvency. On the other hand, too much focus on liquidity will be at the expense of profitability and it is common to find finance textbooks begin their working capital sections with a discussion of the risk and return tradeoffs inherent in alternative working capital policies. Thus, the manager of a business entity is in a dilemma of achieving desired tradeoff between liquidity and profitability in order to maximize the value of a firm. Small businesses are viewed as an essential element of a healthy and vibrant economy. They are seen as vital to the promotion of an enterprise culture and to the creation of jobs within the economy. Small Medium-Sized Enterprises (SMEs) are believed to provide an impetus to the economic progress of developing countries and its importance is gaining widespread recognition.

Equally in Mauritius the SMEs occupy a central place in the economy, accounting for 90% of business stock (those employing up to 50 employees) and employing approximately 25% of private sector employees. Storey (1994) notes that small firms, however, they are defined, constitute the bulk of enterprises in all economies in the world. However, given their reliance on short-term funds, it has long been recognized that the efficient management of working capital is crucial for the survival and growth of small firms. A large number of business failures have been attributed to inability of financial managers to plan and control properly the current assets and current liabilities of their respective firms.

Working capital management (WCM) is of particular importance to the small business. With limited access to the long-term capital markets, these firms tend to rely more heavily on owner financing, trade credit and short-term bank loans to finance their needed investment in cash, accounts receivable and inventory. However, the failure rate among small businesses is very high compared to that of large businesses. Studies in the UK and the US have shown that weak financial management - particularly poor working capital management and inadequate long-term financing - is a primary cause of failure among small businesses.

The success factors or impediments that contribute to success or failure are categorized as internal and external factors. The factors categorized as external include financing (such as the availability of attractive financing), economic conditions, competition, government regulations, technology and environmental factors. While the internal factors are managerial skills, workforce, accounting systems and financial management practices. Some research studies have been undertaken on the working capital management practices of both large and small firms in India, UK, US and Belgium using either a survey based approach to identify the push factors for firms to adopt good working capital practices or econometric analysis to investigate the association between WCM and profitability.

Specific research studies exclusively on the impact of working capital management on corporate profitability of the small manufacturing companies are scanty, especially for the case of Mauritius. The financial management of small firms in developing countries and in particular, Mauritius, a small island developing state is altogether an ignored area of research. Keeping this in view and the wider recognition of the potential contribution of the SME sector to the economy of developing countries, our study is a modest attempt to measure and analyse the trend of working capital investment and needs of small manufacturing firms. This study, therefore, attempts to assess the impact of WCM on profitability of a sample of small manufacturing companies and its results are expected to contribute to the existing literature on working capital and SMEs.

The study objectives are to examine the working capital management of the sample firms, and in particular to:

- To examine the impact of accounts receivables days, inventories days, accounts payable days and cash conversion cycle on return on total assets; and
- To analyse the trend in working capital needs of firms and to examine the causes for any significant differences between the industries.

Nature and Importance of Working Capital

The working capital meets the short-term financial requirements of a business enterprise. It is a trading capital, not retained in the business in a particular form for longer than a year. The money invested in it changes form and substance during the normal course of business operations. The need for maintaining an adequate working capital can hardly be questioned. Just as circulation of blood is very necessary in the human body to maintain life, the flow of funds is very necessary to maintain business. If it becomes weak, the business can hardly prosper and survive. Working capital starvation is generally credited as a major cause if not the major cause of small business failure in many developed and developing countries.

The success of a firm depends ultimately, on its ability to generate cash receipts in excess of disbursements. The cash flow problems of many small businesses are exacerbated by poor financial management and in particular the lack of planning cash requirements. The Management of Working Capital While the performance levels of small businesses have traditionally been attributed to general managerial factors such as manufacturing, marketing and operations, working capital management may have a consequent impact on small business survival and growth. The management of working capital is important to the financial health of businesses of all sizes. The amounts invested in working capital are often high in proportion to the total assets employed and so it is vital that these amounts are used in an efficient and effective way.

However, there is evidence that small businesses are not very good at managing their working capital. Given that many small businesses suffer from undercapitalization, the importance of exerting tight control over working capital investment is difficult to overstate. A firm can be very profitable, but if this is not translated into cash from operations within the same operating cycle, the firm would need to borrow to support its continued working capital needs.

Thus, the twin objectives of profitability and liquidity must be synchronised and one should not impinge on the other for long. Investments in current assets are inevitable to ensure delivery of goods or services to the ultimate customers and a proper management of same should give the desired impact on either profitability or liquidity. If resources are blocked at the different stage of the supply chain, this will prolong the cash operating cycle. Although this might increase profitability (due to increase sales), it may also adversely affect the profitability if the costs tied up in working capital exceed the benefits of holding more inventory and/or granting more trade credit to customers. Another component of working capital is accounts payable, but it is different in the sense that it does not consume resources; instead it is often used as a short term source of finance.

Thus it helps firms to reduce its cash operating cycle, but it has an implicit cost where discount is offered for early settlement of invoices. Review of previous studies Although working capital is the concern of all firms, it is the small firms that should address this issue more seriously. Given their vulnerability to a fluctuation in the level of working capital, they cannot afford to starve of cash. The study undertaken by revealed that small firms tend to have a relatively high proportion of current assets, less liquidity, exhibit volatile cash flows, and a high reliance on short-term debt. The recent work of Howorth and Westhead (2003), suggest that small companies tend to focus on some areas of working capital management where they can expect to improve marginal returns. For small and growing businesses, an efficient working capital management is a vital component of success and survival; i.e both profitability and liquidity. They further assert that smaller firms should adopt formal working capital management routines in order to reduce the probability of business closure, as well as to enhance business performance.

The study of Grablowsky (1976) and others have showed a significant relationship between various success measures and the employment of formal working capital policies and procedures. Managing cash flow and cash conversion cycle is a critical component of overall financial management for all firms, especially those who are capital constrained and more reliant on short-term sources of finance. Given these peculiarities, Peel and Wilson (1996) have stressed the efficient management of working capital, and more recently good credit management practice as being pivotal to the health and performance of the small firm sector.

Along the same line, Berry *et al* (2002) finds that SMEs have not developed their financial management practices to any great extent and they conclude that owner-managers should be made aware of the importance and benefits that can accrue from improved financial management practices. The study conducted by De Chazal Du Mee (1998) revealed that 60% enterprises suffer from cash flow problems. Narasimhan and Murty (2001) stress on the need for many industries to improve their return on capital employed (ROCE) by focusing on some critical areas such as cost containment, reducing investment in working capital and improving working capital efficiency. The pioneer work of Shin and Soenen (1998) and the more recent study of Deloof (2003) have found a strong significant relationship between the measures of WCM and corporate profitability.

Their findings suggest that managers can increase profitability by reducing the number of day's accounts receivable and inventories. This is particularly important for small growing firms who need to finance increasing amounts of debtors. Mauritius provides a good case study for this paper as it looks at the small and medium sized enterprises operating in the manufacturing sector of a small island developing state. Most of the previous studies on working capital management and financial management of small firms have focused on the US, UK and some other developed countries like Belgium and Australia.

Methodology

The primary aim of this paper is to investigate the impact of WCM on corporate profitability of Mauritian small manufacturing firms. This is achieved by developing a similar empirical framework first used by Shin and Soenen (1998) and the subsequent work of Deloof (2003). We extend our study by also analysing the trends in working capital need of firms and to examine the possible causes for any significant differences between the industries. Our study focuses exclusively on the small manufacturing firms operating in five major industry groups which are both registered and organised as proprietary/ private companies. This restriction places a limit on the number of firms qualifying for the study and is further narrowed down following the revised Companies Act of 2001 which requires firms with a given turnover threshold to file only an aggregated financial statements.

Thus the empirical study is based on a sample of 58 small manufacturing companies. The data has been collected from the financial statements of the sample firms having a legal entity and have filed their annual return to the Registrar of Companies. The sample was drawn from the directory of Small Medium Industrial Development Organisation (SMIDO), a database for registered manufacturing firms operating in diverse activities and for which data was available for a 6 years' period, covering the accounting period 1997-98 to 2002-03.

The companies qualified for the two conditions are further grouped into industries based on the classification as listed in the 2003 directory. Thus the data set covers 58 firms from five industry sub-sectors: food and beverages, leather garments, paper products, prefabricated metal products and wood furniture.

This has given a balanced panel data set of 348 firm-year observations for a sample of 58 firms. For the purpose of this study, profitability is measured by Return on Total Assets (ROTA), which is defined as profit before interest and tax divided by total assets. The operating income measure of profitability used in the study of Deloof (2003) is not appropriate for this study. The SMEs is characterised by a low fixed assets base and relied to a large extent on accounts payable to fund its gross working capital.

Thus a comprehensive measure of profitability is best captured by computing the return on total assets which is equal to the total liabilities of the firms, made up mainly of equity capital and current liabilities. Some firms have significant fixed financial assets and were thus excluded from the calculation of ROTA.

The Explanatory Variables

The efficiency ratios, namely accounts receivable, inventory and accounts payable have been computed. The Cash Conversion Cycle (CCC) is used as a comprehensive measure of working capital as it shows the time lag between expenditure for the purchases of raw materials and the collection of sales of finished goods. The longer the cycle, the larger the funds blocked in working capital. The return on assets is a better measure since it relates the profitability of the business to the asset base. There are many ways of managing return on assets but, in principle, key levers are, of course, profit increase and assets reduction. The latter has become more important to many businesses as the former becomes more elusive.

Control Variables

In order to account for firm's size and the other variables that may influence profits, sales a proxy for size (the natural logarithm of sales), the gearing ratio (financial debt/total assets), the gross working capital turnover ratio (sales/current assets) and the ratio of current assets to total assets are included as control variables in the regressions. The regressions also include the ratio of current liabilities to total assets to measure the degree of aggressive financing policy, with a high ratio being relatively more aggressive. Return on total assets is on average 5.6% with paper products industry having the highest return of 11%. The leather and garments industry reported a negative operating profit margin, which could be explained by their high foreign exchange risk exposure and the high labour costs.

Typical to the SME sector, the firms have relied mostly on short-term financing, with the metals industry being more aggressive, with an average of 82%. On average firms collect their receivables after 65 days while they take on average 116 days to pay suppliers. The average CCC is 105 days, implying that typical to the manufacturing sector firms turnover their stocks on an average of 3.3 times a year.

This shows the influence of leather and garments, metals products and wood and furniture industries holding inventories for more than 150 days, with a maximum value of 1688 days. Mean sales value for the sample companies is 10 million rupees, with only the paper products industry having a value twice the amount. On average about 22% of all assets are financed with financial debt. It is also noteworthy that the average firm in the sample has a gross working capital turnover ratio of 3.1, thus indicating a lower operational efficiency.

WORKING CAPITAL ANALYSIS

The major components of gross working capital include stocks (raw materials, work-in-progress and finished goods), debtors, cash and bank balances. The composition of working capital depends on a multiple of factors, such as operating level, level of operational efficiency, inventory policies, book debt policies, technology used and nature of the industry. While inter- industry variation is expected to be high, the degree of variation is expected to be low for firms within the industry. A comparison of inventory composition of industries over the years shows only slight improvement for the food and beverages and the paper products industries. It is interesting to note the consistent improvement in trade debtors share of current assets in all the industries and except for the food and beverages, it represents less that 30% of total current assets.

Thus it can be deduced that the companies have monitored the accounts receivable reasonably well and this could be partly due to their need for generating funds from the operating activities instead of relying from outside funds. Except for the paper products, the other four industries have a greater reliance on short-term funds and this is even more in 2003. The prefabricated metal product is financing 85% of its assets out of current liabilities and this over-reliance may be a threat to the industry's survival.

In terms of liquidity, all the four industries, food and beverages, garments, metal products, wood and furniture are having less liquid assets to meet their current obligations and if this becomes permanent, it may affect supplies of materials and thus production. The proportion of liquid assets to total assets is above 70% for the wood and metal industries, indicating a low fixed assets base. This implies that these two industries can operate with a relatively low investment in fixed assets as compared to the other industries like printing and garments where the production tend to be heavily mechanised. Another plausible reason could be that the Mauritian small manufacturing firms have been more concerned about current operations than about longer term issues like capacity and technology. Weinraub and Visscher (1998), also report industry-wise differences in the level of aggressiveness with respect to working capital investment over time.

Pearson correlation coefficients for the variables used to assess the impact of working capital management on profitability, measured by return on total assets. ROTA is significantly positively correlated with OPM and capital-turnover ratio, but negatively correlated with the measures of WCM, except for the cash conversion cycle. This positive relation for CCC is consistent with the view that resources are blocked at the different stage of the supply chain, thus prolonging the operating cycle. This might increase profits due to increase sales, especially where the costs of tied up capital is lower than the benefits of holding more inventories and granting more trade credit to customers. Also the small manufacturing firms may be able to obtain trade credit from the suppliers and this is supported by the higher proportion of current liabilities to total assets for all the industries except for the paper products. However, care must be exercised while interpreting the Pearson Correlation coefficients because they cannot provide a reliable indicator of association in a manner which controls for additional explanatory variables. Examining simple bivariate correlation in a conventional matrix does not take account of each variable's correlation with all other explanatory variables.

Our main analysis will be derived from appropriate multivariate models, estimated using fixed effects framework and pooled OLS. The different analyses have identified critical management practices and are expected to assist managers in identifying areas where they might improve the financial performance of their operation. The results have provided owner-managers with information regarding the basic financial management practices used by their peers and their peers attitudes towards these practices. The working capital needs of an organization change over time as does its internal cash generation rate.

As such, the small firms should ensure a good synchronization of its assets and liabilities. This study has shown that the paper and printing industry has been able to achieve high scores on the various components of working capital and this has positively impact on its profitability. On this premise this industry may be referred as the 'hidden champions' and could thus be used as best practice among the SMEs. Further, this research concludes that there is a pressing need for further empirical studies to be undertaken on small business financial management, in particular their working capital practices by extending the sample size so that an industry-wise analysis can help to uncover the factors that explain the better performance for some industries and how these best practices could be extended to the other industries. This would also assist policy-makers and educators to identify the requirements of, and specific problems faced by small firms in Mauritius, especially as more emphasis is placed on the sector by the government.

This study has come at an opportune time where the Mauritian government is deploying resources to help the SME sector so that the latter can positively contribute to the Mauritian economy. This analysis has been constrained by the sample size and the nature of the data, which could have well affected the results.

Further studies will aim at increasing the sample size for still better and consistent panel estimates. Many pharma could focus on increasing sales and investing in new markets, without worrying too much about housekeeping. Times have changed and in future, domestic economies will play a far greater part in maintaining profitability in the industry. One area where pharma could create value is in working capital management. Marc Loneux from working capital consultancy REL, the largest US and European pharrna companies have up to US$25 billion tied up in working capital that could be liberated through better management.

The same companies could a further billion by reducing costs and implementing better business practice. His comments are based on research conducted by REL on pharma's practices in this field. Like performance management, working capital management has been a priority for older industries with lower margins, but has been largely ignored by pharmaceutical companies.

However, it is now widely recognised that operating efficiencies will be a major contributor to the long-term value growth in the industry. At the end of 2004, the net operating working capital of the 18 largest pharmaceutical companies in the world (by sales, 13 US and five European) was US$79 billion. US firms had between US$6.4 billion and US$16 billion tied up in working capital.

European companies have between US$4.6 billion and US$0.3 billion that could be liberated. Dealing with this excess would increase the market value of the US companies by between (0.8 per cent and 2.1 per cent. Of the European firms included in the survey, better capital management could increase their value by between 0.9 per cent and 1.8 per cent. The smallest pharma companies in the US, together with Roche in Europe, offer the greatest potential for creating market value, says REL. Although there is a specific working capital model for every business sector, there are general principles that can be applied everywhere, says Loneux. One of The largest US and European pharma companies have up to US$25 billion tied up in working capital these is close collaboration between producers, sellers and wholesalers.

This creates a win-win situation, giving manufacturers a better view of demand, and allowing both parties to manage their inventories more effectively. The automotive industry, in particular, has provided good collaborative models, as has the computer manufacturer Dell, which produces computers only when they are ordered and has negotiated very good payment terms with its suppliers.

Pharma has begun to implement better inventory-management practice over the past two years, with some firms entering inventory management agreements with their wholesalers. As a result, sections of the industry have levelled the quarterly volume fluctuations that once made it difficult to streamline production and reduce inventories.

Improving working capital management also creates savings elsewhere. "We are talking about improved collection, improved logistics and supply chain, further consolidation, more efficient buying and so on," says Loneux. When you implement best practice in working capital, you can cut the number of collectors and people involved in wholesaling and logistics. You can also reduce write-offs in receivables because your inventories are lower. A more general strategy for pharma, says Loneux, is "optimising the commercial". Focusing better on the product mix, ensuring that companies make the most of what they have out there, withdrawing or postponing launches in order to maximise the model.

Such strategies could prove a problem with governments and other healthcare providers, who are seemingly ready to oppose what they regard as manipulation of the market. It appears that pharma industry leaders are increasingly focused on engaging with external agents - governments, healthcare providers and patients - to develop a more collaborative working model.

Loneux acknowledges these difficulties, but thinks public-private collaborations pioneered by the likes of Bill Gates and GlaxoSmithKline are the way forward, ensuring people get medicines they can afford with a decent return for pharma. Asked about the cost-effective ness of outsourcing admin, sales and marketing roles, Loneux is sceptical. He believes this will have a negligible impact on costs and that possible savings in R&D are limited by the quality constraints placed on pharma manufacturing - companies can't place the work just anywhere.

Moreover, he says, outsourcing is often done to serve local demand. Although many companies are opening up in India, where there is a growing market, demand is still largely concentrated in Europe and the US. "There is some outsourcing in India by the big ones," he says, "but I wouldn't say it was a priority." After the research was carried out, REL showed its work to some of the major pharma companies. Loneux comments "Big Pharma recognises that it is something it has just started to address, that there is clearly room for improvement.

8

Translation of Foreign Currency and Financial Statements

A company with operating affiliates in a hundred nations must deal with a hundred sets of generally accepted accounting principles in the consolidation process. The operations of the company must also deal with business transactions and financial reports denominated in a hundred different currencies. A financial reporting and control system, the mechanism by which a global business is managed, must include in its design a means for handling both multiple currency transactions and currency translations of operating affiliate financial results.

GOLD AS A GLOBAL CURRENCY

Dealing in foreign currencies has not always been a major problem in international trade and commerce. Historically, the most common international currency was gold, followed by silver, or a combination of the two. Gold, in particular, has been universally accepted as a monetary means of exchange and a storehouse of value. The purchasing power of an ounce of gold has remained throughout the ages, whereas the purchasing power of paper currencies has eroded with time.

One of the few times when gold lost purchasing power was in the sixteenth century when Spain was inundated with gold from the conquest of the Aztec and Inca empires. This loss of purchasing power is in line with the Webster dictionary definition of inflation as "an increase in the amount of currency in circulation resulting in a relatively sharp and sudden fall in its value and rise in prices; it may be caused by an increase in the volume of paper money issued or of gold mined, or a relative increase in expenditures, as when the supply of goods fails to meet demand."

Gold is associated with times of political and economic stability. During times of upheaval (war, civil unrest, economic turmoil), coins were progressively debased until they contained only common metals. Later, when nations learned to substitute paper that was convertible into gold, instability or turmoil would bring about paper currency that lacked convertibility such as the "greenbacks" during the U.S. Civil War. A sign of the restoration of stability would be the reinstatement of the gold standard and the buying back of "greenbacks" with convertible paper money.

Prior to World War I, major currencies were convertible into gold. The relationship between one currency and another was simply their respective conversion rate to gold. If one unit of currency X was convertible into one gram of gold and one unit of currency Y was convertible into two grams of gold, then the exchange rate between currency X and Y was 2 units of X for 1 unit of Y. The exchange rate was fixed. Indeed, it could not fluctuate.

Suppose, however, that the market rate for currency Y became 3 units of X under a gold standard where Y can be exchanged for 2 units of X in terms of gold. An individual holding a unit of currency Y could exchange it in the currency market for 3 units of currency X. He or she could take the 3 units of currency X to the central bank for currency X and obtain three grams of gold. Then he or she could saunter over to the central bank for currency Y and obtain 1.5 units of currency Y.

Now he or she has 50 percent more of currency Y than what he or she began with—not a bad return for visiting one currency market and two banks. Obviously, an anomaly between currency exchange rates and their respective conversion rates into gold could not exist. The principal advantage of the gold standard is a fixed exchange rate between currencies based on their respective conversion rates to gold. International business is conducted as though there is a single, or global, currency. A global currency, or world currencies whose respective exchange rates are fixed and unchanging, reduces the complexity of both conducting international business and consolidating financial reports denominated in different currencies.

However, the gold standard had its reputed disadvantages. First of all, the expansion of the monetary supply of gold was limited to the amount of new gold mined, which was grossly inadequate when measured against the growth of international trade. Presumably, the benefits of international trade in raising living standards by the exchange of goods between different parts of the world would be difficult to achieve with trade growing at 10 percent per year and the gold supply expanding by 2 percent per year. In time, and in theory, there would be inadequate monetary reserves to support the volume of international trade. One argument against gold as a medium of exchange is the potential of an inadequate supply of gold inhibiting commerce.

Under the gold standard, trade imbalances between two nations eventually required a movement of gold between two nations. As a consequence of World War II, much of the world's gold ended up in U.S. bank vaults for safekeeping. Following the war, transfers of gold between nations were accomplished by moving gold from one location in a bank vault to another, signifying the settling of trade imbalances between nations. Photographs of these quaint scenes supposedly showed the apolitical disciplinarian nature of the gold standard: a nation with a trade deficit better have some gold in its corner of the vault.

In theory, under the gold standard, nations with chronic balance of payment deficits in international trade could not paper over their economic difficulties by turning on the monetary printing press. Continuing deficits in trade would result in a loss of gold reserves. A nation whose paper currency was convertible into gold would suffer a loss of its money supply. Less money in circulation would induce a recession. Loss of jobs would cut demand for goods and reduced demand would cause prices to fall. The contraction of business activity would last until prices had fallen to the point where the nation's products became competitive in the world market. More competitive prices enhanced exports and the pickup in the volume of goods sold to overseas markets created job opportunities for the factory workers. Gold would flow into the nation as its trade balance turned positive, increasing the nation's money supply and fueling the continued expansion of the economy. Unfortunately, an expanding economy fostered higher wages and prices. When wages and prices once again became out of line with the world market, product exports would shrink, imports would grow, the trade surplus would be transformed to a trade deficit, setting the stage for a repeat of the cycle.

Another argument against gold is that the gold standard induces cyclicality in business activity through the self-correcting mechanism of an endless series of contractions and expansions accompanying the tidal movement of gold in and out of the central bank's vault. Although the expansion phase of a business cycle is enjoyed by labour and capital alike, the contraction phase is not—thus, the battle cry of those against the gold standard of "mankind being crucified on a cross of gold."

Lastly, no nation is eager to be bled of its gold reserves. This goes beyond the consequences of a loss of money supply. It is a point of national pride to have an increasingly larger pile of gold bars in the central bank's vault and a matter of national concern when the golden security blanket is threatened. Having gold as a medium for settling accounts between nations has a tendency to induce government officials and rulers to favour a trade policy that results in an ever growing stack of gold bars in the central bank's vault. Consequently, they are motivated to take whatever actions are necessary to enhance the inflow, and restrict the outflow, of gold, the success of which can be easily measured by counting the gold bars. Adam Smith called this economic practice, or behaviour pattern, mercantilism.

Mercantilism declared that the winner in international trade was the nation with the largest hoard of gold. Adam Smith realized that an economic system in which every nation is trying to maximize the inflow and minimize the outflow of gold is not conducive to international trade. Such conduct leads to encouraging exports, which adds to the stack of gold, and discouraging imports, which reduces the stack of gold. This contradictory behaviour pattern results in the erection of trade barriers and the contraction of international trade. Adam Smith believed that the material welfare of the people is enhanced if every community, and every nation, specializes in what it does best and relies on domestic and international trade to satisfy its other needs. Anything that inhibits trade eventually lowers the living standards of the people. The last argument against the gold standard is that it encourages rulers and governments to maximize their gold reserves by erecting trade barriers against imports, which impede international trade and lower living standards.

Some say that this lesson taught by Adam Smith over two hundred years ago has yet to be learned by Japan. Japan has been criticized as the world's greatest mercantilist nation by its insistence in accumulating the world's largest hoard, not of gold, but of U.S. dollars. This is done by pushing its export industries while at the same time making it difficult for imported finished products to reach Japanese consumers. Accumulating a hoard of U.S. dollars may be of comfort to the Japanese government, but it is having a deleterious impact on the U.S. economy. This condition cannot continue indefinitely because the ultimate outcome is a "rustbelt" of unacceptable and unparalleled proportions.

In fairness, Japan has reinvested a large portion of its surplus in direct investments in the United States, totaling $104 billion at the end of 1989. These included the building of transplant factories and the acquisition of real estate properties plus investments in Treasury securities. Japan is under intense pressure to open its markets to non-Japanese-made products, and has done so in a limited way.

U.S. DOLLAR AS A GLOBAL CURRENCY

The twentieth century was a tough time for the gold standard. World War I, the Great Depression, and World War II forced nations off the gold standard. Being off the gold standard did not necessarily save mankind from being crucified on a cross of gold, a cross of paper could do the job just as nicely. The inflation of the German mark during the Weimar Republic destroyed the savings of the German people, caused the economy to collapse, and paved the way for Hitler. In 1944, the principal nations of the world met at Bretton Woods, New Hampshire, to hammer out a new international monetary system. The Bretton Woods Agreement created the International Monetary Fund (IMF), whose purpose was to promote international monetary cooperation among the member nations, to encourage growth in international trade, and to promote stable currency exchange rates between various nations.

The system envisioned fixed exchange rates between various currencies and the U.S. dollar, with the dollar alone being convertible to gold. This made good sense in that the United States, as a result of the war, was the holder of much of the world's gold. The Bretton Woods Agreement provided the essence of the gold standard in that the exchange rates between the primary world currencies and the U.S. dollar were fixed. Therefore, each unit of currency was convertible into a known quantity of dollars, and dollars could be converted into gold at $35 per ounce. Again, international trade could be conducted in what amounted to a global currency as long as the exchange rate between a currency and the dollar was constrained to trade in a narrow range about a fixed exchange rate.

However, the amount of currency in circulation was not fixed by the Bretton Woods Agreement. Individual nations, not the IMF, controlled the speed of the monetary printing presses, and therefore, the amount of money in circulation. It was also the responsibility of each nation, not the IMF, to maintain its currency exchange rate within plus or minus 1 percent of the official exchange rate with the dollar. If the lower limit of the allowable band was about to be pierced, the central bank was expected to purchase its own currency to increase its value. If the currency exchange rate was bumping against its upper limit, the central bank was expected to sell its currency to decrease its value. As attractive as this may sound, two problems immediately arose. The lesser problem was exceeding the upper limit of a permissible trading band. A nation was expected to sell its currency to depress its value.

Ultimately, this meant turning on the printing press to create a sufficient quantity of currency to suppress its exchange rate with the dollar. But a national government might not be eager to do this if it had concerns about the inflationary consequences.

Following the war, the West German mark strengthened with the reestablishment of the nation's industrial base and the mark began bumping against its upper limit with respect to the dollar. Remembering the inflation during the Weimar Republic, the West German central bankers and political leaders were reluctant to print marks to depress its value. The mark began to trade above its upper limit. A potentially knottier problem was dealing with a currency trading near its lower limit. This meant that a nation must buy its currency to enhance its value with relation to the dollar. A nation cannot purchase its currency with its own currency. The Italian central bankers cannot purchase lira with lira to bolster its value.

A nation must use its gold or foreign currency reserves to purchase its currency. Without these, a nation cannot offer anything in exchange for its currency. With nothing to offer in exchange for their currencies, both the Italian and British bankers could not prevent their currencies from falling below their lower trading limits. Therefore, the IMF permitted, with proper consultation, a nation to change the exchange rate of its currency with respect to the dollar. A lowering of the exchange rate was called a devaluation and a raising of the exchange rate was called a revaluation. As long as devaluations and revaluations were not common occurrences, the Bretton Woods system functioned reasonably well, which it did for a quarter of a century as a substitute for the gold standard.

The undoing of the Bretton Woods system was not caused by the disruptions occasioned by devaluations and revalua-tions, but the growing number of dollars in circulation. It was the U.S. printing presses that were running full tilt to paper over its chronic balance of payments deficits with other industrialized nations that provoked an international financial crisis. These vast holdings of U.S. dollars were partly the result of the outflow of dollars to support the rebuilding of war ravaged Europe and Japan (the Marshall Plan).

But much of the dollar overhang was a consequence of a chronic U.S. trade deficit caused by Americans buying more products made overseas than American made products were being sold overseas.

By 1969, it was readily apparent that the holdings of dollars in foreign hands, that is U.S. dollar deposits in non-U.S. banks, far exceeded the amount of gold in Fort Knox. The first patch sewed on to the tearing fabric of international finance was the creation of Special Drawing Rights (SDRs), or paper gold. SDRs were to be a substitute for gold.

A nation could cash in excess dollars and supposedly be indifferent whether it received an ounce of gold or a slip of paper declaring itself to be equivalent to an ounce of gold. In fact, SDRs were not even a slip of paper, but an entry in a computer data base. Proponents of SDRs desired such a system to show once and for all that mankind no longer had to resort to that "barbaric relic," gold, as a means of settlement between nations.

Apparently, it did make a difference. One ounce of gold did carry more weight than an entry in a computer data bank declaring itself to be an ounce of gold. This forced President Nixon, in 1971, to "close the gold window." No one could turn in dollars to the U.S. government and expect to receive a specified amount of gold. Although holders of U.S. dollars could buy gold in the open market, the price paid for the gold would be determined by the laws of supply and demand, not by government fiat backed up by gold reserves. This undid the Bretton Woods Agreement.

During the crisis, the monetary authorities of the industrialized nations hammered out the Smithsonian Agreement. The Smithsonian Agreement turned out to be a short-lived stopgap agreement that, by 1973, gave way to a totally free floating currency exchange system.

LIVING WITHOUT A GLOBAL CURRENCY

In a floating currency exchange system, only the central bank knows a nation's target exchange rate with other nations and the band in which it is permitted to float without intervention by the central bank. Those in commerce may guess at what this target exchange rate and its associated trading band are, and even if they are good at second guessing, they still cannot conduct international trade with confidence. The central bank may change its mind on the target exchange rate, or may choose not to intervene in the currency exchange market to keep its currency exchange rate within some prescribed trading band. A "clean" float exists when a country permits the forces of supply and demand to determine its exchange rate with other currencies. A "dirty" float implies government intervention to maintain some control over the exchange rate of its currency with other currencies. Most exchange rates between major currencies are managed, in that central bankers intervene in the currency exchange market to keep their currencies within certain desired limits. Intervention is forced on the central bankers because currency exchange rates have a major impact on the volume of international trade, the monetary balance between imports and exports and the health of the domestic economy.

Suppose that one unit of currency X is fixed at 2 units of currency Y. Two manufacturers make widgets, one in the nation whose currency is X and the other in a nation whose currency is Y. Widgets are a common industrial item, a mature product where manufacturers' profit margins are about 5 percent of sales. In the respective countries, widgets sell for 10 X's and 20 Y's, and the manufacturers' profits are 0.5 X and 1 Y. From the point of view of the manufacturer in the nation whose currency is X, he can sell widgets in the domestic market and receive 10 X, or he can export and receive 20 Y. Upon receiving 20 Y, he exchanges the proceeds for 10 X, pays out his total costs of 9.5 X and nets 0.5 X just as if he had sold the goods in his own nation (assuming for now that transportation costs are the same for both the domestic and international markets, and ignoring taxes).

Now suppose that the market price and the cost of manufacture do not change, but that a floating exchange rate system comes into being. After some period of time, the exchange rate is floating at 1 X to 1.5 Y. The same manufacturer can still receive 10 X in the domestic market or 20 Y in the foreign market. However, when he sells in the foreign market, the 20 Y can now be exchanged for 13.3 X—13.3 X less 9.5 X in manufacturing costs is 3.8 X in profits as compared to making 0.5 X in the domestic market. It is much more profitable to sell in the foreign market. His predictable behaviour pattern is to increase production to the greatest possible extent and dump his "excess" production into the Y market.

Assuming efficient production where there is little leeway to cut costs, the only way for the manufacturer in the nation whose currency is Y to respond to this flood of imports is to cut his price. But he can only cut his price to the point of covering costs. This is 19 Y. This price cut can be matched by the exporter. Now he receives 19 Y, which when exchanged for X at the rate of 1 X for 1.5 Y, nets him 12.7 X. His cost is still 9.5 X, so his profit selling in the foreign market is 3.2 X versus 0.5 X in the domestic market. Thus, he continues to flood the Y market by operating his plant at maximum capacity and by building new plants to take advantage of this favorable situation. As long as he can convert his foreign sales to an equivalent of something more than 10 X, he is making more profits in the export market. The manufacturer, as a profit maximizer, would expand his productive capacity until the price for a widget is depressed to 15 Y, which nets him 10 X, the same as selling in the domestic market. In so doing, he will be a hero to his workers as their numbers expand. He will be a hero to the municipal government for the benefits that accrue to the local economy in building new factories and hiring more workers. He will be a hero to the national government for expanding foreign sales. He will be a hero to the shareholders for enhancing the profitability of the company.

Meanwhile, the manufacturer in the nation whose currency is Y is selling in a market where the price is 15 Y and where his manufacturing costs are 19 Y.

He will appeal to the national government for subsidies, trade restrictions, and anything else that may save him and the jobs of his workers. In a world more or less committed to free trade, subsidies and trade restrictions may be difficult to obtain. If this is the case, and if he cannot cut his costs, then the most probable outcome is that the manufacturer, and the entire widget industry in the Y currency nation, will go out of business.

Of course, if the floating rate moved in the opposite direction, the cast of characters would be reversed. The manufacturer whose costs are denominated in currency Y would wipe out the manufacturer whose costs are denominated in currency X. As the floating exchange rate moves up and down much as waves on the open sea, manufacturers in different nations can take turns bludgeoning one another. Floating currency exchange rates open up a whole new dimension of risk that was not present under a fixed currency exchange rate system. In a world of global commerce, an adverse change in the floating exchange rate means a loss of both domestic and international sales. A company whose market is located within walking distance of its factory can lose it to a company located on the other side of the world by an adverse change in currency exchange rates. Alternatively, its market may explode through no effort of its own because of a favorable change in the floating exchange rate. A meaningful change in the exchange rates between two nations is apt to be a bonanza for one set of manufacturers and a disaster for the other. And a floating exchange rate system means that change in currency exchange rates occurs continually.

Consequently, there is a real incentive for national governments to stabilize their currency exchange rates with other nations, particularly those nations that figure prominently in their international trade. The European Joint Float was established in 1972 by France, West Germany, Italy, the Netherlands, Belgium, Luxembourg, the United Kingdom, and Denmark to maintain their currencies within a narrow band, which, at that time, was called a "snake." They also agreed that the snake could wiggle with a greater degree of freedom with respect to other currencies—dubbed the "tunnel." The idea of the snake was to ensure that trade among the European nations would not be severely impacted by wide swings in the floating exchange rates among the European currencies. The snake wiggling in a tunnel permitted the European currencies, as a group, to fluctuate more widely with respect to the currencies of the rest of the industrialized world, which would not have such a severe impact on the European economies.

A snake wiggling in a tunnel was the progenitor of the European Currency Unit (ECU). The ECU is a "basket" currency made up of European Community currencies weighted in relation to the size of their economies. The ECU tends to be more stable than any of its individual currencies, making it a desirable currency for conducting business and financing companies.

It is possible that the ECU might become the only currency in Europe, with the full implementation of the European Monetary System (EMS) later in the 1990s, if the Maastricht Treaty is approved by the member nations. The progression of the snake wiggling in a tunnel leading to the ECU as a single currency under the auspices of the

EMS manifests the desire of national governments to stabilize currency exchange rates with their major trading partners. Whatever benefits accrue from stable currency exchange rates, the plain fact of the matter is that currency exchange rates have been anything but stable. The highest exchange rate for the indicated year between a currency and the U.S. dollar, was taken from the U.S. Statistical Abstract.

Table. Highest Exchange Rate-U.S. Cents per Unit Foreign Currency

	Australian Dollar	**Canadian Dollar**	**British Pound**	**French Franc**
1989	87.1	86.1	177.4	16.8
1985	81.5	75.5	144.5	13.0
1980	117.4	86.8	241.6	24.8
1975	135.9	100.5	241.8	25.0
1970	111.8	98.4	240.6	18.1
	Swiss Franc	**German Mark**	**Japanese**	**Yen S. Africa Rand**
1989	64.0	57.5	0.79	49.9
1985	47.5	39.8	0.49	51.5
1980	62.7	58.0	0.48	133.2
1975	40.5	43.1	0.35	148.7
1970	23.3	27.5	0.28	139.8

Interestingly, an adverse change in currency exchange rates need not be accompanied by an industrial retreat. The Midwest "rustbelt" in the United States was not caused by an adverse currency exchange rate change between the dollar and the yen. Quite the reverse, the Japanese yen appreciated with respect to the U.S. dollar.

This means that U.S. firms had a clear pricing advantage in selling their goods in Japan. The aforementioned economic model would suggest that U.S. firms should have transformed Japan into a "rustbelt" if changing currency exchange rates were entirely responsible for shifts in the competitive position between nations.

However, the economic model did not include an effective ban of U.S. and other nation's manufactured goods in Japan, which may not have been purchased by Japanese consumers even if they were available.

Another assumption violated in the model was the ability of Japanese manufacturers to improve their productivity, which reduced the cost of production, partly compensating for the appreciating yen. The model did not take into consideration the possibility of the Japanese being able to raise prices in terms of U.S. dollars and still gain market share because of a marked preference by U.S. consumers for higher quality Japanese goods.

QUOTING RATES

An American watching the financial news on television sees currencies reported as follows:

British pound	1.77
French franc	5.53
German mark	1.62
Japanese yen	127.70
Canadian dollar	0.84

This presentation of various currencies mixes two ways of quoting rates. A direct quote is made in terms of the number of domestic units for a foreign unit. An indirect quote is made in terms of the number of foreign units for a domestic unit. In the preceding example, the British pound and the Canadian dollar are direct quotes, where 1.77 U.S. dollars purchase 1 British pound and 0.84 U.S. dollars purchase 1 Canadian dollar. The French franc, German mark, and Japanese yen are indirect quotes, where 5.53 French francs, or 1.62 German marks, or 127.70 Japanese yen purchase 1 U.S. dollar. Currency exchange rates published in the *Wall Street Journal*.

The South African rand has two quotes: a commercial and a financial rate. The central bank of South Africa examines requests for conversion of the South African rand into other currencies and divides these requests into three categories: commercial, financial, and all others. If a transaction is deemed commercial, the bank exchanges the South African rands at a rate of 2.8098 rands per U.S. dollar. If the transaction is deemed financial, the central bank of South Africa exchanges rands at a rate of 3.62 rands per U.S. dollar. Obviously, it is very important for a holder of South African rands to have a currency exchange transaction deemed commercial rather than financial because more U.S. dollars are received with the former classification than with the latter. If the transaction does not fall into either classification, the central bank of South Africa may not convert the currency. The holder of the currency has to exchange it by some other means. How he does it and what he receives for the rand is no longer a central bank, or official, transaction.

Multiple currency exchange rates are not unusual. In 1983, Venezuela had three official rates—4.3 bolivars per U.S. dollar for essential imports, 6 bolivars for nonessential imports, and 7 bolivars for other purposes. Multiple exchange rates open the door for corruption, as government officials are enticed to declare.

The Mexican peso was fixed at 8.65 pesos for one U.S. dollar for a generation. In April 1954, the peso was devalued to 12.5 pesos to the dollar, which held until 1971 when the central bank of Mexico ran out of dollars to maintain the official rate of exchange. The Mexican peso began to float against the U.S. dollar. The rate between the peso and the dollar floats "cleanly" in response to the laws of supply and demand at more than 3,000 pesos to the dollar. Both the Venezuelan bolivar and the Mexican peso are considered "soft" currencies, where people have little, or no, faith in the currency as a storehouse of value. Any currency left over from spending on goods and services is not placed in a bank savings account or kept in a drawer, but is either invested in tangibles (land, inventory) or exchanged for stronger currencies. In essence, these currencies have been repudiated by the people.

The U.S. dollar has undergone a significant revaluation with respect to the Venezuelan bolivar and the Mexican peso. Venezuelans and Mexicans who switched their holdings to U.S. dollars have done much better in maintaining the purchasing power of their cash reserves than those who steadfastly held on to bolivars and pesos. Although fleeing from a currency is understandable, it does not help the economic development of a nation because unspent currency, in the form of savings, is no longer available as a source of funds to support trade and commerce.

The currency of Chile is listed at the official rate of 336.73. The day before, the official rate was 337.22 pesos per dollar. Because it requires fewer pesos on the given day to buy one U.S. dollar than on the prior day, the official rate of the currency is being revalued. The real question is to what degree is the central bank of Chile permitting the exchange of its currency with dollars at the official rate. It is possible that the official rate may simply be a quoted rate without any underlying transactions. If that is the case, then the true exchange rate is being established in the back alleys of Chilean marketplace, where there is a clean float determined by the supply of, and the demand for, a currency.

Most rates are not listed as floating or official rates, such as the Austrian schilling at 11.42 per U.S. dollar. This implies that there is intervention by the central bank to maintain a predetermined relationship between the schilling, the dollar, and other currencies, a so-called dirty float. It is possible that the Austrian central bank is primarily concerned with the relationship between the schilling and the deutschemark. If so, then the exchange rate between the schilling and the U.S. dollar is established indirectly. The rate between the schilling and the deutschemark and the rate between the dollar and the deutschemark establishes the rate between the schilling and the dollar.

Lastly, the *Wall Street Journal* Currency Trading table publishes exchange rates for two "basket" currencies—Special Drawing Rights and the European Currency Unit. SDRs is a basket of U.S., German, British, French, and Japanese currencies, whereas ECUs, as previously mentioned, is a basket of European Community currencies. Since the currencies making up SDRs and ECUs are exchangeable for U.S. dollars at published rates, the value of an SDR and an

ECU can be calculated in terms of U.S. dollars. Once expressed in dollars, an SDR and an ECU can be valued in terms of other currencies. SDRs and ECUs are quoted in the financial press because some transactions are denominated in basket currencies. Companies have financed their operations with ECU-denominated bonds and ships passing through the Suez Canal pay tolls in SDRS.

The published quotes are for conversion of $1 million or more of one currency to another. The "retail" market handles currency exchanges for smaller amounts where the quotes may differ from those published in the financial press. Tourists rely on the retail market where exchange rates tend to be less favorable than the quoted rates, and may even be negotiable. Two rates are usually quoted to a prospective customer such as $1.80/$1.95 for a British pound. This means that the retail trader is willing to buy a British pound for $1.80 and sell a British pound for $1.95. The difference, or spread, in the rates is the retailer's profit margin.

CROSS RATES

The rates published by the financial press in this country are in terms of U.S. dollars. These can be used to develop "cross rates" between two currencies by removing the U.S. dollar from the equation. For instance, the German mark, or deutschemark (DM), is quoted at 1.623 per U.S. dollar and the Swiss franc (SF) is quoted at 1.458 per U.S. dollar. For dealings between German and Swiss companies, the appropriate German mark/Swiss franc exchange rate can be calculated by dividing 1.623 DM per U.S. dollar by 1.458 SF per U.S. dollar for a cross rate of 1.113 DM per SF. In European currency markets, cross rates are usually in terms of direct quotes, but sometimes the liquidity of the dollar market is such that it is easier to exchange two currencies in a two-step process where one currency is exchanged for dollars and the dollars are then exchanged for the other.

FORWARD RATES

The rates quoted in the *Wall Street Journal* are for delivery within 2 business days. A few nations have quotes for forward rates—Britain, Canada,

France, Germany, Japan, and Switzerland. These are "hard" currencies, where individuals or banks are willing to quote a rate where the delivery is not in 2 days, but in 30, 90, or 180 days. The forward quotes are not the same as spot quotes, but represent the belief on the part of currency traders and investors as to what spot rates will be when the currency is "delivered" to the buyer in the future.

From the *Wall Street Journal* listing, the spot rate for the British pound is $1.7725 and the 180-day forward rate is $1.7216. Those quoting the 180-day forward rate are expecting the spot rate of the British pound to decline by $0.0509 over the next six months. The annualized rate of decline can be calculated from the following formula where *N* is the number of months of the forward contract. The forward rate contains an implied forecast of an annualized decline of -5.7 percent in the exchange rate between the British pound and the U.S. dollar.

Those quoting a forward rate between two currencies have implicitly considered the relative rates of inflation, trade imbalances and interest rate differentials, and central bank reserve positions. Past trends in the exchange rate between the two currencies play an important part in the process of setting forward rates. Facts can only provide guidance on what is the appropriate rate for forward delivery of a currency. Although there is data available for past and current inflation and interest rates, and on the past balance of trade and bank reserves, what is more pertinent are changes to these economic and financial measures and how they impact on the future relationship between two currencies.

Moreover, one has to guess at how much of central bank reserves might be committed, and how eager the central bankers are in defending against a devaluation of a currency or in fending off a revaluation.

Internal events, such as the outcome of an election, can change currency exchange rates. External events also have a bearing on exchange rates. The United Kingdom and Norway are oil exporters from crude produced in the North Sea. The British pound and the Norwegian krona have at times been called petrocurrencies because of shifts in the balance of payments in the United Kingdom and Norway induced by changes in oil prices. Currency relationships are also influenced by changing economic developments between nations.

The value of a currency must ultimately be linked to the political and economic health of a nation and the relative growth of its industrial base with respect to other nations. Both Germany and Japan emerged shattered from World War II only to successfully challenge the industrial supremacy of Great Britain and the United States in succeeding decades. Switzerland exercises more fiscal restraint than Great Britain and the United States by running its government operations without enormous budget deficits. There are sound economic reasons why there has been a long-term trend of an appreciating deutschemark, yen, and Swiss franc in relation to the British pound and the U.S. dollar. Forecasting the future direction of one currency with respect to another is both an art and a science. It is an unavoidable exercise for those who are willing to commit themselves to a future delivery of currency in the form of a forward contract.

DEVELOPING FORWARD CONTRACT QUOTES

Although there is no organized forward market for the Brazilian cruziero, suppose, for purposes of illustration, that an individual, or some institution, felt that the Brazilian cruziero would depreciate by 20 percent over some period of time, and was willing to quote a contract for forward delivery. If such a person existed, his calculation to determine the forward rate, with a current spot rate of 1,392.44 to the U.S. dollar, would be as follows:

$1{,}392.44 - x = -.20x$ or $1392.44 = 0.80x$ or $x = 1{,}740.55$

If an individual, or a collection of individuals and companies making up a market, anticipated a 20 percent devaluation of the Brazilian cruziero in relation to the U.S. dollar over the period of a forward contract when the spot rate was 1,392.44 cruzieros to the U.S. dollar, they would quote a forward contract at 1,740.55 cruzieros to the U.S. dollar. As a counter example, if the Swiss franc was expected to be revalued by 5 percent over the period of a forward contract with respect to the U.S. dollar, and had a current spot rate of 1.4580 Swiss francs to the U.S. dollar, then the forward contract would be calculated as follows:

$1.4580 - x = 0.05x$ or $1.4580 = 1.05x$ or $x = 1.3886$

The spot rate of 1.4580 Swiss francs to the U.S. dollar and the forward rate of 1.3886 Swiss francs to the U.S. dollar anticipates a 5 percent revaluation between the Swiss franc and the U.S. dollar over the contract period. Cross rates would be more applicable for direct dealings between firms in Brazil and in Switzerland. The cross rate for the spot market between the cruziero and the Swiss franc is 1,392.44 cruzieros to the dollar divided by 1.4580 Swiss francs to the dollar or 955.03 cruzieros to the Swiss franc. The cross rate for the forward contract between the two currencies is 1,740.55 cruzieros to the dollar divided by 1.3886 Swiss francs to the dollar or 1,253.5 cruzieros to the Swiss franc. The spot and forward cross rate quotes do not reference the U.S. dollar, although the dollar is the reference currency for measuring the relative degree of devaluation and revaluation between the two currencies.

ROLE OF ARBITRAGERS

The presence of various money centers gives rise to various quotes for different currencies depending on the balance between buyers and sellers at each money centre. Suppose that there are active centers of currency exchange in New York, Frankfurt, and Zurich where the following exchange rates are being quoted.

	$/DM	$/SF	DM/SF
New York	0.6161	0.6859	—
Frankfurt	—	0.6932	1.1133
Zurich	0.6204	—	1.1202

The New York market has individuals willing to buy German marks and Swiss francs for dollars, but there are no individuals interested in exchanging francs for marks or marks for francs. Therefore, there is no quote for this transaction. Suppose, for purposes of illustration, that individuals in Frankfurt are not interested in exchanging German marks and dollars, but are willing to exchange Swiss francs for dollars and marks. There is no quote available for the former transaction, but there are quotes for the latter transactions. A comparable situation holds for Zurich. These quotes reflect an active market of those interested in buying and selling the respective currencies for commercial purposes. An individual with no commercial interest in dollars, marks, and francs can examine these rates and play a "what if" game. What if 1,000 marks are sold in Zurich for dollars and the dollars are then exchanged for marks in New York?

Step 1: Sell marks in Zurich for dollars.
DM 1,000 × 0.6204 $/DM = $620.40

Step 2: Sell dollars in New York for marks.
$620.40 × 1/0.6161 $/DM = DM 1,006.98

Ignoring fees associated with these transactions, an individual can set up a round robin of selling marks in Zurich for dollars and buying marks for dollars in New York and make a 0.7% return on every round. Before doing this, he might want to play another what if game. What if marks are sold for Swiss francs in Zurich and the Swiss francs are then sold in Frankfurt for marks?

Step 1: Sell marks in Zurich for Swiss francs
DM 1,000 divided by 1.1202 DM/SF = SF 892.70

Step 2: Sell SF in Frankfurt for DM
SF 892.70 × 1.1133 DM/SF = DM 993.84

The trader, in this instance, would not enter into this last transaction, because it generates a loss. A profit would result if the nature of the transaction was reversed. Be that as it may, the three markets afford a large number of alternatives to play what if, including those with a greater degree of complexity. The best alternative for making money by taking advantage of disparities in currency exchange quotes between markets can be identified by examining every combination of trades.

An arbitrager is an individual who examines the rates of exchange in various markets seeking out those combinations of trades on which he or she can earn a profit. His or her purpose in the market is not to trade currencies to complete a commercial transaction, but to profit from price disparities between markets. As there are many markets, and many currencies, computers can be programmed to monitor exchange rate quotes on a real time basis, to identify those combinations of currency exchange trades that can be profitably executed net of trading costs. Naturally, such a painless way of making a living is going to attract a number of eager participants. The presence of arbitragers continually seeking currency exchange rate disparities and taking advantage of these disparities is vital in ensuring that every market consistently prices its exchange rates with others. Whenever disparities appear, the "arbs" will place orders to take advantage of the situation and will continue to do so until the disparity disappears. Arbs keep currency markets "in sync" with one another.

ACCOUNTING ASPECTS OF MULTIPLE CURRENCIES

There are two separate issues regarding accounting associated with multiple currencies: transactions and translations. Transactions are associated with the buying and selling of goods involving multiple currencies. An international transaction that is denominated in terms of a domestic currency does not differ, from an accounting viewpoint, from a domestic transaction.

If a U.S. firm sells an item to a consumer in France and receives U.S. dollars in payment, the accounting for the transaction does not differ from selling the item to a consumer in Kansas. A currency transaction would result if the French buyer paid for the goods in francs. Translations, on the other hand, are part of the consolidation process whereby balance sheets and income statements expressed in non-domestic currencies are consolidated into a single financial report in the domestic currency.

TRANSACTIONS

Three dates are important in accounting for transactions that involve a currency, or currencies, other than the domestic currency. One is the date that a transaction was initiated by the rendering of service or the shipping of goods. The second is the settlement date when payment is made. The third is any interim reporting date for accounting purposes. For example, a U.S. company buys goods valued at 1,000 Canadian dollars from a Canadian manufacturer on 15 December. The goods are received with payment due on 31 January.

An interim financial reporting date is 31 December. Each of these three dates may have a different exchange rate between the U.S. and Canadian dollars. Suppose that the Canadian dollar was worth $0.84 on 15 December, $0.86 on 31 December, and $0.88 on 31 January.

The initial transaction of 1,000 Canadian dollars was recorded at $840 on 15 December when the order was placed, $860 on 31 December for financial reporting purposes, and $880 on 31 January when the payment was made. Three different liabilities are now associated with a single transaction. There are two accounting methodologies for handling this situation-the one- and two-transactions views.

One-Transaction View

The one-transaction view takes the position that the financial impact of exchange rate changes should simply be charged or credited against the purchase price of the goods or the receipt of a sale. The initial accounting record is considered temporary because the ultimate exchange rate in effect on payment or receipt of funds is not known at the time the transaction was initiated. In this example of buying goods for 1,000 Canadian dollars, the initial entry on 15 December would be $840 both for goods purchased and for accounts payable. Both these accounts would be increased to $860 on 31 December, and to $880 on 31 January, reflecting changes in the exchange rate between the U.S. and Canadian dollar.

The initial accounting records are temporary in the one-transaction view. The entry made on 31 January finalizes the accounting treatment of this transaction. The ordering of the goods and the subsequent changes to the exchange rates are handled as a single item.

Although the one-transaction view is simple in its administration, currency exchange gains or losses are not explicitly recognized, because they are hidden by making direct adjustments to accounts receivable or payable. Financial reports incorporating the one-transaction view do not permit the reader to judge the management of a company with regard to their handling of currency exchange risk.

Two-Transactions View

Whereas the one-transaction view hides currency exchange losses by direct adjustments to accounts receivable or payable, the two-transactions view separates the currency exchange portion of the transaction from the transaction itself and views both as separate events. The cost of goods purchased is locked into the accounting records at the exchange rate on the initial transaction date. Subsequent changes to the exchange rate are separately handled as currency exchange gains or losses. The appropriate journal entries for the previously described transaction follow. Note that "foreign" exchange is used rather than "currency" exchange in the captions in agreement with Financial Accounting Standards Board (FASB) terminology. The desired goal of global business is to eliminate the words "domestic" and "foreign," but it is not clear what words would differentiate between "domestic" and "non-domestic" or "foreign" currencies when such differentiation is necessary.

The purchased goods remain at $840 in the two transaction view regardless of subsequent changes in currency exchange rates. In this case, the $40 increase in the cost of these goods is recorded as a currency exchange loss apportioned over two accounting periods. The first is at the end of the current accounting period on 31 December where the actual currency exchange loss is $20. The second reported loss, coincidentally another $20, is reported at the end of the succeeding accounting period. An alternative accounting treatment when the amounts are immaterial, which is less frequently employed, is to defer transaction gains or losses from one accounting period to the next until they are finally determined. Had the Canadian dollar lost value in relation to the U.S. dollar with a value of $0.81 on 31 December and $0.77 on 31 January, the accounting for the transaction would have resulted in the following currency exchange gain.

TRANSACTION ASPECTS OF FASB 8 AND 52

The United States has long been a leader in accounting for currency exchange gains or losses. Most nations, in adopting such standards, look to the United States for its handling of currency exchange gains and losses as a reference point in their deliberations on setting accounting standards. Prior to 1975, U.S. accountants could choose between the one- or two-transaction views when dealing with currency exchange fluctuations. In 1975, FASB 8, "Accounting for the Translation of Foreign Currency Transactions and Foreign Currency Financial Statements," required the use of the two-transactions view. FASB 8 stipulates international transactions denominated in a foreign currency be translated into dollars at the exchange rate prevailing on the transaction date. Thereafter, foreign currency receivables and payables are "marked to the market" at the end of subsequent accounting periods with currency exchange gains or losses flowing through net income.

In 1981, FASB 52 introduced changes in accounting for foreign currency translations, but the aforementioned FASB 8 provisions for accounting for foreign currency transactions were not changed. However, FASB 52 permitted currency gains and losses for transactions denominated in foreign currencies to be deferred if the company insulates itself from the risk of exchange fluctuations by entering into a forward or futures contract. The forward or futures contract must be tailored to satisfy a specific commercial transaction in order to avoid currency exchange gains and losses flowing through income. A forward or futures contract is an agreement between two parties who wish to exchange a certain amount of one currency for another at a prescribed date in the future. The words "forwards" and "futures" are frequently used interchangeably. Technically, two parties tailor the details of the forward contract to suit their needs. A futures contract differs from a forward contract in that a futures contract has standardized terms, requires margin deposits, and is traded on organized exchanges. The principal difference between the two is that a futures contract can be more readily traded or liquidated, whereas a forward contract has less liquidity because it is usually tailored to fit a given situation. Regardless of the semantic differences between forwards and futures, the accounting treatment is the same.

ACCOUNTING FOR FORWARD CONTRACTS IN HEDGING

Forward contracts have proven to be very useful in hedging against currency exchange risks. The effective cost of goods increased from $840 to $880 in the previous case of purchasing goods with Canadian dollars because of an adverse change in currency exchange rates when the Canadian dollar appreciated in value with respect to the U.S. dollar. Forward contracts can fix the value of an outstanding receivable or payable whose date of receipt, or payment, is in the future and neutralize the risk of loss from an adverse change in currency exchange rates.

Suppose that the U.S. buyer of the Canadian goods also purchased a forward contract for 1,000 Canadian dollars on the day of buying the goods. Suppose that the spot rate on 15 December was $0.84 for a Canadian dollar and the forward contract rate for delivery on 31 January was $0.85. The purchase of the forward contract for the amount of 1,000 Canadian dollars satisfies the criteria associated with FASB 52 that the foreign currency commitment be firm and that the forward contract be specifically designated to a particular foreign currency transaction.

The following journal entries of 15 December are associated with a straight purchase of goods for 1,000 Canadian dollars and with the hedge associated with the forward contract.

Purchase of Goods	Hedge
12/15 Purchases $840	12/15 Can $ Receivable $840
Accounts Payable $840	Premium on Forward 10
(Can $ @ 0.84)	Accounts Payable $850
	(Spot.84, Fwd.85)

These entries record the purchase of the goods, the resulting liability to the supplier, and the company entering into a hedge agreement to receive $1,000

The Canadian dollar appreciated in value to $0.86 and the company records the resulting loss of $20 and increases the amount owed to the supplier by $20. The company also amortizes the premium based the number of days that have elapsed. The premium of $10 represents the difference between the spot and futures rate on 15 December. There are sixteen days left in December and thirty one days in January for a total of forty-seven days. The sixteen days of December represents 34 percent of the total time, which supports amortizing 34 percent of the premium, or $3.40. The gain in the value of the Canadian dollar receivable of $20 is also recognized. The hedge is working because the loss on currency exchange of the liability to the manufacturer is exactly offset by the gain on currency exchange related to the hedge.

The foreign exchange (FX) loss has been neutralized for a cost of $10, which preserved the purchase price of $840. If the forward contract had not been purchased, or if the conditions surrounding the purchase of a forward contract set forth in FASB 52 were not satisfied, the foreign exchange loss would have flowed through income. Foreign exchange gains and losses affecting the income of a company are not looked on with favour by financial managers. Currency exchange gains and losses become "wild cards" that can upset a financial forecast and influence corporate planning activities.

In the above example, the hedge provided protection against a currency loss that would have occurred because the Canadian dollar appreciated, or increased, in value. Had the hedge been in effect and had the Canadian dollar depreciated in value to $0.81 on 31 December and to $0.79 on 31 January, the outcome would have been as follows.

12/15 Purchases $840	12/15 can $ Receivable $840
Accounts Payable $840	Premium on Forward 10
	Accounts Payable $850

These entries record the purchase of the goods, the liability to the supplier, and the fact that the company has entered into a hedging agreement to receive 1,000 Canadian dollars on 31 January.

12/31 Accounts	12/31 Premium Expense 3.40
Payable 30	Premium on Forward 3.40
Gain on	Loss on Foreign
Foreign	Exchange 30
Exchange 30	Canadian $
	Receivable 30

The Canadian dollar has depreciated to $0.81 and the company records the resulting gain of $30 and decreases the amount due to the supplier by $30. The company amortizes the cost of the premium based on the number of days that have elapsed as previously described. The value of the Canadian dollar receivable has decreased by $30, and the loss is recognized. The gain on foreign exchange relating to the liability of the manufacturer is exactly offset by the loss on foreign exchange related to the hedge. The overall effect of the hedge follows.

	Purchase Of Goods	Hedge Combined
Asset Purchase	$840	$840
FX Gain	(50)	
FX Loss	$50	—
Prem Expense	10	10
Cash Paid	790	60 850

In this case, where the Canadian dollar depreciated, the cost of goods remains at $840, but the purchase of the forward contract for $10 prevents the company from enjoying a foreign exchange gain of $50. This would have reduced the liability to the manufacturer to $790. The hedge worked in the sense of fixing the cost of goods at $840, but at the cost of giving up the currency exchange gain.

To recap the first example, on December 15 a liability of 1,000 Canadian dollars was booked at the current spot rate of $0.84 resulting in a total liability of $840. At that time, management believed that the Canadian dollar was likely to appreciate in value during the next six weeks.

This would have caused the liability to the manufacturer to increase from a currency exchange fluctuation. To guard against this, management entered into a hedge, agreeing to purchase Canadian dollars at $0.85 on 31 January. This resulted in a cost to the company of $10 (0.01 × $1, 000). This limited the company's downside exposure to $10 if there were an adverse change in currency exchange rates, which, in this case, would occur if the Canadian dollar appreciated in value during the six-week life of the contract. The hedge worked when the Canadian dollar appreciated because the company was protected from a currency exchange loss.

In the second example, when the Canadian dollar depreciated, the company did not enjoy the gain associated with a lessening liability because the gain was offset by a currency exchange loss related to the hedge.

The company had, in effect, foregone a currency exchange profit to protect itself from a currency exchange loss. One might maintain that the true cost of the hedge to protect against an adverse change in currency exchange rates is the premium for the hedge plus the opportunity foregone for a currency exchange gain.

ACCOUNTING FOR SPECULATIVE FORWARD CONTRACTS

In the foregoing example, a forward contract was purchased for the purpose of hedging a specific commercial transaction. If the conditions surrounding the purchase of a forward contract do not meet the stipulations contained in FASB 52 for being considered a hedge, then the purchase of the forward contract is treated as a speculation. According to FASB 52, a speculative position is taken when the forward or futures contract is not associated with a specified commercial transaction.

The rules that now apply stipulate that the premium or discount associated with the forward contract be ignored when initially recording the contract. At the end of each succeeding accounting period, the value of the contract is "marked to market" by reference to the applicable forward rate, and any resulting gain or loss flows through income.

Suppose that the deutschemark has the spot and forward values on the indicated dates shown in Table. Only those forward contracts for delivery at the end of October have been included in the table. Note that 29 October is exactly ninety days from 1 August.

DEUTSCHEMARK SPOT AND FORWARD VALUES

The financial market expects the DM to appreciate in value, which can be seen by comparing the forward rate with the spot rate. The financial officer, for any number of reasons, feels that it is in the company's interest to purchase a forward contract. However, he does not have a specific commercial transaction in mind when purchasing the forward contract. In accordance with FASB 52, the currency exchange position is treated as speculative in nature. On August 1, a 90-day forward contract is purchased to buy one million DM for $0.6078 per DM for a total contract cost of $607,800. The initial journal entry follows.

August 1 Contract Receivable (DM)	$607,800
Contract Payable ($)	$607,800

Thirty days later at the end of August, the next monthly accounting period, the forward contract is examined for any gains or losses, which must be immediately applied to income. The applicable forward contract to judge the original 90-day contract is a 60-day contract that expires at the same time. The 60-day forward contract is quoted at $0.6211 per DM.

August 31 Contract Receivable (DM)	13,300
Gain on contract	13,300
(0.6211-0.6078) × DM 1 MM	

At the end of September, the original futures contract can now be best matched with a 30-day futures contract, which is quoted at $0.6217 per DM.

Sept 30 Contract Receivable (DM)	600
Gain on contract	600
(0.6217-0.6211) × DM 1 MM	

On October 29, the forward contract is delivered, and the transaction is wrapped up with the following journal entries.

Oct 29 Contract payable	607,800
Cash	607,800
Dollar Value of DM	615, 500
(spot on 10/29) Loss on Contract	6,200
Contract receivable	621,700

On October 29, the dollar value of the receipt of DM 1 million is determined by the current spot rate and is recorded as $615, 500. The contract receivable was originally recorded on August 1 as $607, 800, then was increased by $13, 300 on August 31 and again by $600 on September 30 as forward rates changed.

These gains were added to the company's income at these times. At the maturity date of the contract, a loss of $6, 200 was generated and was recognized as such in the company's monthly income.

Summing up, if a forward or futures commitment does not meet the requirements of a hedge, both the forward or futures contract exchange rate and the amounts due to the broker are initially recorded at the forward rate. Neither the premium nor the discount is separately reported. Transaction gains and losses are measured by the difference between the forward rate in the contract and the forward rate for a comparable forward for the period remaining until settlement.

Any resulting currency gains or losses flow immediately through income.

This accounting treatment of "marking to market" differs radically from that accorded to hedges. Forward exchange contracts that are classified as hedges are initially recorded using the current spot rate and the premium or discount is amortized over the life of the forward contract. Transaction gains or losses are keyed to changes in the spot rate with no currency gain or loss flowing through income.

The same forward contract classified as a speculation is initially recorded using the forward rate, and is marked to market using comparable forwards with regard to time to maturity.

Transaction gains and losses flow through income because, unlike a hedge, there is no offsetting change in valuation of an associated asset or liability. In the United States, the Financial Accounting Standards Board requires that currency exchange gains and losses that are not hedged be treated as normal operating items for inclusion in income. In many other countries, gains and losses from foreign currency receivables and payables are not recognized until the transactions are finalized.

There are no interim mark-to-market currency exchange gains and losses affecting income. Even then, there are a number of countries that do not require the explicit recording of such gains or losses in the income statement.

Adjustments are made directly to the related asset or liability accounts as described under the one transaction view. Therefore, readers of the financial statements do not "see" currency exchange gains and losses because they are embedded in line items in a balance sheet, nor can they judge management performance in handling currency exchange risk.

TRANSLATION

Translation is the process whereby a financial report of a branch, affiliate, or subsidiary in one country is expressed in the currency of the parent company for financial reporting purposes. Three translations may be required for financial statements prepared by local accountants whose language, accounting practice, and currency are different from the nation of domicile of the parent company. The language translation is relatively straightforward.

The accounting standard translation is handled line by line with suitable adjustments to take into consideration differences in accounting practices between the two nations.

Several issues must first be resolved before the third, or the currency, translation can be performed. They are the selection of the appropriate currency exchange rates, the choice of which exchange rate applies in the translation of each line item of a financial report, and the accounting treatment for translation gains and losses arising from using different exchange rates. Three currency exchange rates are common in the translation process: the current, historic, and average rates. The current rate is the currency exchange rate at the end of the accounting period. The historic rate is the currency exchange rate in effect when a transaction took place. The average currency exchange rate is a single rate that applies for the accounting period, which may be a month, a quarter, or a year.

Suppose that a factory was built when the exchange rate between the U.S. dollar and the British pound was $1. 90 and the exchange rate at the beginning of the accounting year was $1. 50 and $1. 60 at the end. The current exchange rate is $1. 60, the historic exchange rate associated with the fixed asset is $1. 90, and the average exchange rate for the year $1. 55. The average exchange rate may not be exactly $1. 55 if the averaging process is performed on a quarterly, monthly, or some other basis.

A number of methods, briefly summarized below, have been associated with currency translation of financial statements.

Current-Noncurrent Method

The essence of the current-noncurrent method is that all items that are easily convertible to cash, or are to be paid out or be paid within a year, are translated at the current exchange rate. Balance sheet items classified as current assets and liabilities are translated at the current rate and the remaining items are translated at the appropriate historic exchange rate. This method was widely employed until 1975.

Monetary-Non-monetary Method

This method examines the nature of each element of a financial statement to be translated into the reporting currency. Monetary items are those financial assets and liabilities that can be expressed in currency units such as cash, receivables, and payables. Any item on a balance sheet not given a monetary classification is then considered non-monetary. The principal non-monetary items are inventories and fixed assets. One major difference between this model and the current-noncurrent model is the treatment of inventories.

Inventories can be divided into three categories. One is raw materials and components inventory that is first transformed into semi finished goods, or in process inventory, by a manufacturing process before becoming finished goods inventory. Generally speaking, cost of goods sold is translated at the current rate under the current-non-current method and at the historic rate under the monetary-non-monetary method. The former method translates the cost of raw materials and components consumed in the manufacturing process at the exchange rate applicable when they were transformed into finished goods. The latter method translates the cost of raw materials and components consumed in the manufacturing process when they were acquired.

Temporal Method and FASB 8

During the 1950s and early 1960s, neither the level of international trade nor the ownership of operating affiliates in other nations was a major factor in corporate America. The method of translation was not a significant accounting issue, particularly when most currency exchange rates were fixed and changes in exchange rates were infrequent. The issue of standardization of the methodology of translating financial reports for consolidation purposes for American based multinational corporations was addressed in 1965 when the Accounting Principles Board suggested that the monetary-non-monetary method be preferred for translating financial statements. However, companies were free to select their preferred methodology.

The most common choice was the current-non-current method, but it was not the dominant methodology. Some companies selected the modified current-non- current method where long-term receivables and payables were translated at the current, rather than the historic, rate. Other companies used the monetary-non-monetary approach in its pure form or in a modified form where inventories were translated at the current rather than the historic rate. A few companies preferred the temporal method, which, with some minor differences, is the same as the monetary-non-monetary method, and others relied on the current rate method.

There was a striking lack of consistency in translating financial statements after the suggestion of a preferred method by the Accounting Principles Board. In 1975, the issuance of FASB 8, "Accounting for the Translation of Foreign Currency Transactions and Foreign Currency Financial Statements, " was the first comprehensive accounting standard dealing with non-domestic operations of American companies including importing, exporting, foreign borrowing and lending, forward contracts, and translations of foreign affiliate financial statements for the equity and full methods of consolidation. FASB 8 stipulated that the foreign financial statements must first be recast to conform to American generally accepted accounting principles (GAAP) and then be translated into U. S. dollars using the temporal method. Any currency gains and losses from translation flowed through income.

FASB 8 was a contentious accounting document. American firms were restricted to one particular model for translating financial reports to U.S. dollars. The requirement that inventory be translated at historic, rather than current, rates, which was the prevalent choice, meant that record-keeping activities had to be expanded to keep track of the currency exchange rate at the time of each inventory purchase. Many objected to the fact that accounts payable, which often arose from the acquisition of inventory, was to be translated at the current rate, whereas the items that gave rise to the accounts payable, additions to inventory, were being translated at the historic rate. In theory, accounts payable is a natural hedge against currency exchange gains or losses associated with inventory.

Others objected to the requirement that cost of goods sold be translated at the appropriate historic rate, while revenue was being translated at the average rate. Different exchange rates being applied to revenue and costs distorted the measurement of gross margin of an operating affiliate. The gross margin of an operating affiliate was not the same before and after translation. In addition, there was widespread opposition to translation gains and losses flowing through income.

The dollar was losing value during the years following the issuance of FASB 8. Profits made in non-U.S. affiliates in nations whose currencies were appreciating with respect to the dollar were diminished when translated in accordance with FASB 8. There were instances of local profits being transformed to losses by the translation process.

As such, FASB 8 was not "directionally sympathetic" to changes in currency exchange rates. One would expect that an operating affiliate in a nation whose currency was appreciating with respect to the U.S. dollar should be gaining economic value. Its profits should be enhanced, not reduced, by the translation process. American executives found themselves in a position of having to explain to their shareholders why a profitable enterprise in Germany was showing a loss, or to be more accurate, why a loss on the financial reports was really a profit.

The loss, of course, was a non-cash translation loss arising from the use of multiple currency exchange rates in the translation of a financial statement from German marks to U.S. dollars. A translation loss could have been a gain had the mark weakened against the dollar. The earnings of American corporations were being buoyed up and driven down by shifting exchange rates and these swings were opposite to what one might logically expect. Reported earnings became more volatile as translation gains and losses flowed through income.

Management had difficulty explaining the added volatility of earnings to the shareholders; particularly when a reported non-cash translation loss was actually a real cash profit. Some firms made economic decisions to reduce the volatility of earnings based on the method of translation stipulated in FASB 8, by selling profitable operating affiliates to avoid translation losses. This is the tail wagging the dog. The purpose of accounting is to fairly represent the happenings of a company in the form of a financial report. FASB 8 created a situation where avoidance of translation losses on the financial report, and not the economics of the situation, were sometimes driving business decisions.

Current Rate Method and FASB 52

Efforts were underway to correct the situation soon after the publication of FASB 8. In 1981, FASB 52 "Foreign Currency Translation" was issued with a three year "window," giving corporations time to convert to the new rules on currency translation. The thrust behind FASB 52 was to ensure that the process of currency translation was directionally sympathetic to the real economic effects of changes in currency exchange rates and to ensure that the translation process would preserve financial relationships or ratios, such as the gross margin or liquidity ratio. Currency gains and losses from the translation process were no longer to be charged to income, but to a new component of stockholders' equity called Translation Adjustments.

FASB 52 stipulates that all assets and liabilities be translated at the current rate, with equity accounts translated at historic rates. Financial relationships, such as the liquidity ratio, are preserved in the translation process because the same currency exchange rate is applied to current assets and liabilities. The gross margin is preserved in the translation process because revenues and expenses are translated at the same currency exchange rate. Another advantage of FASB 52 is that the translation process is directionally sympathetic with regards to changes in exchange rates. If a U.S. company has an "asset exposure" in an operating affiliate where assets exceed liabilities, then such an operating affiliate's value is enhanced as its currency of operations appreciates against the dollar.

FASB 8 eliminates the "roller coaster" impact on income from changing currency exchange rates because gains and losses in the translation process no longer flow through the income statement but are recorded as a separate component of equity on the balance sheet. The methodology of translation set forth in FASB 52 is inherently simple and in harmony with translation practices in many other nations. One disadvantage of FASB 52 is the "disappearing asset" problem that results from applying the requirements of FASB 52 in hyperinfla-tionary economies.

After the financial statements of a foreign subsidiary are recast in accordance with U.S. GAAP, the next step is currency translation. FASB 52 defines various categories of currencies for translation purposes. The "functional" currency is the currency of prime economic environment in which a company operates. A "foreign" currency is any currency other than the functional currency. The "local" currency is that of the country in which a subsidiary operates and the "reporting" currency is the currency of a company's financial reports. The functional currency of an entity is the currency of the primary economic environment in which the entity operates and generates cash flows. It may be either the local currency of the foreign entity or a different foreign currency or the currency of the parent, assumed to be the U.S. dollar. The choice depends on many considerations. No single consideration determines the selection of the functional currency as the final choice encompasses all of the following:

- If cash flows are principally in the foreign currency, the usual situation, and do not have a direct bearing on the parent company's cash flow, the functional currency would probably be the local currency. If the subsidiary's cash flow is readily available for remittance to the parent company, the functional currency would probably be the U. S. dollar.

- If the market for the entity's goods is primarily local, the functional currency would be the local currency. If the market for its goods is principally in the parent's country, and/or the sales contracts are principally denominated in the parent's currency, then the functional currency would be the U.S. dollar.
- If the selling prices are mainly driven by local competition, or possibly by government regulation, and not by short-term fluctuations in exchange rates, then the functional currency would be the local currency. If sales prices are driven by international prices and competition, and also fluctuate with the dollar exchange rate, then the functional currency would be the U.S. dollar.
- If costs and expenses for labour, raw materials, and other items primarily represent local costs, then the local currency would be the functional currency. If costs and expenses primarily represent items obtained from the parent company, then the functional currency would be the U.S. dollar.
- If financing for the local company is mainly raised locally and denominated in the

local currency, and if debt service is expected to be covered by cash flows generated in the local currency, then the local currency would be the functional currency. If financing, including debt service, is provided by the parent, or is denominated in the currency of the parent, then the functional currency would be the U.S. dollar.

In summary, a foreign entity whose operations are integrated within its country and who is relatively self-sustaining would normally use the local currency as its functional currency. A foreign entity whose operations are essentially an extension of the U.S. parent would normally use the U.S. dollar as its functional currency. A foreign entity whose operations are essentially conducted in another foreign country would normally use the currency of the other foreign country as its functional currency. If an operation is located in a "highly inflationary economy," defined as cumulative inflation of 100 percent or more over a three year period, the functional currency is the U.S. dollar.

The reporting company must examine all these aspects for each foreign branch, affiliate, or subsidiary to decide on the functional currency. Once this decision is made, it may only be changed if the underlying economic circumstances clearly show that a change can be justified. After foreign financial statements have been adjusted to conform to U.S. GAAP, assets and liabilities are translated from the functional currency to the reporting currency (in this example, U.S. dollars) at the current exchange rate. Revenue, expenses, and other gains and losses such as asset disposition of the foreign entity are translated from the functional currency to the reporting currency at the weighted average exchange rate for the period. Transaction gains and losses, unless associated with a hedge, are recognized as a part of income statement currently. Transaction gains and losses associated with hedges are not included in income.

Dividends remitted to the parent are translated at the exchange rate on the day of declaration. Shareholders' capital accounts, including Stock and Paid in Surplus, are translated at historic rates of exchange. Retained earnings are determined by a calculation, not by translation.

The translated amount of retained earnings at the beginning of the period is added to the translated amount of income or loss during the current period less the translated value of dividend payments. Differences arising from translating financial statements using various exchange rates are recorded in a separate shareholders' equity account called Translation Adjustments.

This is deferred as a separate component of shareholders' equity until the foreign entity is sold or otherwise liquidated. When it is sold or liquidated, the deferred translation adjustment associated with the entity is included in the net gain or loss of the disposition of the foreign entity. If the cumulative inflation in a country is 100 percent or more over a three year period, the currency of that country is unsuitable for a functional currency. In this case, financial statements of the foreign subsidiary must be re-measured into the functional currency of the parent. If the foreign entity's records are not maintained in its functional currency, they must first be re-measured into the functional currency before translation. Gains or losses resulting from the re-measurement are included in the income statement of the foreign entity.

The following example illustrates the current rate method of translating the financial statements of a foreign subsidiary for consolidation in a U.S. parent corporation financial report. The local currency is the functional currency, which is the usual situation. In this example, Global Corporation, a U.S. multinational enterprise, acquired all the outstanding common stock of Small Company, which is located in a country where the currency is the LC (local currency), on 2 January 1991. The LC is the functional currency of Small. For 1991, the exchange rates for the LC were as follows:

2 January	$0.20
31 December	0.40
Average	0.30

The average exchange rate for the year is used to translate the income statement, resulting in net income of $15,000. Retained earnings at the beginning of the year are translated at the historic rate of $0.20, the rate in effect when Global acquired Small. Net income in U.S. dollars ($15,000) is then added to retained earnings at the beginning of the year ($14,000). A dividend was declared and paid during the year and is translated at the actual spot rate on the day of declaration ($7,600).

Retained earnings at the end of the year are calculated in dollars amounting to $21,400. This is not the result of translating the LC retained earnings, but represents the dollar equivalent of retained earnings at the start of the year plus the dollar equivalent of net income, less the dollar equivalent of dividends. Retained earnings on the books of the subsidiary at the beginning of the next year will be LC 100,000 and will be reflected in the U.S. dollar consolidated financial statements of Global as $21,400.

All assets and liabilities are translated at the end-of-year exchange rate ($0.40). The shareholders' capital accounts, consisting of Common Stock and Paid-in Capital, are translated at historic rates. In this case, the historic rate is that of 2 January 1991, when Global acquired all the outstanding shares of Small. These translated dollar amounts will not change in the future.

The dollar amount of Retained Earnings ($21,400) is determined in the Statement of Retained Earnings and then appears in the equity section of the balance sheet. The Translation Adjustment in U.S. dollars ($84,600) is derived by subtracting the dollar amount of liabilities and equity from the dollar amount of total assets ($408,000 less $323,400, or $84,600). The gain of $84,600, which occurred from the revaluation of the LC from $0.20 to $0.40 during the year, is deferred.

This discussion is based on the acquisition of Small Company at the beginning of the year. In succeeding years, the process of calculating the Translation Adjustment is repeated and added if a gain, and subtracted if a loss, from the start-of-year value of the Translation Adjustment. All else being equal, an appreciating LC will increase the Translation Adjustment, whereas an LC undergoing devaluation will reduce the Translation Adjustment. If the devaluation is large enough, the Translation Adjustment may become negative.

TRANSLATION PRACTICES OUTSIDE THE UNITED STATES

Despite, or because of, the disputes associated with the development of translation practices within the United States, the United States is considered a leader in addressing translation issues. Some nations use the current method of translation and others use either the monetary-non-monetary or the temporal methods.

In the European Community, the Fourth and Seventh Directives merely require disclosure of the translation methodology incorporated in the consolidation process. There are no specific directions in Germany as to which translation method should be employed, however, the selected method should be disclosed and it should not affect net income. This latter requirement is necessary because financial reports in Germany may also serve as tax reports. There is no specified methodology in the Netherlands other than its identification and that it should have no impact on the profit and loss statement. Switzerland has no legal requirement to prepare consolidated financial reports. If a company desires to do so, it is free to select any translation method.

Japan has no specific guidelines as to the appropriate method of currency translations. Canada has accounting requirements similar to FASB 52, except that deferred taxes are translated at the historic rate. In July 1983, the International Accounting Standards Committee required the use of the current rate method for translation purposes (IAS 21).

QUESTIONS PERTAINING TO TRANSLATION

Is a single translation methodology applicable for all situations? Should a company's financial statements be translated? Suppose that a company has no intent of repatriating cash from a foreign entity, and the foreign entity's bank accounts are all in the local currency. Is it appropriate for the parent to continually increase and decrease the reported U.S. dollar value of the cash holding in the foreign entity as exchange rates change? This, of course, is just one aspect of the problem. Every line item on the balance sheet of a foreign entity changes in response to changing currency exchange rates. Yet, in the final analysis, little or none of these assets and liabilities will ever be converted into U.S. dollars. Is translation appropriate between stable and unstable currencies?

If a currency is " soft," and essentially unconvertible to U.S. dollars because of currency exchange restrictions, should the entity be consolidated at all? Would it be preferable to "deconsolidate" these entities from those located in countries with more stable currencies that are convertible to U.S. dollars? In extreme cases of is "soft" currency nation, earnings must remain within a nation because they cannot be repatriated. Moreover, earnings cannot remain as cash without rapidly losing value. Usually, profits from operations are invested in tangibles to preserve purchasing power. Would it be preferable to "deconsolidate" such entities and reflect income in the financial statements of the parent only when actual cash is received from the foreign entity? FASB 52 permits translation adjustments to be made directly to equity. What effect does this have on reported income and on price/earnings ratios? These gains and losses, which may be substantial, are excluded from the determination of income and may escape the notice of readers of the financial reports.

9

The Evolution of Banks and Financial Intermediation

The Case of Asia: The Asia crisis has revealed a number of weaknesses in the supervision of financial institutions in Asia. Coincidentally, this has taken place at a time when supervisors in mature economies are confronted with new risks and are revising their approach.

By and large, Asia's financial intermediaries still operate as fairly unsophisticated moneylenders and rely on antiquated risk management tools. While the new financial tools that are presently the focus of supervisors and raters in mature economies have yet to pose a serious threat to the balance sheets of Asian financial institutions, enough of those tools have become accessible to them for Asian supervisors to take notice. But this matter in fact represents considerably more of a danger in Asia than in regions with advanced banking systems, simply because there is, among Asian financiers, a general lack of skill in risk management and control.

An impending financial crisis in the early 1990s and how new financial tools and broader access to international financing have compounded the problem. The sorry state of risk management in Asia, on the failure of many local authorities to rehabilitate the banking system and on why simple but drastic solutions are disregarded.

Moneylenders are highly geared companies that enjoy the recognition of and a degree of protection from supervisors in exchange for the provision of financial services to the community under strict rules. The rules take the shape of capital and liquidity ratios, while a number of regulations affect the risk profile of the financial institutions' assets, especially their loan assets. On that front alone, supervisors made considerable mistakes in Asia prior to the 1997 crisis. Perhaps would it be useful at this point to clarify that the 1997 crisis was in reality a market panic that, through the transmission belt of exchange rates and stock market valuations, served to reveal the weaknesses of many Asian countries.

But the banking crisis started well before the 1997 panic. Japan's banking crisis started in 1991. The Korean banking system was on its knees as early as

1993 or 1994. The liquidity profile of Thailand's banks was so fragile that by 1995 a major rating company-Thomson Financial Bank Watch-took the unprecedented step of gathering the 15 Thai banks for tea and cookies to tell them that a major crisis would hit them sooner or later. That the banks survived until the July 1997 crisis is simply a miracle. Malaysia was less of a problem, and the misallocation of capital would only have hit the country in about 1999, if not for the 1997 contagion. The same goes, paradoxically, for Indonesia where the local banks, for all their mistakes and the flouting of some prudential rules, were not in immediate danger. The Philippines banking system was not scheduled to crash until the year 2000. Taiwan had-and still has-a remarkably fragile banking system in an otherwise healthy economy. Most banks in China, Vietnam and the Indian subcontinent have been happily operating with negative equity for years.

How did the regulators fare? The regulators' job is to keep the banks on the straight and narrow. They must catch delinquent institutions before their mistakes start to costinflict depositors, creditors or taxpayers. When a private-sector bank is about to lose its last chunk of free equity, it should be forced to mend its ways and inject fresh capital funds.

Should it fail to do so, the authorities should step in, force a reduction of capital and, if no fresh investment funds can be located, nationalise the institution partly or entirely. It comes as a surprise that, after the mid 1980s when Malaysia acted that way in respect of three small banks, no Asian country used such powers to clean the banking system until Thailand made a belated attempt in 1998. The regulators failed in their duties, but in all fairness it should be stressed that politics went into play and they were largely prevented from doing their job.

Beyond control by the ratios, the regulators failed in another way: they disregarded the all-important risk management and control. This is where the new tools-the new toys is perhaps a more appropriate description-came into play: derivatives and large international risk-taking activities. It would be possible today for relatively small financial institutions to go bankrupt within two weeks, and there would be little the regulators could do. But it would also be possible for them to collapse suddenly under the weight of accumulated mistakes that no external observer could have foreseen. Managers themselves often fail to acknowledge the existence of such mistakes. Beyond the ratios, regulators should be able to gauge the skills and the tools of the risk managers in the financial institutions they control.

If the managers of a bank adequately control the bank's risks, there should be no need for external supervision, beyond basic ratios. If the bank managers know what they are doing, there should be no risk-except at the tail end of the risk spectrum-that they could not manage and contain. A major weakness of the Asia banking systems in recent years is that financial institutions have been allowed to take risks that they do not understand and have been unable to control. From Thai banks borrowing short-term dollars to finance long-term baht investments in unneeded real estate, to tiny Korean merchant banks lending dollars to unsafe Brazilian or Indonesian corporate borrowers, to Hong Kong-based banks lending to Malaysian companies for risky investments in the steel industry of the Philippines, the list is long of obvious mistakes in risk management.

The huge losses posted by many banks in the aftermath of the 1997 crisis should have at least prompted the authorities to take a fresh look at those matters, and to start a new era of better controls, beyond traditional ratio monitoring. But here also the countries have failed: the rehabilitation of the banking systems has been far from harmonious.

Governments and bank regulators across much of Asia have been desperately trying to fix banking systems that in many cases are arguably beyond repair. Efforts to date amount to little more than creative accounting techniques designed to mask insolvency. Regrettably, received wisdom has centred on the principle of merging unsound banks with those perceived to be sound, with the expectation that reducing their number will somehow give rise to miracles. I would suggest that, to the contrary, now is the time to allow the creation of brand new commercial banks across the region. A case could be made that it would be best to create new banks rather than rehabilitate moribund financial institutions. Asian governments, swayed by international trends in the consolidation of banking systems, do not seem interested in the idea, but that is another story.

The capital funds that are presently missing from commercial banks represent between 15 per cent and 45 per cent of GDP, depending on the country. It is simply not realistic to expect that the missing capital funds can be easily found. So banks must cook the books. In truth, using stringent international accounting practices, most banks in Thailand, Indonesia and Korea would exhibit negative capital ratios. In many cases they are beyond repair. This has a number of implications.

From an investor's point of view, it would theoretically be more appropriate to start a new bank rather than to invest in a bankrupt financial institution and see the best part of the fresh injection of capital devoted to writing off bad loans.

From the bank owner's point of view, there is nothing more to lose. With no more downside risk, moral hazard is at its highest. The temptation exists to increase both reward and risk. Little fresh lending is likely to be directed at safe borrowers.

From the regulator's point of view, it is preferable to let the owners of the ailing banks make an attempt at rehabilitation. This is because liquidating the bank at this stage would carry social and perhaps political implications. Once the capital funds are exhausted, depositors, creditors and taxpayers will share the cost of the failure. It is often the case that a bank operating as a going concern, in the hands of those who wrote the credits in the first place, is likely to be more successful than liquidators in pursuing recalcitrant borrowers. It is also likely to be more successful than government bodies taking over such assets.

The Basle Committee's approach to capital ratios, in its original 1988 form and with subsequent revisions, may exhibit some weaknesses, but it is an important step forward. Its adoption in Asia, however, has become a source of creative accounting for banks in that, since it is the focus of all rehabilitation gauging, no effort is spared to fake solvency. The valuation of assets is inaccurate and the regulators often conspire with banks to conceal the extent of the damage. Banks post inflated capital ratios. Loan losses are concealed that, if recognised, would eat away at Tier I, the most precious part of capital funds, as opposed to the more fuzzy capital attracted under Tier II.

Now that capital funds have become acutely restricted, the banks will, for the first time in Asia, face trade-off decisions between various risks that may lead them to lending decisions that could become socially undesirable or economically suboptimal, simply because they have lost the power to choose.

Meanwhile problem loans in aggregate have reached catastrophic levels and created a huge gap in equity. Compounding this difficulty is the very manner in which problem loans are identified. The classification of problem loans is not only changing, being lenient and inconsistent across the region, but is also often subject to unwholesome influence by authorities. The same problem applies to the provisions that these banks need to put aside against such loans. Provisioning decisions seem to be dictated not so much by prudence or the recognition of loan defaults, but by what banks can afford without recording embarrassing losses.

Banks have traditionally hidden huge amounts of non-performing loans simply by rescheduling the terms of their interest and/or principal payments, despite the bleak future prospects of such repayment. There can, of course, be, valid situations in which borrowers have legitimate cause to seek a restructuring of their obligations. In Asia, however, such reasons are generally rare. Rescheduling allows banks to skimp on prudent provisions while simultaneously recording interest income that never was, and is never likely to be, earned. This explains why a bankrupt bank can often look profitable. While acknowledging that improving economic conditions could restore the cash flows of some distressed borrowers and their ability to service their debt obligations, the banks' practices remain an unacceptable gamble.

Another expedient-and more acceptable-practice involves the transfer of non-performing loans to asset management companies. The main characteristic of such financial vehicles in Asia is that, beyond the liquidation of loans in a more efficient manner, they ensure the transfer of wealth from taxpayers to banks in a discreet and seemingly painless way.

Most banks in South Korea, Thailand, Indonesia and Malaysia are now at the mercy of their governments for their very survival. Either the governments own the banks outright, or they have a moral obligation to support them, sometimes as a price paid to the banks for their help in rescuing the weaker constituents of the financial system. Such Faustian arrangements are not new to Asia. The governments of Indonesia, South Korea, the Peoples' Republic of China, Vietnam and the countries of the Indian subcontinent have long controlled most of the larger commercial banks. Under government control, banks can more easily fake solvency. They conceal bad loans. In lieu of capital, government bonds are lodged on the books.

The aforementioned practices are merely accounting illusions. At best they allow banks to post the minimum regulatory ratios to keep them alive, so that they can fulfil their role as moneylenders. At worst they perpetuate mediocrity and moral hazard.

However viewed the present efforts to rehabilitate banks in Asia are but a transfer of enormous wealth from the many to the few. The major shareholders and managers of failed banks have not only escaped just punishment generally but often profit from the artificial rescue of their banks.

Clearly the regulators have been forced to go along with expedient decisions dictated by political and often practical considerations. Beyond capital ratios, there are many pressing problems to fix in the financial systems throughout Asia; namely credit culture, transparency, disclosure and corporate governance. More important still, Asia should pay more attention to the development of its capital markets. Meanwhile substantial efforts are needed for a quick resolution of the present credit crunch. Asia needs ruthless regulators and supervisors who will not allow private sector banks to resume their wild chase for market share or elusive profits. One possible development would be the creation of brand new banks, an option to which nobody gives serious consideration. The sad truth, perhaps, is that the lessons of the painful Asian crisis will not translate into any substantial improvement in the way banks are supervised.

THE ROLE OF THE FINANCIAL STABILITY

INSTITUTE OF THE BANK FOR INTERNATIONAL SETTLEMENTS

The height of that concern the G-7 has supported a number of actions to put in place disciplines to promote greater stability, and the worlds economic growth prospects are now substantially better. To some degree a sense of complacency has grown that should cause concern. We must not forget that the instability of 1998 saw the fastest growing economies in East Asia suffering contractions in output that were even greater than that experienced during the Great Depression of the 1930s; Russia going into default beneath its cloud of corruption; in the US, the mounting of one of the biggest ever emergency refinancings, not for a bank but for a hedge fund; free enterprise Hong Kong taking publicly owned stakes in all of its private companies; and Japan nationalising its banks.

The causes of the problem, about which there is general agreement, include excessive indebtedness, both public and private; the inappropriate nature of that indebtedness, with its tilt towards short-term maturities in non-domestic currencies; high levels of leverage, not just in the financial system, but also in the debt to equity ratio in the industrial sector; and the nearly universal weakness of developing nations' domestic financial systems. It is almost impossible to pick up a newspaper or magazine these days without confronting another set of proposals to reform the 'international financial architecture', proposals that sweep the horizon of reform and include:

- The creation of an international deposit insurance corporation.
- The formation of an international bankruptcy courts.
- A rethink of the generalised antipathy towards controls on capital outflow.
- Chilean-style controls on inflows.

The creation of a single global super-regulator of financial markets and institutions. The creation of a world central bank with responsibility for overseeing a new global. The selection of the IMF to perform the functions of a lender of last resort, a suggestion packaged along with a wide range of improvements to the existing structure of the international financial institutions (IFIs).

The Council on Foreign Relations created a task force (of which the author was a member) and recently published its findings in a report entitled 'Safeguarding Prosperity in a Global Financial System: The Future International Financial Architecture', which put forward seven key recommendations:

- The IMF should lend on more favourable terms to countries that take effective steps to reduce their crisis vulnerability, and should publish an assessment of these steps so that the market can take note.
- Emerging economies with fragile financial systems should take transparent and non-discriminatory tax measures to discourage short-term capital inflows.
- The private sector should promote fair burden sharing and market discipline.
- Emerging economies should reject pegged exchange rates.
- The IMF should adhere consistently to normal lending limits and abandon huge rescue packages.
- The IMF and the World Bank should revert to their basic historical roles.
- Political support for financial reform should be generated.

Most of these schemes have fatal flaws. Some suggestions, ranging from the unrealistic to the surreal, are politically infeasible given the absence of a supranational legal authority; some could substantially increase costs to lenders or add protection for borrowers, and thus would lead to a sharp contraction of capital flows to developing nations; and those that shift risk away from creditors, thus leading to an increase in capital flows, are likely to be followed by a wave of greater risk taking, followed by another wave of defaults.

It seems to me that all these suggestions possess bits that could be recalibrated and, if taken together, would be helpful in designing solutions. However any attempt to find a sweeping one-size-fits-all answer is bound to fail. After all, each situation is different and needs to be evaluated in light of its particular circumstances. In my view solutions must be designed on a case-by-case basis, combined with smaller packages from the IFIs and accompanied by a reduction of bailout expectations (the moral hazard issue); more private sector involvement early on with terms that incentivise the private sector to participate; the recognition that solutions cannot be forced, since countries make their own decisions, the acceptability of which are priced into the market; and limit restructuring to the most difficult cases when insolvency threatens. There is of course considerable disagreement about any and all of the solutions save one the need to strengthen the financial sector of developing nations. All commentators, all committee reports, public and private, agree that this is key to financial stability. Since the mid 1970s we have seen time and time again that:

- Poor macroeconomic policies coupled with a weak financial sector is a recipe for disaster.
- Even when a country has a reasonably decent macro policy mix, if it has a weak financial sector any external shock is quickly transformed into disaster.
- A country may have a poor macro policy mix, but if it has a strong and vibrant financial sector there may be big problems, but disaster is averted.

The financial sector should be a stabilising influence, but as we have seen in Asia, Russia and elsewhere it has acted as a multiplier, making bad problems worse.

Since there is general agreement that strengthening the financial sector is critical, there is an unfortunate tendency within the official community to assume that sufficient attention and resources are being paid to fixing this problem. Some efforts along these lines have been made in the past and are being made by a variety of central banks and international financial agencies- but not nearly enough.

Improving the financial sector fundamentally requires substantial upgrading of financial supervisory systems. Theoretically, change could and should be implemented by the private sector in recognition of best practice and in response to competitive pressures. But this has not happened. Many reasons have been cited-including structural and cultural issues, which are usually used as an excuse for not meeting best practice-for their inability to change. The fact remains that those institutions wished to enjoy the benefits of global markets without accepting global standards.

In recognition of the need to improve the functioning of financial intermediation, the Basel Committee on Banking Supervision (BCBS) adopted the Core Principles of Banking Supervision, which were designed to guide supervisors on the standards they should require when examining a bank in order to judge the safety, soundness and prudent management of that institution. Since the private sector had abdicated the role of self-improvement, the financial supervisors recognised that it fell on their shoulders to become the agents of change.

Upgrading financial supervision in any country is a long-term project, one that will take years of diligent implementation to succeed. In the US it takes about five years to train a good bank examiner. And good bank examiners are exactly what are needed. On-site supervision is key to determining the strength or weakness of any individual financial institution, and on-site means on-site bank examiners. Off-site examination, favoured by some, is only valid if off-site is the sum of skilled on-site examination. If it is not, then off-site calculations are often corrupted by incomplete and often misleading information.

In many of these countries there is an overwhelming shortage of trained and experienced bank examiners. Furthermore many of these supervisory agencies are starved of the financial resources needed to provide a competitive wage for professional staff and purchase support mechanisms such as information technology. These agencies do not receive the necessary political support, which precedes financial support, to upgrade their capacity to do the job.

Many of the G10 central banks and banking supervisory agencies have been active in training bank examiners from developing nations. This has been helpful, but not all the G10 banking supervisory agencies have a similar view on the techniques needed to implement the core principles. Furthermore the training provided has been coloured by the practices and procedures used in the country in question.

As a result, hundreds of men and women have been sent back to their home countries with some element of training but, as a group, without a common understanding of techniques and goals. It is imperative that we create a broad set of international standards that are accepted, implemented and enforced across the global financial system. We need a common understanding of the root meanings of the Core Principles and a common measure for their implementation and enforcement. It is to be hoped that this will be furthered by the final adoption of the Core Principles Methodology by the BCBS. The Financial Stability Forum (FSF), under the chairman-ship of Andrew Crockett, the general manager of the BIS, and in cooperation with the IMF and the World Bank, has begun to collect data on the various training courses being offered to banking supervisors. Prior to this effort, no compendium of courses was available. This is an important first step in the process of providing assistance for financial supervisory improvement.

The IMF has agreed to undertake, in the course of its Article IV consultations, a review of the state of financial supervision. That should prove to be enormously helpful, but much more is needed. Identification of problems is an important first step towards their correction, but it must be accompanied by sources of education, training and assistance to which countries can turn in order to improve financial supervision. It is towards this end that the Bank for International Settlements (BIS) and the BCBS created the Financial Stability Institute (FSI) of the BIS.

The FSI's mandate is to help improve and strengthen financial intermediation in the developing nations and those in transition. For the most part this means working with banking supervisors, since financial intermediation in these countries is heavily concentrated in the commercial banking system. For the most part capital markets are virtually non-existent or are only in the earliest phases of development.

The FSI is pursuing this task through a variety of symposia, meetings and workshops for the leaders of financial supervisory agencies. Leadership is key. We know that we must convince the agency heads of the validity and timeliness of our programmes so that they will encourage, even order, their associates to attend the courses that have been designed for them.

An integral part of the FSI's programme is the holding of workshops and meetings, many of them regional, for middle-level members of the supervisory agencies-the men and women who are responsible for the examination process. The programme began with the leadership, but it must reach out to professional staff so that they too can receive the benefit of FSI programming.

At the very heart of the FSI's work will be the Core Principles and the Core Principles Methodology, when finally adopted by the BCBS. This is particularly important since the IMF's Article IV consultation will include an assessment of adherence, implementation and enforcement of the methodology.

During 2000 the FSI held a series of workshops on methodology in Basel and the regions. It has also offered workshops on fraud detection, consolidated supervision, governance, asset and liability management, information technology, financial innovation, deposit insurance, capital flows and, last but not least, risk management, credit risk, and market risk.

It is the FSI's practice to use supervisors from around the world to lecture on subjects that are primarily supervisory in nature, and for the private sector to provide the lecturers for subjects that are directly market related.

The FSI recognises that at this stage much of what it is doing is somewhat experimental. Early in its existence it sent a survey to the heads of supervision and the central bank governors of all the non-G-10 countries to find out what they needed. Most encouragingly, it received a response rate of slightly over 75 per cent. This impressive result overwhel-mingly indicated the need for assistance. The programme for 2000, which focused on risk management, consolidated supervision and core principles methodology, reflected their priorities.

Prior to 2000 the FSI had held four workshops, attended by 129 persons from 74 countries. Their level of sophistication and experience was broadly spread from a very few with near state of the art capacity to those who had just begun seriously to improve their supervisory skills. Nearly all of those with whom the ESI has been in contact have been seeking a substantive upgrade for their agencies.

They wished to have the same basic competence as that which presently exists within the G10. And they realistically recognised that it would take some time to get there.

Therefore the task of the FSI is twofold: to give supervisors a grasp of the end result they wish to achieve; and to provide them with the tools that will help them to achieve that goal, not only in the long term but in the short term as well. It is not good enough just to outline the landscape of the promised land of banking supervision.

They have continuing responsibilities and must examine and pass judgement on banks tomorrow. The FSI must provide them with the necessary tools to help them manage their ongoing responsibilities as they travel the long road to the promised land. This is easier said than done. Whatever is suggested for immediate implementation must be in concert with long-term, presently unachievable goals.

The FSI is attempting to resolve this dilemma by stressing basics, coupled with techniques for an immediate assessment of an institution's ability to meet minimum standards. The FSI's course on market risk explains the benefits of and the techniques for stress testing and measurement tools such as VaR-all of this done by private sector experts, complemented by supervisors with this particular expertise-and simultaneously provides them with questions that will help them to determine the scope and reach of an institution's market risk management.

In many countries, supervisors simply do not have enough trained professionals to evaluate the more sophisticated techniques designed by the G10 supervisors.

Therefore the questions the FSI gives them are designed quickly to reveal the state of management's capacity to manage risk without requiring the supervisor to field an army of experienced examiners backed up by state of the art technology. For example, at the beginning of an examination the examiner could ask the CEO the following questions (there are follow-up questions depending upon the answers):

- What is the tolerable level of loss your board of directors has agreed is an acceptable level of risk?
- Please show me how you decompose your profit and loss statement between risk- and non-risk-related activities. Also, may I see your log of extraordinary gains and losses for the past six or 12 months with the accompanying explanations?

These questions are simple but not simplistic. If the board of directors has not set a tolerable loss limit, the supervisor knows there is a basic governance issue. If the profit and loss statement is not decomposed and if there is no log of extraordinary gains and losses, then the supervisor knows there is no effective risk management in that institution even if a risk management box appears on the organisation's chart. Since most supervisors have the power to inspect the institution's records, including board minutes, the answers given are easily verified by inspection. The FSI recognises that the path to global improvement of financial supervision is long and arduous. Most nations with which it has been in contact seem serious about improving their financial supervisory capacity. But no doubt some of those who say they are will not commit the necessary resources to accomplish the task. Adherence to principles is not necessarily compliance with principles. The FSI does not prejudge the motives of any nation in this respect. Over time it will become apparent to the FSI and the international financial community which nations are seriously trying to improve and those which are just paying lip service. As that becomes apparent, and it surely will, then international financial institutions and the capital markets will take progress, or the lack of it, into account and act accordingly.

TURBULENCE, CRISES AND RISK MANAGEMENT

Balance sheets are opaque concepts. In more than one way, the individual instruments in a balance sheet have no meaning by themselves. What is more, most large financial institutions carry a very large number of diverse instruments on their balance sheets, in many different branches and subsidiaries around the world. Even a careful analysis of financial tables and balance sheets will not show the exact positions and exposures the financial institution has taken. This is even before one can ask how one would value these positions.

Quantitative methods of risk management are perhaps the only reasonable way of assessing the potential losses institutions may face in the event of financial turbulence. In this introduction we illustrate why this is so by discussing the difficulties of managing risks using non-quantitative approaches. We do this using two examples, both of which relate to options. Options exist in explicit and implicit form. They are often implicit in very common contracts that never draw attention. For example, annuity contracts often contain significant optionality. Another case in point is bonds, most of which usually come with call or put options. Call loans on the other hand, are loans that contain complex implicit options. Looked at from this angle, explicit options that are either written over the counter or traded in organised exchanges are an exception.

All these aside, some of the more popular derivatives that have attained a huge volume contain options. Caps, floors and swaptions form the largest part of derivatives books in financial institutions.

They are basically options on interest rates. Selling or buying an option appears to an outsider as a very risky activity. After all, the seller of a call on interest rates or currencies faces the (gross) payoff at expiration.

Clearly it looks as though the trader who is short faces very high risks and may lose unlimited sums if the interest rates move against him or her! Yet this way of looking at option risks is misleading. As soon as a trader sells an option he or she buys an appropriate amount of the underlying asset. For example in this case he or she buys Eurodollar futures, whose value is:

$$Ft = 100(1-0.\ 25r_t)$$

where r t is the three-month Libor for example. If the contract is entered into when, say $r_{t'} = r$, then this position looks like the one. Here the slope of the payoff is 0. 25 times the number of futures contracts sold, which in general is equal to $C_3^0/0.\ 25$ the slope of the option position at point C^0.

The two quantities are approximately equal, especially if r is small. This means that the option buyer (seller) has hedged his or her risk.

Hence if we look at the balance sheet of this institution we will see a long position in options, which we may think is risky. We will also see a short position in the underlying asset, which we may also find risky. But put together these risks cancel out. Does this mean that the positions are not risky? Nothing could be further from the truth. The option holder faces volatility, or vega risk. If the actual volatility in the market turns out to be less than expected, the trader may lose money.

The trader is long the underlying asset, he is long an at-the-money put and short an at-the-money call. Considered separately, the instruments appear to be very risky and the trader has a high probability of losing money. But put together the position is not risky at all. In fact traders use these types of riskless positions to arbitrage between markets. They will 'buy' an instrument and, using appropriate call and put options, 'sell' it at a higher price. The spread is their profit. Their position is not any riskier than the activity of a new car dealer.

Yet suppose the prices move and the trader mistakenly sells the put, which has become profitable. Then the whole position reduces to a short put, which carries unlimited risks. This shows that the closing of a position may affect the risks of other assets in the portfolio

How can the institution tell whether such indirect exposures are created by the thousands of transactions carried out on a given trading day? Clearly this is not an easy operation.

The current methods of risk management and provides one answer to the above questions. The main concepts and tools. The next section discusses some standard ways of measuring risk.

This is followed by a discussion of the types of assets financial institutions deal with and their relevance from the point of view of risk management. The next two sections deal with the complications that one may encounter when applying these tools, and with the new avenues.

MANAGING RISKS

Risk management can be seen as having two broad branches. The first, and the one with which we are mainly concerned, is market risk management. The second, and equally important, is credit risk management-we shall comment on this rapidly developing domain as well.

We begin by considering a simple example in order to define the basic concepts, which are essentially the same across markets and credit risk management. Consider a default-free zero coupon bond with price B 0 with maturity T and yield R T. This could be a treasury bond, or more exactly a STRIP. Because the bond is default-free the holder of this instrument is guaranteed to receive 100 units of a certain currency at T, which for simplicity we assume is the US dollar. Assuming that the future default-free short rates are given by (*r t*, *t* = 0, 1.., *T* 1), the arbitrage-free price of this bond will equal,

$$B_0 = E^P \left(\frac{100}{(1 + r_0)(1 + r_1)..(1 + r_{T-1})} \right)$$

where P is the risk-neutral probability measure. This price can also be written in terms of the corresponding yield.

Here the R T, r t and the exchange rate, e T, between the US dollar and some relevant variables will alter the value of the asset in question. Market risk has to do with losses that may be caused by changes in these market risk factors. There are in fact three major ways in which changes in risk factors can affect the value of a portfolio.

We shall discuss these within the context of the same example. The first effect is the portfolio or asset's delta. The yield, R T, is a random variable and it will change by R T as time t passes. This change can be large and may cause significant drops in the value of the bond. In a portfolio that has long bonds, the losses will be proportional to increases in R T. This proportion (called the delta of the instrument) will be greater the longer the maturity of the bond.

Here we see the first type of market risk, namely the first order price risk of the bond portfolio, and this is clearly caused by random movements in the risk-free yield.

The secondary effects of movements in risk factors is the gamma effect. An institution that is long (short) the bond, or some other instrument, may have hedged the delta risk, however. This can be done by selling (buying) T-bonds, T-bills or other appropriate interest rate futures. But in some cases, such as Eurodollar futures, the futures price is a linear function of the interest rates, whereas the bond price is a non-linear function of R T, as can be seen from the formula above. Thus the institution may have exposure to the second derivative with respect to yield: This risk is called the gamma risk and is another type of market risk created by the inability of a linear instrument to hedge fully for the nonlinear effects of random changes in the risk factor R T. Note that in this particular case the gamma risk is of the opposite sign to the delta risk. Hence if one has exposure to a particular delta, ignoring the gamma risk will be equivalent to adopting a conservative approach.

CREDIT RISK

THE NEW FRONTIER OF RISK MANAGEMENT

The art of market risk measurement and control has reached a state today that is impressive by any standard. Recent academic developments (notably based on option pricing), new tools (VaR and its variations), new instruments (with the continuously renewed derivative contracts), new institutions (for example the importance assumed by risk management departments in banks) have all converged to provide a remarkable understanding and mastery of market risk, whether interest rate, foreign exchange or stock markets. Of course our deepened understanding has also confirmed what we cannot understand-forecasting and asset pricing have particularly been under stress.

But overall the advancement of finance in market risk is both obvious and a guarantee of further advancements in the field, and other the clear promise of rocket science discoveries continuously to upgrade our knowledge and techniques. It is thus unfortunate that what is arguably the largest single risk class in volume today ($4. 6 trillion of public debt in the US in 1996 alone and easily $2. 9 trillion in corporate loans in the same country) and arguably the major risk for all economic agents in the business world-the risk of default-is far from being as well understood.

Credit risk is also very pervasive. Most of the huge derivatives markets, for example, are OTC (over-the-counter) contracts and as such present a credit risk-the possibility of default by one counterparty. Banks have had to manage credit risk (risk of default on the loans they provide) for centuries. The fact that they are much less sophisticated at doing this than they are at managing their (comparatively more recent) FX or interest rate exposures, and also lack advanced techniques and instruments to do so, may therefore come as a surprise-but actually it should not do so. Credit risk is a complex topic that requires all our intellectual, technical and institutional abilities, and even then it does not lend itself to easy solutions. What should also be clear is that hoping to manage risk without managing credit risk is hopeless.

This is the risk to manage. It pervades all financial contracts and it perverts market risk, for example a portfolio believed to be fully hedged with swap or forward contracts against an FX or an interest risk may suddenly find itself at risk again because of credit risk.

What we propose to do here is to give a sense of why credit risk is so difficult to apprehend, what traditional methods are telling us, how modern techniques, inspired by the most advanced market risk techniques, are being used to look at the problem from a new angle, and how new instruments and new institutions are emerging that may help us to manage credit risk better in the near future.

THE COMPLEXITY OF CREDIT RISK

Credit risk is extremely complex and presents a greater challenge than both market risk (one needs to understand market risk in order to predict when and under what conditions a counterparty might default) and purely exogenous risks such as operational risk.

Indeed credit risk depends on market risk, but while market risk can be made homogeneous by category (interest rate, FX and so on), credit risk is deeply fragmented. First, credit risk is fragmented by product. For example banks hold loans while mutual funds hold bonds on what might appear to be the same credit risk (a company) but it actually leads to a very different outcome in the event of default (technically, while the probability of default may be similar across products for a one company exposure, the loss given default, and thus the credit risk that is a combination of these two dimensions, will differ widely and is usually not well determined ex ante but a consequence of complex negotiations).

Second, credit risk is fragmented geographically. Most institutions lend and invest primarily in their own back yards. Global players, and those trying to design management techniques that will be applicable worldwide, have long discovered that default in the US, default in Switzerland and default in Japan are three very different things, with different economic outcomes and different uncertainties about the outcome, not to mention the complex interaction between the credit risk of the country and the credit risk of the company.

Third, credit risk is fragmented in time. On the investor's side it is fragmented by maturity horizon. Bank loans often mature within five years, while life insurance companies invest in 10- to 30-year bonds. These exposures are usually analysed by means of the same long-term rating system. The relationship between credit risk and time is not well understood, but as we shall see later, credit risk can increase or decrease with maturity, in a highly non-linear fashion.

This fragmentation can lead to excessive risk taking and inefficient pricing. If one adds to this fragmentation the proliferation of credit enhancement methods (from collateralisation to AAA subsidiaries via credit risk insurance), which make the issue even more confusing, the problematic heterogeneity of this risk starts to become evident.

On a more technical note, most market risk models (such as asset selection and the efficient frontier, the CAPM and other asset pricing models, and more recently most of the models in the option pricing literature) are based on an assumption of normal distribution. Unfortunately this assumption (and the rather simplified mathematical conclusions it produces) does not carry well for credit risk.

A holder of a credit instrument such as a bond can expect to receive the principal plus interest if the instrument is held until maturity, or even to have a limited upside if the credit instrument is upgraded in rating. The downside occurs, usually with a low probability, when either the obligor defaults or the instrument is downgraded in rating. Therefore the return from a credit instrument is highly skewed. In contrast the return from an equity instrument is fairly smooth and symmetrical and can be assumed to be normally distributed. Because of the highly skewed nature of returns from credit instruments, the calculation of value-at-risk (VAR) requires a different approach from the traditional market risk methods (from derivative pricing to VaR), where a normal distribution of returns is assumed. Note that this difference in statistical behaviour is linked to the relationship between credit risk and market risk and to the nature of credit risk itself.

One way of looking at credit risk, which those used to option theory will recognise, is to plot the profile of a bond that is subject to credit risk versus the value of the assets of the firm. The profile differs between a bond that is subject to interest rate risk and the reimbursement value of the same bond, depending on the capacity of the firm to honour its commitments. To these conceptual issues we have to add a practical consideration: lack of data. While there are some data on ratings, these are not frequently updated, nor are they necessarily a good representation of default probability.

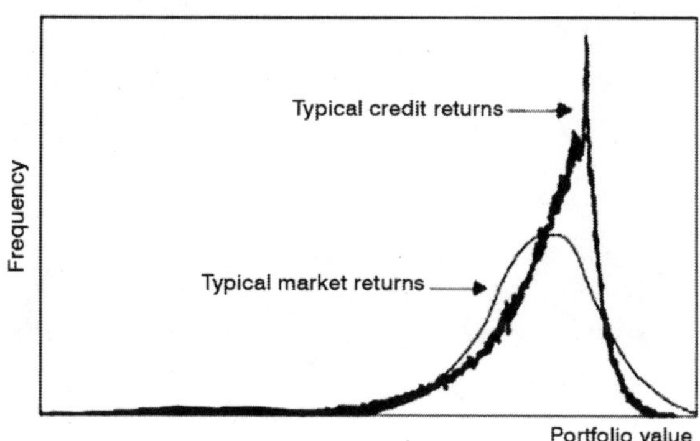

They have no explanatory power for loss, given default. Yields on publicly traded instruments can be observed but they are instrument-dependent. Also, unlike with market risk, the correlation between the returns on credit instruments is not directly observable, which makes it difficult to calculate the credit risk of a portfolio. The current lack of data (something that could be partly remedied by effort on the part of banks and regulatory bodies) thus makes a conceptually difficult task even more problematic.

It is therefore to the credit of those working in the field that our knowledge and techniques have advanced dramatically since the late 1990s. Before examining these techniques we shall look at the difficulties that arise with the most frequently used traditional instrument: ratings.

DIFFICULTIES THAT ARISE WITH RATINGS

Traditionally ratings have been used as the starting point in credit risk analysis. Ratings are a simple way to transform a discrete event (default) into a more continuous variable (rating changes). It is well known that continuous variables are easier to handle and to obtain the dynamics of than discrete events. This transformation is thus welcome if it is valid. The following brief example illustrates the functioning of ratings. Suppose you have a long position in a bond that is rated AA. The risk you face is that of being downgraded. Hence to calculate the credit risk of your position you need to calculate:

- The probability of a downgrade.
- The bond's value in the event of a downgrade.
- The recovery rate in the event of the ultimate downgrade: default.

Hence the use of transition matrices, which plot the probability of moving to another rating. They are useful for measuring and managing credit risk in that they can be used to ascertain the dynamics of ratings over time.

The transition matrices can be calculated from past data by calculating (over a period of 15-20 years) the number of AAAs that have remained AAA, the number of AAAs that have become AA, and so on. More recent work tries to integrate the credit cycle instead of using only historical data, but obvious challenge of the methodology is its dependence on the latter (and its failure to consider outside factors such as macroeconomic variables).

How good are ratings at capturing credit risk information? Several researchers have addressed the problem, with mixed results. For example Lucas and Lonski analysed the ratings of 6000 issuers over the period 1970-90 and found that ratings are not stable, and that even their instability is not stable. Ratings volatility doubled from 6 per cent of changes per calendar year in the 1970s to 12 per cent in the 1980s.

There was a clear downward trend in quality that makes credit risk analysis all the more important today. The ratio of downgrades to upgrades went from 1. 17 (almost balanced) to 2. 17 for long-term debt over the period in question, that is there were twice as many downgrades than upgrades at the end of the period. Some authors defend the idea that there is no useful information to be obtained from ratings as they are too slow to adjust and reflect rating agencies' management as much as true credit changes. Others have strongly defended ratings as the only true source of information available. Using a sample of 1500 industrial firms during the period 1985-95, that there is little information content in rating upgrades (all the information has already been incorporated into market prices) but there is some in rating downgrades. This study shows that neither the antirating nor the prorating lobbies are right-the reality is more complex.

Several studies have shown that neither of the two agencies truly dominates the other as far as the information content of their ratings goes. Indeed, if one considers split ratings, it can be shown that taking into consideration the two ratings has more information content than taking either one. Stability (or instability) of rating migrations and established a methodology to adapt rating migrations to changes in the business cycle, the country or the industrial sector.

In short, the information content of credit ratings is minimal at best, even in the US, where ratings are extensive.

Note that credit risk depends not only on the probability of default (captured to a certain extent by ratings) but also on the recovery rate (or conversely the loss, given default), and information on this variable is even hardly to crime. There are huge differences across industries-for some industries the recovery rate can be as high as 80 per cent while for others it barely goes over the 10 per cent mark. Different recovery rates should lead to different credit risks, a fact not well represented in ratings and for which we lack even the most basic information, especially in Europe. From a practical viewpoint, the usual instruments of credit risk measurement seem limited and their relationship to actual pricing is difficult to assess as complex, non-linear relationships are sure to be present.

RECENT THEORETICAL LITERATURE ON CREDIT RISK PRICING

During the last few years, academic research has shed new light on the complexity of the credit risk problem and on ways to approach and treat it. Two major lines of research have evolved (with some overlap): the contingent claim approach and the reduced form approach.

The first approach was pioneered in 1974 by Robert C. Merton (who won a Nobel Prize in 1997). Merton proposed that in a simple setting (a firm with only one issue of zero-coupon debt) the stock of the firm can be seen as a call option on the assets of the firm and hence the credit risk on the debt issue can be compared to a short position on a put option. Thus contingent claims analysis (option pricing) can be used to value the component parts of a firm's liability mix. In general, the value of each component will depend upon the stochastic variables that determine the evolution of the firm's asset value, the evolution of the interest rate, the payouts (dividends, coupons and so on) to the various claimants, and the division of the firm at any point of reorganisation (for example bankruptcy). The method makes it possible to analyse and measure the impact on credit risk spreads of a change in asset volatility, a change in interest rate volatility, different maturities of debt and so on.

The payoff structure for levered corporate equity is isomorphic to the one for a call option on a share of stock where the maturity date of the firm's debt, T, corresponds to the expiry date of the option, the promised payment on the debt, B, corresponds to the exercise price of the option and the firm's value, V, corresponds to the underlying security. As a consequence the terminal payoff to debt is functionally equivalent to owning the assets of the firm and being short a call option on those assets with an exercise price of B. (Alternatively the debtholders can be considered to have lent money risklessly at face value B and gone short a put option on the assets of the firm with an exercise price of B.)

We can thus use option pricing to value credit risky bonds. The theory provides for interesting and unexpected consequences, such as the fact that volatility and credit spreads may be two contradictory measures of credit risk (they may rank instruments differently as to their risk) and the fact that in high-yield debt, longer maturity may be associated with a lower credit risk, all else being equal.

The methodology has been extended in various ways to take into account non-constant interest rates, several debt issues, more complex instruments (including credit derivatives), the presence of collateral, the presence of gaming when there are bankruptcy costs and so on, but it becomes very difficult to handle mathematically when these different complexities are cumulated. It is nonetheless a full theory of credit risk with, notably, an endogenous recovery rate.

The reduced-form approach is quite different. Although it focuses on arbitrage-free models (and thus differentiates itself from the plain actuarial ratings-based approach), it treats bankruptcy as an exogenous rather than an endogenous process. From a theoretical point of view this is not a welcome departure, but it does allow for easier treatment of practical cases (with the weakness of ignoring the financial economics behind the determination of the bankruptcy process).

Many recent papers have followed this assumption. The papers allow for somewhat easier pricing of complex instruments. They also allow models to be fitted in a clean way to past data. On the other hand the models are limited to exogenous times to default and exogenous recovery rates. Although very sophisticated mathematically and of great use in practice, the models do not provide a full theory and thus may be taken to be at fault in a highly unstable environment. Put together the two theories give us a much better picture of what credit risk is about and how this risk moves with different variables. They allow for a more precise pricing of credit risk and should prove highly useful as the market for credit risk evolves (notably with credit derivatives such as credit default swaps).

CREDIT RISK MEASUREMENT FOR PORTFOLIOS

Financial institutions are required by the regulatory authorities (The Bank for International Settlements and the national governing bodies) to hold a certain amount of funds in reserve to cover the risk of their assets. Determining the amount to be held is an important regulatory challenge, but knowledge of the amount of risk an institution is ex manage their portfolio and risks.

Since the financial performance of a company is influenced to a large extent by market conditions, the credit risk of the company (the possibility of downgrade or default) depends on market conditions.

Simply adding together market risk and credit risk may lead to double counting. At the same time a sudden increase in the riskiness of large 'market makers' can influence the overall market conditions. Ideally, therefore, in order to quantify the amount of risk there should be a holistic approach to risk measurement, capturing both aspects. Since the theoretical models for this are too complex for easy implementation, financial institutions are using separate models to evaluate the two aspects of risk.

Of the many models available to evaluate credit risk, the following four are dominant.

CREDITMETRICS

Creditmetrics, which was initially promoted by J. P. Morgan and is now marketed by an independent company (Riskmetrics), measures changes in the value of an asset due to the migration of its credit rating.

It starts by assigning a credit rating to an asset/obligor. The range of changes in the value of the asset is calculated on the basis of the probability of the asset changing its credit rating or defaulting over a certain period. Than the value at risk at a given confidence level is derived as the value of the return on the asset at that confidence level. Credit rating agencies such as S&P and Moody's publish data on the credit ratings of assets, their transition probabilities and the recovery rates in case of default.

CREDITRISK

Credit Suisse's CreditRisk+ is derived from the model used by insurance companies to evaluate their risks and relies on a two-state model of an asset-the asset is either in default or not in default. In this sense it is close to reduced-form models. The model does not consider risks due to the downgrading of the credit rating of the obligor. No assumption is made about the causes of default: obligor A is either in default, with probability P A or is not in default, with probability. Losses (exposures, net of recovery) are divided into bands, with the level of exposure in each band being approximated by a single number. Default rates, their volatility and the recovery rates of obligors are obtained from the credit rating charts published by rating agencies or the financial institution itself. To calculate a loss due to the default of a portfolio of assets, the model divides the assets into bands, based on exposures. The total portfolio is then regarded as a portfolio of these bands. Value at risk at a certain confidence level is then calculated as the expected loss due to default at that confidence level.

CREDIT MONITOR MODEL

The Credit Monitor model is based on Merton's option model of a firm, where both the stockholders' and bondholders' claims on the firm's assets are considered as options. If the volatility of a firm's equity is known, its value and the firm's capital structure, value of the firm's assets and its volatility can be calculated. The value of the risky debt can then be calculated using the option pricing model.

Using historical data on the behaviour of defaulting firms, the credit-measuring company KMV has concluded that the critical threshold for default (The 'default point') is not the point where the value of a firm's assets falls below the value of its liabilities, but where the firm's value reaches the par value of current liabilities to be serviced over a time horizon plus half its long-term debt.

The model then computes the index, distance to default (DD) as the number of standard deviations between the mean of distribution of the asset value, and the default point. Unlike the Creditmetrics model, where firms with the same credit rating are expected to have the same default and transition probabilities, which are equal to the average historical rate, the Credit Monitor model allows us to look at the default probability of a specific firm.

Also, since rating agencies take time to upgrade and downgrade the credit ratings of firms, the default rates they report may not accurately reflect the actual default rates. In fact there are examples of the EDF (expected default frequency) becoming the leading indicator of default or a tall in the creditworthiness of obligors.

CREDITPORTFOLIO

The CreditPortfolio model incorporates macroeconomic factors into the calculation of default rates and the probability of credit rating transitions. The probability of default is calculated as a function of various macroeconomic factors and the speculative grade of the obligor. Provided there is enough historical data to calibrate the model-that is to establish coefficients for the influence of a particular factor on probability-this model can be used to calculate the riskiness of assets in any country or industry. The econometric consistency of the model thus becomes essential, but its theoretical base is weaker than those of the other models.

It should be noted that none of these models can deal with market risk at the same time as credit risk (for example none can deal with non-constant interest rates) and none can deal with non-linear instruments such as options, hence they are very limited. However, they do represent an important advance on the usual practices. For example they allow for portfolio optimisation of high-yield portfolios, something that has not been done before. When new instruments to manage credit risk emerge, such as credit derivatives, knowl

edge of how to manage portfolios and transform their exposure to credit risk will offer a major competitive advantage as the flexibility of exposure management becomes increasingly important. The most widely used credit derivatives (credit default swaps-basically default insurance-and total return swaps, whereby a safe return is swapped for a credit risky return) as well as new instruments (default spread options and futures) will render the credit risk exposure of financial intermediaries more flexible than they have ever been. Understanding what they want in terms of credit exposure and the value of that exposure are thus becoming essential concerns for financial intermediaries in respect of competitiveness.

PRESSURE TO INNOVATE AND RESTRUCTURE

The financial sector will face tremendous challenges in the coming years. Globalisation and information technology are the twin forces transforming the industry-indeed the world economy-at a pace never experienced before.

GLOBALISATION

It might sound like a cliché, but we are in the midst of the greatest economic transformation in the history of mankind. Since the early 1980s, thanks to new technology and globalisation, around one billion people have been lifted from abject poverty to some kind of global middle-class status. Globalisation has proceeded in steps: via freer trade, deregulation of the capital markets to today's rapid transformation and diffusion of technology to all corners of the world.

As a result the old trade-off between quality and quantity is changing. Some decades ago, when deciding on their production base global companies could choose between high-cost, high-quality production in industrialised countries and cheap, low-quality production in Third World countries. Today, however, courtesy of globalisation, new information technology and the collapse of communism, it is quite possible to produce high-quality goods and services in emerging economies-and much more cheaply than in industrialised countries.

This of course means more rapid global growth, but also new challenges to the industrialised world and its old companies.

For the small and open economies of this new world there is no control room in the Ministries of Finance, where ministers can push buttons or pull levers and feel certain of controlling their national economies. As a matter of fact most national economies are merging into a single, comprehensive global economy.

In this new global economy the Anglo-Saxon free market model has triumphed over the planned economy, and also over the welfare state and the Asian model. Hence there is increasing pressure for deregulation and free markets in just about all countries. Tax structures are converging as tax bases become more mobile. The number of independent currencies is diminishing, due to currency unions, currency boards and dollarisation. New fashions and cultural trends are spreading rapidly via new media, global television, fax machines and the Internet-even to the remotest villages. Young people are increasingly influenced by global trends and by other young people all over the world, rather than by their local elders. We are truly becoming one world.

THE IT REVOLUTION

In this global environment a new revolution is taking place in information technology, a revolution that is in turn helping to propel both growth and globalisation. In my opinion the IT upheaval is a third industrial revolution-following the first industrialisation process, based on the steam engine, and the second wave, based upon the electrical motor and the internal combustion engine. There is of course no scientific or exact definition of what constitutes an industrial revolution. However economists and historians seem to agree that one important characteristic is the development of a generic technology, which is then exploited and employed in numerous sectors, creating spin-offs and 'developmental blocks' in important ways that were totally unforeseen by the original innovators.

We all know the story of the dynamo and the electrical motor; how it started as a big, clumsy machine at the centre of the factory floor but gradually evolved over decades to become more efficient, smaller and universal. Today there are literally hundreds of electrical motors in each home, in our kitchen appliances, vacuum cleaners and other gadgets that have transformed everyday life. The same is true of the internal combustion engine, which radically transformed transporta-tion, distribution, housing and living. And in time the manu-facture of cars, the construction of houses and the production of television sets, refrigerators and so on created economic growth and mass prosperity on an unprecedented scale.

I believe the same thing will happen again as a result of the IT revolution. Its symbol is the silicon chip and the glass-fibre cable. Some 20 years ago, when computers started to be used in industry, they were rather bulky and slow and were usually handled-in closed-off rooms-by men in white coats, speaking unintelligible techno-lingo. The productivity effect was low or hardly discernible. I guess we all remember Solow's quip: 'Computers are everywhere but in the productivity statistics'. Now, however, computers are literally everywhere and the man-machine interface is much easier to handle, and when millions of computers are interconnected through high-speed cable the productivity effects are much greater.

They are bound to be even greater in the future. While the engines of the earlier industrial revolutions simplified physical human work or replaced it with machines, the chip and the cable will replace or simplify mental and intellectual work. In doing so they will transform our lives in ways we cannot imagine today.

HEADING TECHNOLOGY

The technical change brought about by the IT revolution has just begun. Over the next few years we will see rapid development in several areas.

- Moore's law (exponential growth of computing capacity) will apply at least for the next couple of years. Processors will be faster, and memory capacity will rapidly increase. Computers and chips will become even smaller and smarter.
- Bandwidth will expand. The sending and receiving of immense amounts of information via the Internet is increasing much more rapidly than was thought possible only a couple of years ago. The bottleneck is the last thread out to the individual household, but here also experimentation and innovation are moving fast.
- The man-machine interface will become even simpler and easier to handle. We have become used to a screen, a mouse and a keyboard, but in the near future we will be able to interact with the computer through speech (or even via sensors applied to our bodies). The screens will be thinner, bendable or foldable and transportable. This means that e-mail and Internet connections will be easier to handle and will function faster from any place in the world with the help of a number of gadgets.
- All this opens up true interactivity. Not only will we be able to interact sequentially, but together we will be able to work on the same project or design, in real time, irrespective of where in the world we are.
- The communication explosion will propel the rapid development of filters, screening and push technologies.
- IT will, in simpler and less conspicuous ways, become embedded in all kinds of products and processes, which will become 'intelligent' or at least self-regulated, like thermostats. We can already see this in durable consumer goods, for example antilocking brakes and automatic traction systems in cars. In the financial markets we can see it in automatic trading programs and their various selling and

buying orders. In manufacturing, electronics are being gradually linked to electromechanical micromotors with sensors and switches, which work in a mechanical environment in machines and products of all kinds.

- Huge resources are being spent on combining such techniques with medical technology. Self-regulating medication and medical treatment, even operations, via remote control is already here. Simulations and similar technology can also be utilised to revolutionise education.
- In manufacturing and the service sector it is increasingly possible to mass produce tailor-made products, paradoxical as that may sound. Compute-rised control of production, inventories and supplies is being used already and is spreading to more and more industries.

Generally, means of group communication and communication over large distances will be more widely available and easy to use, as well as more sophisticated.

GROWTH-BUT STILL LOW INFLATION

All of this has already affected the macro economy, and it will have an even greater impact in the future. In the words of Joseph Schumpeter, earlier revolutions started long waves of growth and credit expansion.

The pattern is not completely clear, and it has repeatedly been disturbed by external shocks (wars and political disruption) and internal boom-bust cycles. Nonetheless, beneath the surface of day-to-day events it is quite possible to see a secular trend. Consequently, part of the rapid growth of the postwar period can be explained by the transformation of society through commercialisation of the electrical motor and the internal combustion engine.

The gradual economic retardation during the 1970s and early 1980s was partly due to external shocks (oil crises) and politics (deficit financing and inflation), but it can also, or at least partially, be explained by the fact that these technologies had matured to such an extent that they had lost much of their creative and transforming effects.

If the hypothesis about a third industrial revolution proves correct, we are now on the threshold of a new period of growth, but nobody knows how lasting or how strong it will be. Even though there will certainly be setbacks every now and then, I believe that it will take decades for the new technologies to make enough breakthroughs to lose their power. If such optimism is justified, we will see a better-functioning economy for several years in the western economies:

- Technical development will cut costs.
- Consumers will be stronger, better informed and more likely to shop around for the best buy.

- Quality of information and the more rapid processing of information will help cut transaction costs.

There is a clear possibility that the next decade will be characterised by strong growth and low inflation in many countries outside the US. It is impossible to quantify the growth effect, not least because statistical aggregates have a hard time capturing the development of the service sector. In particular, national accounts tend to underestimate improvements in the quality of goods and services. This is crucial to the knowledge-based economy that is now emerging. Nonetheless it is a good bet that growth in Europe and elsewhere will be stronger in the first decade of the twenty-first century than it was during the last 25 years of the previous century.

Furthermore there is a fair chance that inflation will stay low. Central banks have become more independent and they are likely to continue their inflation-bashing. They will be supported in this by the breakthrough of new cost-cutting and competition-enhancing technologies. More rapid productivity growth, improved market transparency and globalisation all speak in favour of low inflation. It is true that serious and stringent academic economists are uncertain of the quantitative effects, telling us sternly that this is not really a retardation of inflation rate per se, but rather a one-off effect on the price level. They may be right-in theory. But in real life it will take years for these one-off effects to make their full impact, and to any non-economist, therefore, they are naturally interpreted as a lower rate of inflation. All practical businessmen see the effects in real life in the increasing difficulty of raising prices. We can no longer push cost increases onto the consumer; instead we have to increase productivity. It is difficult to see this trend being reversed in the foreseeable future.

The combination of tight monetary policies, rapid industrial transformation (the scrapping of obsolete capital) and stiffer competition will also transform wage formation and labour markets, not least in Europe. The labour market will become more fragmented as union power decreases. Salaries are being set according to productivity rather than determined by distribution or egalitarian quarrels. Clearly, cost pressures from the labour market will tend to decrease as a result.

All in all it is fair to assume that growth can be strong without inflation picking up as a result. This does not necessarily mean that a 'new economy' is replacing an 'old' economy or that old economic laws have suddenly stopped working. Rather, old patterns are being stretched somewhat because of the great number of technological and structural changes. There is nothing strange about that.

It should be stressed that the effects of these new technologies, although beneficial at the global level, will not be perceived as beneficial by some people. Schumpeter aptly coined the term 'creative destruction' to depict the turbulent forces that tear down and build up in one single process. Rigid companies will be severely hit by industrial transformation. Regions that are highly dependent on such old companies will experience increased unemployment. On average, people with poor or old-fashioned educational backgrounds will fare worse than highly educated people.

Wage differentials will change as new professions are created and old ones become obsolete. The leaders and stars of the new markets and technologies will be able to heap huge rewards, while others fall behind. Equity valuations will soar-and crash, as they always do during period of intense innovation and creative destruction. Of course, this will cause strains-for individuals as well as for elected politicians. There is a risk of political turbulence and short-sighted political reactions.

Market change at the micro level In many respects the micro effects on individual markets will be more far-reaching than the macro effects. Many markets will function more efficiently. As already stated, improved information and lower transaction costs will make it possible for consumers to shop around, choosing suppliers in a more efficient way. But beyond that it is interesting to note that markets in the communication and information sectors often tend to show more fundamental changes. In this new 'network economy', markets often show four characteristics:

- Products are more valuable if many people have access to them. A single phone or fax is not worth anything. But the more common they are, the more valuable they become since they can be linked to each other and communicate. This is a fascinating example of how the traditional textbook rule of declining marginal utility is turned on its head-utility actually increases sharply as more machines are linked to the network.
- Economies of scale cause unit costs to drop in several of these markets. The first product (software programme, musical recording, computer game and so on.) is expensive to manufacture, whereas mass production-that is, digitally copying the first product-is extremely cheap. Here also the traditional hypothesis about decreasing returns seems to be wrong.
- In order to enable users of fax machines, computers, cellular phones, pagers and so on to meet and communicate, the various products and systems must be able to communicate with each other. Thus industry standards must be established, spontaneously or through regulation.
- All this creates strong incentives for the emergence of (perhaps temporary) monopolies. Individual companies that conquer a dominant market position can set market standards and hence make it virtually impossible for any competitor to challenge them. This makes it profitable to act extremely aggressively in order to gain market share as fast as possible.

It can be said that the supply and demand relations of network markets are different from those prevailing in ordinary markets. If the value of a product increases with the number of people who have access to it, the demand curve is upward sloping. Consequently large economies of scale mean that the slope of supply curves may be negative. Some analysts see these peculiarities as so important that we should accept a 'new economy' paradigm-alas with a new economic theory as well. Most economists, however, see such network markets as special cases of the all-encompassing traditional micro theory of economics.

MANAGEMENT FACES NEW CHALLENGES

Obviously, these huge changes will have a profound impact on management. Developments in information technology will affect the very core of management as well as the company itself. Information is a decisive factor for client relations, brand name and the value chain of production. Until now information on the corporation and its products has primarily been embedded in the products themselves. But as the electronic networks evolve, information can be decoupled from the physical content and location of the products. This entails new business opportunities as information and products can be separated and reconnected in new combinations. In management literature this is called 'unbundling'. The traditional value chain is broken up and put together again in new ways.

In this respect the IT revolution constitutes a disruptive change to existing business on a scale never seen before. One effect is that the success and market capitalisation of firms can undergo sharp swings. In times of rapid change, new technologies and new products can suddenly ruin even very well-managed and successful companies, which just happen to be on the losing side of the new technologies. The other side of the coin is that upstarts that happen to be at the right place at the right time can suddenly be extremely successful and rewarded with a market capitalisation that-at least for a while -looks downright ridiculous. Such evaluations need not be long-lived; in this uncertain world new information rapidly has an effect on market capitalisation. But even though stock market valuations are volatile, the long-term economic and social effects of the new technology remains-as do the effects on business models and management.

There are many consequences for management emanating from these facts. One glaringly obvious conclusion is that hierarchical companies will tend to become less efficient. On the other hand flat organisations with a rich flow of information in easy-to-access networks will foster creativity; independent and small business units are the natural building blocks of the modern corporation. But the link between the corporation and its clients will also be affected. It is possible to provide more customers with information all over the world, irrespective of where production takes place or the products are sold. Consequently the role of the middleman or intermediary has abruptly changed. The customer and the supplier can find each other faster and easier, provided the information system can screen, filter and select. Traditional wholesale middlemen will soon be a defunct species unless they transform themselves into electronic information specialists and navigators. However, if they are successful in this, there is a new, booming market to catch.

One extremely important aspect of the new information technologies is the possibility of 'data mining', that is, exploiting all the new possibilities to learn about the customer. Intelligent data information systems make it much easier to collect information about clients' needs and purchasing patterns, making it possible to customise advertising, target special offers and adjust the product mix in an ever-more fragmented world. It also opens the possibility of price differentiation, which is all the more important in a world of cut-throat competition.

Given the high costs of information systems and the emergence of (albeit short-lived) technological monopolies, there are high risks involved in being locked into dependence on systems that become both costly and obsolete far more rapidly than expected. The obvious conclusion is to avoid such a locking-in. As product cycles get shorter it is also important to be more flexible in as many areas as possible.

It is quite dangerous to put all one's eggs in one basket; firms that are dependent on a single technology are extremely vulnerable. The conclusion is that experimentation is vital. The firm must test many solutions and be prepared to incur losses in the process. It must allocate resources to make such experiments possible. To encourage creativity and overcome resistance from established departments, it is often advisable to set up special units to develop and test new technologies. This should be done even if they compete head-on with the (former) core activities of the firm.

STRONG TRANSFORMATION PRESSURE IN THE FINANCIAL SECTOR

The financial industry is one of those sectors that will see the greatest and most rapid upheavals. The reason is obvious. The sector's bread and butter is to process information and the IT revolution makes it easy to unbundle its products. The new technology makes it possible not only to change old patterns, but also to create totally new products and channels of distribution.

Retail banking is facing huge changes. Yesterday's banking was a vertically integrated value chain, where a number of different products were packaged, distributed and sold via a system of branch offices. This has been changed by electronic banking. It is seen by many as mainly a new and cheaper channel of distribution. But if my description of the trends facing us is correct, the changes will be much greater. As the networks grow and become more sophisticated, more customers will be able to access information through new channels and to choose more freely among various services. The supply of personal financial management software is rapidly improving, while at the same time advanced analysis and updated information in real time is available more or less free from several sources, often via the most popular portals. It is probably only a question of time before alliances are formed between software producers, portals and other Web-sites on the one hand, and a number of banks and financial institutions on the other.

Free software and direct access to banks, as well as streaming video and audio will make it possible to see and listen to different financial advisers on the Internet-and to compare their advice. This makes the customer's freedom of choice much more real.

The customer will soon be able to choose all sorts of services on the Internet. Until recently the general perception was that the market would be segmented into two main groups: cheap and quick transactions via the Internet; and more sophisticated, personalised and expensive financial advice, sold for a (hefty) fee in special, plush branch offices. However, the borderline between these markets is becoming increasingly blurred as clients are demanding to pick and choose between services and combinations of services.

It seems as though all big players must be able to provide their customers with all kinds of Internet-based services. Consequently the most sophisticated financial advisory services are being subjected to intense pressure to transform themselves. Commercial banking and corporate banking have already experienced great changes. Previously stable relations between banks and corporate clients have been severed as disintermediation and niche strategies have fragmented the markets. E-commerce is creating new channels for corporate clients of all sizes, which can now find each other easier and faster without traditional intermediaries. The new technologies that are transforming the financial sector

- Three enabling techniques. Advances in the performance and cost-efficiency of three interrelated technologies (computing power, data storage and data transmission bandwidth) are dramatically reducing the cost of collecting and processing information.
- Exploding connectivity and plummeting transaction costs. The fall in the cost of information is reducing transaction costs and increasing the demand for improved connectivity, creating a self-reinforcing cycle of reducted transaction costs.
- Substitution of information for hierarchy. The falling cost of delivering information instantaneously through-out the organisation is resulting in formal organisa-tional hierarchies giving way to more nimble, decentralised, network-based structures.
- Interactive customer relationships. The plummeting cost of interaction and connectivity is enabling companies to capture unprecedented

amounts of data on their customers and to deliver increasingly individualised value propositions.

- Transformation of value chains to value webs. Lower transaction costs, increased connectivity and open standards are reducing coordination costs among multiple, disparate entities; as a result the traditional value chain is being replaced by web-like structures of coordinated, value added activity.
- Scale economies are increasing-and decreasing. Increasing connectivity, increasing information intensity of production factors and declining transaction costs are undermining traditional scale economies in marketing and distribution, while increasing economies of scale in digital production.
- Network effects and serial monopoly. There is an increase in the prevalence of network effects, which exist when the utility that a user derives from the consumption of a good increases with the number of fellow users, leading to monopolistic business systems-until replaced by rival product systems with displacing network effects.
- Digitial substitution and unbundling. The Information component of physical (or analog) products and services is being replaced by digital substitutes, often with radically different development trajectories, cost structures and distribution capabilities.
- Disintermediation and reintermediation. Some middlemen (retailers, agents and distributors) are being disintermediated or displaced by direct (typically electronic) buyer-seller trade; others are reintermediating markets by expanding their role as third-party information brokers or market makers.
- Channel disruption. Traditional physical or personal sales channels are being disrupted by lower-cost e-commerce alternatives and by consumers' increasing preference for scattering purchase activities across multiple channels.
- Infomediation. Traditional sales and distribution intermediaries that exploit information asymmetries are being replaced by electronic intermediaries that provide information and match buyers and sellers.
- Demand aggregation. The Internet and other information networks are enabling buyers to aggregate individual purchasing and 'put out to bid' transactions, transferring pricing power to the demand side and transforming suppliers into explicit price takers.
- Trading is obviously undergoing similar changes due to the introduction of electronic trading. Markets have become more transparent and information is flowing more freely, so traditional full-service brokers have become increasingly squeezed.

As a result of these changes-and of low interest rates and low inflation-it has become more difficult to make a profit on payments systems, using the float. Instead credit analysis is becoming more important as low inflation puts pressure on interest rates and corporate restructuring takes giant leaps.

THE SEB'S EXPERIENCE

The Skandinaviska Enskilda Banken (SEB) has undergone a rapid transition during the past few years. It has traditionally been the dominant commercial bank for large Swedish exporting companies, as well as the bank of choice for many wealthy Swedes. It is the biggest trader of currencies, bonds and securities in the Nordic region, and consequently is at the centre of the current reshaping of the financial markets due to globalisation and the IT revolution. In terms of size, it is large by Nordic standards but small in global or even pan-European terms. The pressure to transform is extremely strong and the SEB is facing this pressure head-on. It has embarked on a path of rapid technological renewal and transformation, concentra-ting on the booming savings markets and the possibilities offered Internet banking, in which area it intends to exploit its expertise in a European perspective.

The bank's Nordic focus is visible in the sense that it has acquired the Swedish insurance company Trygg-Hansa (and then divested the non-life operations) and Gyllenberg, a Finnish private bank. It entered Denmark through an alliance with Codan, an insurance company, and expanded into the Baltic region through ownership of three banks in the three Baltic countries, and recently also by acquiring a Polish bank. As a result its assets under management have more than trebled in three years, from SEK 190 billion in 1996 to SEK 950 billion in the third quarter of 2000. At the same time the number of Internet clients has increased 70-fold, from 10 000 to almost 700 000.

This last development illustrates the SEB's relentless pursuit of technological advancement, new distribution systems and new products. To a large extent its acquisitions have been prompted by its wish to channel its new products into new markets, for instance it is busy setting up an Internet bank in Denmark. It has also bought BfG Bank, the fifth largest privately owned bank in Germany, which the SEB hopes will create a platform for rapid expansion into Internet banking in Europe.

This is well in line with its (albeit short) Internet tradition. The SEB was among the very first to set up an independent Internet bank (in December 1996), although to a certain extent it cannibalised existing business and the retail branch offices. It was deliberately created as a separate entity to ensure its independent growth and aggressive expansion, even at the expense of other business of the bank. This reflects the experience in other areas, where new, disruptive technologies can threaten the entire business unless new units are allowed to be creative and to experiment, even though their activities seem to be at odds with the rest of the organisation. Now that e-banking is well established and more mature, it is being integrated into the different business areas more fully. The SEB e-banking activity offers a complete range of banking and insurance services to private clients and small businesses alike-from account information to bill payment mutual funds and stock brokerage. The results have exceeded the bank's expectations. The bank now has more customer visits on the web than in its branch network in Sweden.

Even in the Baltic region, which is very small and has a far lower average income than Scandinavia, there has been a surprisingly rapid increase in e-banking. This demonstrates the possibility of starting from a 'low' technological base and moving directly to the most modern forms of production and distribution, that is, skipping a few of the normal steps of technical development and going straight for the frontier.

Encouraged by these events, and in order to sharpen its focus even further, the bank has set a high goal for its Internet service: it intends to have 5 000 000 Internet clients by 2005. This may sound overly optimistic; but the point is that setting such a seemingly impossible target will force the entire organisation to rethink its full range of processes and products. It will foster creativity, since it will demonstrate that the old ways of doing business will not suffice if the bank is to survive, let alone thrive, in the new global economy.

One example of the bank's high-tech approach is the development of an Internet Trading Station. This is an on-line service directed at all corporate clients, but perhaps is most beneficial to medium-sized trading clients that lack large financial departments. Physically, this is simply a computer terminal, but the client has access to all of the SEB's research, trading services and facilities.

When using the Trading Station the customer can be certain that deals will be automatically passed to clients' financial systems via a common system interface. Decision support and the execution of deals are available globally through one channel, the Internet. Controlled deal entry enables clients to let administrative staff execute trades. As a result, human errors are reduced and costs are cut as real-time financial information is provided to all users within the company at low cost. In effect the Trading Station moves the bank's trading floor-the largest in Northern Europe-right into the office of the client.

Here, growth has been even more spectacular than in private banking. After only two years, the Internet accounts for some 50 per cent of total FX transactions in Sweden. Great interest has been expressed by other banks in franchising this service. During my 25 years in finance I have never seen technological breakthrough as rapid as this one. According to analysts the SEB is one of the world leaders in the use of modern IT in banking and financial services, and it intends to maintain its technological lead. One obvious task is to launch its IT distribution model in Europe. This can be done through mergers and acquisitions, using acquired firms as vehicles to spread the bank's knowledge. It can also be achieved through organic growth. Both these strategies are currently being used.

FROM BANK TO PORTAL

All these activities are tied together in a long-term e-centric strategy. The breakthroughs in IT are applicable on a global scale, whereas the existing banking systems and client bases are still largely local. The SEB's aim is to link global technological change to local clients by introducing new technologies through several channels. It intends to create a standardised Internet platform with three main characteristics:

- An Internet bank that offers private clients a wide range of services-payments and transactions, savings and borrowing, advice and investment.
- An interface that is easy to use, takes advantage of the bank's global technological expertise and is adapted to local needs.
- Technical solutions to payment and transaction systems tied to local/ national payments systems.

This means that the bank's global system must be standardised and able to cope with local solutions, which may initially look different. Local solutions and interface, linked to data mining, will reduce customer acquisition costs and lead to long-term growth of the client base. Technically the process is intended to move from the local to the global as banking and financial markets become more integrated.

In a somewhat longer-term perspective, one task is to evolve from a service channel to a valuable portal, supplying clients with investment services, on-line banking and advisory services, but also leveraging the bank's valuable client base to other services and providers, financial as well as non-financial. This process has already started. The bank has launched a 'travel square' on its Web site as a first step. It is based upon a partnership with the Amadeus booking system and supplies its Internet banking customers with the opportunity to search, book and pay for travel on-line. It offers the bank the possibility of broadening its client base, it provides clients with additional services, and it provides airlines with the possibility of selling more tickets, not least excess capacity tickets, to an attractive customer segment. The bank's clients enjoy lower-priced tickets, and both the bank's and the booking system's client bases become more valuable.

This is seen as only the starting point. More services will be added, and the bank plans to cooperate more closely with a number of other service providers, leveraging each other's services. New technology and the links to existing client groups will be used to create new affinity groups, where the bank's will act as an entry point for special client groups to gain access to numerous other service providers. One example of this is the recent creation of a 'Senior Net' for older clients with special needs and demands in respect of housing, travel, medicine and so on. Another aspect of the recent developments is the increasing speed and accessibility of services. Currently, most electronic transactions go via PCs, but an increasing amount of business will soon be carried out via cell phones. The new WAP technology will make it possible to use mobile phones not only for conversation, but also for e-mail, automatic market updates and the transmission of buy and sell orders to stockbrokers. It will soon be easy to programme WAP phones to carry out just about everything that a top-of-the-range PC with modem can do today, no matter where you are in the world. At this point the trading floor will have moved not only to the office of the corporate client but also to the coat pocket of private customers-the branch office and the portal to many other services will literally be in the client's pocket.

10

Competency Loss: Financial Statements

Thus far we have concentrated on ways of honing the capabilities of more or less gifted men in order to enable them to reach higher levels of competence. That is an essential but in itself insufficient strategy for organizational survival. It is also necessary to deal with the erosion of competence, which is perhaps more of a problem for ordinary men than it is for the unusually capable.

The man of promising potentialities is often provided with what amounts to an insurance policy against a decline in his abilities, simply because he is more likely to repay an investment in developing those potentialities than is someone of more ordinary talents. But in terms of overall productivity, small ways of preserving the value of the ordinary man's contributions can be at least as important as dramatic ways of enhancing the contributions of exceptional men.

The point could probably be argued endlessly, but it can hardly be doubted that the *cost* of inefficiency among the rank and file becomes inflated, in most companies, by a much larger multiplier than can be applied to the activities of so-called key men. Hence it seldom makes good financial sense to base an organizational development plan solely on the flowering of the ablest people available. Neither does it make good psychological sense to plan solely for increasing competence. Unhappily, competence can also decline. We therefore have to find ways of preserving it, along with ways of enlarging it.

The problem of decline in competence is older than it may seem. During the past several years both management and labour have become concerned with the tendency for certain skills to become unnecessary, owing to the displacement of one product or process by another. But this so-called skill obsolescence is only part of a larger, less obvious problem that has been with us for a long time — the tendency for some people to become *less competent*, under certain circumstances, than they have been. True, the productivity of the average worker has been increasing for years, owing mainly to rising educational standards and to improvements in tooling. What is not so widely recognized is how often declines or standstills in individual productivity have acted as a brake upon the rising averages.

Competence is, after all, a relative rather than an absolute quality. It is a matter of being able to do what is expected of one. But these expectations change, and sometimes the things one is able to do change too — in either direction. So competence itself is essentially changeable, not fixed, and we can reasonably expect it to fluctuate to some extent during the course of any man's career. Nevertheless, we have traditionally regarded competence as being rather like a beard; that is, something not acquired until adulthood and never really lost thereafter. Regrettably, it is becoming increasingly clear that competence is more like the hair on top of a man's head, in the sense that it is not necessarily there to stay.

The changeability of competence has been obscured for several reasons. One is that the acceleration of technological change has only recently approached the point at which a man can no longer take it for granted that he will spend his entire working lifetime in one career. Another reason is that in an era when change came more slowly, losses in speed, strength, and adaptability could usually be offset by increases in wisdom. Still another reason is that motivation used to be considerably more stable over a lifetime than it has since become.

That is, until fairly recently most men were never really free of the fundamental pressures of job security and income, and accordingly they were unlikely to knowingly permit their income producing skills to wane. Today income per se is a less crucial problem, and men tend to become concerned with such esoteric motivators as dignity, recognition, and a sense of fulfillment in their work. Like it or not, the tendency is to demand more of one's job and less of one's self; and the result is sometimes a gradual decline in output.

We will have more to say about this later, but for the moment it is important to clarify one point: When productivity declines because men are less motivated to produce, the fault is seldom with their moral fibre or with the climate of ideas around them. Rather, the fault is usually with a management that is unable to harness the reservoir of latent motivation that such men represent.

What we will refer to here as "competence loss" has a variety of causes and therefore calls for a variety of remedies. It is a class of problems rather than a single problem for which a single solution can be sought. For convenience' sake, we can refer to a variety of related problems under this single label, but it is neither convenient nor possible to handle them all in the same way. Perhaps it would be best to begin by reviewing what competence loss is *not*; since, despite its relatively recent discovery, it has already begun to be obscured by a mythology of its own.

First and most important, competence loss is not a well-studied, well-understood phenomenon. Despite the tendency of some writers to prescribe for it confidently, it is still very much in the discovery and definition stage. Useful research is only beginning to be reported, and we therefore have to rely heavily on both common sense and a cautious interpretation of common experience. Second, it is already clear that competence loss is not the inevitable fate of anyone.

In many cases it is preventable. To let it occur by default, which is why it usually occurs, is a gross squandering of human talent. Further, the shadow of competence loss can be just as devastating as its substance. This is because managers tend to overreact to it, relegating men who appear to have suffered some degree of loss to positions that are often of considerably less consequence than they are still prepared to handle. This practice is, if anything, more wasteful of talent than competence loss itself.

In particular, competence loss is *not* the lot of older workers in general. To be sure, age is no longer the advantage it once was, since education increasingly offsets experience (rather than vice versa), and wisdom is often no match for being technically up to date. But while older people may, as a group, be more susceptible to competence loss than other age groups, the majority of them compensate quite well for whatever handicaps age itself carries with it.

Therefore the apprehension that is often felt for the older worker in an increasingly sophisticated economy is seldom justified by the available facts. To write off a man's ability to rise to a significant new challenge merely because he has passed a particular birthday is one of the most profitless ways to create a self-fulfilling prophecy.

A third fallacy about competence loss is that it is both epidemic and incurable. Managers tend to diagnose it rather casually — and probably too frequently. We have no satisfactory way of measuring competence loss, and for that reason it often appears to be a much more formidable problem than it really is. To say that it often exists chiefly in the eye of the beholder is not to minimize it, but to place it in a more realistic perspective. The problem is bad enough without making a nightmare out of it.

It is useful to remember that there has been what amounts to an educational revolution in the United States during the lifetime of many men who are still working. Only two generations ago, a high school graduate was considered an educated man. Today college degrees are commonplace and graduate degrees are by no means uncommon. The education that was considered ample to equip an entrant into the labour force in the 1920's and 1930's is, in other words, considered minimal today.

And thereby may hang a good deal of what appears, at first blush, to be competence loss. The jobs that are being created in today's economy often presuppose a more extensive exposure to formal education than the jobs that are being eliminated. Consequently, many of the men who are considered incapable of being retrained to handle the newly established jobs may, in reality, never have been educated to the point of readiness to learn them. Their deficiencies are, in short, remediable. That deficiencies in education are remediable was illustrated in a careful study at International Business Machines Corporation conducted by Walter J. McNamara. The company had embarked on a programme of upgrading factory employees from various electromechanical tasks to inspection jobs on computer systems. This programme involved 12 weeks of formal training in such subjects as computer organization, transistors, and printed circuits. As might be expected, the trainees selected for this rather costly training were among the best-qualified employees in the plant, from the standpoint of both ability and performance. McNamara's interest, however, was in whether employees who would ordinarily be considered poor risks for such programs — the less well educated and even the less able — could be trained successfully. He therefore deliberately chose a class of trainees from among the *least* promising employees available. They were well below the plant average in tested aptitudes and knowledge. However, since they had all volunteered for a course in which they knew they would be severely challenged, it is reasonable to consider them more strongly motivated than the average employee in similar circumstances.

In addition to the built-in motivational advantages that this class had, McNamara provided two additional educational advantages. One was to lengthen the total classroom time by about 25 percent over the regular courses. This was partially in recognition of the fact that the regular programme had been paced for faster learners. However, the main reason for the added time was to permit a special precourse training programme in arithmetic fundamentals and basic electricity.

These were the subjects on which the training course itself was to be built and in which the trainees' own formal schooling had not given them an adequate background. In effect, the pretraining course brought this class up to the same educational starting line that the regular classes had been able to begin from, simply because they had had the benefit of better schooling. Not surprisingly, the special class did not do quite as well in the main part of the training programme as the regular, better qualified trainees. But they did considerably better, as a class, than would ordinarily be expected of a group that had begun with such handicaps. About twothirds of them completed the programme successfully, which is a very respectable result indeed in view of the problems they faced. Those failures that did occur were due to loss of determination nearly as much as to inability to handle the subjects that were taught.

There is nothing really new in the demonstration that presumably unpromising workers can, given a somewhat greater-than-usual investment and some extra motivation, be upgraded to handle relatively complex work. But McNamara's experiment demonstrated a great deal more than its most obvious finding. What is new and important in this study is its implication about the nature of the handicap that so-called unpromising workers carry.

In many cases, this may be, not so much a matter of adaptability that time has taken away from them, as a matter of never having been given certain essential adaptive tools in the first place.

The defect may, in other words, have dated from the time they discontinued their schooling and went to work, rather than from a slow erosion of learning ability as they grew older. There is reason to believe that many an oldtimer could acquit himself reasonably well in advanced training if he were given some of the basic schooling that he either never got or has forgotten — schooling which the modern youngster with whom he must compete is given more or less routinely. In this sense, a good deal of what seems like irreparable competence loss may be largely a matter of a few missing but easily supplied prerequisites.

If a man cannot be built up to a skill level within reach of the job, sometimes the job can be brought within reach of the man. This was shown in another study at IBM, this one by Ernest F. Bairdain. Once again, the problem was to upgrade the skill level of a group of workers who had been hired and trained for simpler tasks so that they could work on a considerably more sophisticated product line. Most of the workers in this plant were able to make the adjustment to their new jobs without much difficulty. However, Bairdain was concerned about the workers whose abilities did not seem to present a suitable match to the apparent requirements of the new jobs. He approached the problem from the job side by challenging the assumptions that had been made about the skill and ability levels they required.

Detailed analyses were made of the actual demands which various tasks made upon the abilities of the men who performed them. In many cases it was found that the requirements which had usually been assumed were, in fact, unnecessarily high. For example, in one process involving microminiaturized parts, it had usually been considered necessary to perform about 80 percent of the work under microscopes. This meant that most of the employees working in these departments had to have nearly perfect vision. But the new analysis revealed that only about 20 percent of the work really needed to be done with the aid of microscopes and that this portion could be consolidated into a limited number of the jobs. In this way, more jobs could be opened to workers whose vision would have disqualified them under the original distribution of work. Findings such as this in many kinds of jobs enabled the company to take great strides toward overcoming the problems attendant upon the apparent mismatch between people and jobs.

The tendency to overestimate the skill and ability requirements of a job is especially common in new jobs which, because there is little precedent for them, often appear to be more demanding than they really are. Sometimes exaggerated skill requirements persist for years simply because it has never been necessary to challenge them. For example, Bethlehem Steel Company completed a new mill in the Chicago area at about the time that a shortage of skilled labour became acute. The company was therefore obliged to begin operations with many inexperienced and supposedly marginal workers. The mill achieved efficient production much more quickly than had been expected, simply because many of the new workers were able to master their jobs faster than had been anticipated. The point is, of course, that many of them weren't really marginal at all; the requirements of their jobs had been overrated.

So it is clear that men can be underrated or that jobs can be overrated, or both; and for any of these reasons men may seem to be obsolete or incapable when in fact they are not. Even granting the possibility of these errors, there are of course many situations in which the gap between what the individual can really do and what the job really requires is too great to be bridged. In plenty of situations this dilemma is not at all illusory. Bairdain faced the dilemma by trying to change the only element in the picture he could change: the job itself.

Those jobs that seemed to be beyond the capabilities of available workers were analyzed, broken down into their components, then restructured in new combinations so that the same manufacturing process was accomplished by a combination of redesigned jobs. Some of these jobs were within the skill limits of workers who might otherwise have been excluded by the original job designs. There is, of course, nothing sacred about *any* job designs; yet somehow they rapidly acquire a thick coating of tradition, and we tend to forget that alternative ways of getting the work done may be just as effective. By assuming, in effect, that jobs *have* to be done in the way they would be done by highly qualified or experienced workers, we relegate many potentially effective workers to an undeserved and at least partially fraudulent category of "incompetence."

The two IBM studies show that the real dimensions of obsolescence and competence loss may be considerably less than they might at first appear, even in processes involving highly sophisticated technologies. It is therefore vitally important to keep the problem in perspective and to avoid leaping either to excessively pessimistic conclusions about human capabilities or to excessively awed conclusions about jobs. Having issued this necessarily lengthy *caveat*, we can proceed to consider forms of competence loss that are neither illusory nor easily corrected.

It is useful to distinguish between three kinds of competence loss. They are all serious, but we will deal with them in descending order of the difficulty of doing anything about them. First, we will consider the person who is no less capable than he ever was, but who works in a field where the standards of productivity have been rising, so that they now exceed his abilities; second, the person whose ability to handle his work has actually decreased; third, motivational problems which, while they last, have the effect of reducing productivity. One seldom encounters a pure case of any one of these problems. They are likely to occur together; like locusts, they bring their relatives with them and thus worsen an already bad situation. But, even though any given individual could suffer simultaneously from more than one of these forms of competence loss, we will consider them separately for the sake of clarity.

Rising productivity standards that eventually have the effect of making a man's output marginal, thereby pricing him out of the market, are usually the result of technological changes of one kind or another. Work may arrive at his bench faster than it did before, or it may require more precise handling than it did before, or the workers to whom his finished work is sent may now be able to handle a larger volume of input than before. For these or similar reasons, an individual whose output has not changed may gradually become less competent, in the sense that he is no longer able to do what is expected of him. When this happens, he is likely to be regarded as an unfortunate but unavoidable victim of progress — rather like the dinosaur that, although just as big and powerful as its earthruling ancestors, perished anyway because it could not adapt to climatic changes. The worker in this situation is, in other words, regarded as one of a species headed for extinction, with little if anything that can be done about it.

This rather common point of view has led to much hand wringing over the plight of the ordinary man who either is no match for today's technology or will be no match for tomorrow's. But that whole line of reasoning is very loose. It is by no means a foregone conclusion that the average worker or even the marginal worker must be caught, sooner or later, in the rising waters of technology. Whether this happens may depend as much on management policy as on the limitations of the individuals involved. When a job demands more in an intellectual or physical sense than an individual is able to contribute to it, his continued employability depends on how readily he can apply his abilities to other jobs. Thus the switching or transfer process, in which capabilities that have been invested through training and experience in one set of skills are reinvested in another set, becomes crucial.

This switching process was seldom necessary in the days when a single set of skills sufficed for a lifetime. Consequently, management has had to learn relatively little about them. But it is now clear that a man's ability to transfer to another job what his hands or his eyes or his brains have learned in one job is nearly as important as his ability to learn those same skills in the first place. It is in preparing for one's second job, and for all subsequent jobs, that the ability to capitalize upon prior learning becomes crucial.

If learning transfer is new to industry, it is not new to the psychological laboratory, where it has been studied for years. It has laws of its own, and these laws have two fairly clear-cut implications for management that could minimize this particular form of competence loss. One is rather obvious: The more there are of common elements, or at least similar elements, between the old job and the new, the more easily the transfer occurs. The second is less obvious: The more experience one has had with learning transfers, the more readily they occur. It would be difficult to overstate the importance of this second point. The ability to learn is not unlike the tone of a muscle, in the sense that if it is not exercised it becomes flabby.

People who are not required to learn gradually lose much of their ability to learn. Therefore, any job in which an individual remains for too long (provided it is not inherently varied and changeable) can eventually become a trap, regardless of whether it was originally set at or below the theoretical limit of his capacities.

In other words, a good deal of the form of competence loss that is a concomitant of rising productivity standards is the result of eroded ability to make a transition from old to new skills. And this erosion is the indirect consequence of not having had to make enough transitions in the past. This clearly works against the long-term interests of anyone who has been highly specialized for any length of time, or who has not been exposed periodically to an opportunity to enlarge his skills or knowledge. This form of competence loss is plainly easier to prevent than to cure; but its prevention demands a continual battle with inertia, tradition, and the perfectly natural tendency to leave well enough alone when the penalty for doing so is remote and unclear.

The problem, in brief, is to *avoid* letting too many people learn their jobs too well. Paradoxical as it may seem, it is contrary to the best interests of both the employee and his employer to let a man become so familiar with his job that he can handle it flawlessly. (Actually, this idea is paradoxical only if we forget that the premises have changed: The crucial ability today is the readiness to acquire new skills, not the burnishing of old ones.) Thus the man who can handle his job "with his eyes closed" or "with one hand tied behind his back" is in danger of forgetting how to learn. If he does forget, only luck can save him from eventual obsolescence.

Management policy must therefore be directed toward the preservation of what might be called the "learning attitude" — a disturbing awareness of one's ignorance, a fascination with the way fragments of knowledge fall into place, and a confidence in one's ability to master what is not yet understood. This naïve frame of mind is the best possible preserver of adaptability. But how can it be maintained when the learning process itself tends to reduce ignorance, turn the fascinating into the familiar, and build such confidence in what has been learned that further learning seems unnecessary? Does not, in other words, the normal psychology of a man who has held a job for any length of time work against his ability to learn a new one?

To some extent it does. But it would greatly oversimplify human nature to suggest that the learning process eventually turns itself off or that only the naïve are capable of growing and adapting. Some people manage to keep the spark glowing by themselves, usually in hobbies or interests far removed from their work; others may find that an encounter with some new experience reawakens a taste for learning that they had not felt in years. But management cannot afford to assume that its investment in human assets will somehow preserve itself. It cannot expect to maintain its people in a state of adequate readiness to learn new jobs through good luck and nothing else. There must be a definite policy that creates an environment in which most people will encounter enough experiences of the kind that keep the learning attitude alive or that can rekindle it. Without such a policy, the likelihood that changing productivity norms will eventually make people "obsolete" is more than just a danger; it is very nearly a certainty.

A number of specific programs have helped to maintain this kind of environment. The list offered here is intended to be suggestive rather than exhaustive. In all probability, the list will grow considerably longer as managerial ingenuity comes to grips with the problem in various companies and contexts. One useful technique is what is often referred to as "work simplification. " Groups of workers are periodically assigned the task of analyzing their own jobs -functioning, as it were, as their own industrial engineers. They examine the jobs they know better than anyone else for the purpose of making them more efficient. This kind of exercise is usually undertaken primarily for the sake of productivity, secondarily to enlist the support of the workers in implementing any changes in methods that may be agreed to by management. But sessions of this kind, if they occur often enough, can have another result that could be more important, in the long run, than today's productivity and cooperation. By requiring men to think analytically and to look for relationships that may not be apparent, work simplification techniques provide them with invaluable practice in skills that must be in good working order if they have to learn new jobs later on.

Another useful technique is what the British sometimes refer to as "seconding"; that is, periodic assignments to tours of duty in job environments wholly different from the one in which the bulk of one's career is spent. There are many variations on this, but they all have the same effect — to present the individual with the necessity of learning enough about a new specialty to be able to function effectively in it. Some examples are assignments to temporary task forces that are organized to deal with particular problems, such as production bottlenecks; assignments as an instructor, troubleshooter, or consultant; or assignment to a wholly new function.

Still another technique involves formal instruction. There is little doubt that the most important thing gained from most refresher courses is not the material that is taught but the refurbishing of learning skills. Technical updating courses, reviews of recent developments, seminars on related technologies or even on wholly nonjob-related topics — all these can provide the needed leavening. Timing is perhaps as important a consideration as course content. Courses that are held too rarely are not much better than no courses at all as far as maintaining the learning attitude is concerned. They may, of course, succeed in teaching exactly what they were supposed to teach;

but it is not likely that widely separated courses will deliver any bonus benefits. The problem is to time formal instruction, or any other stimulus, in such a way that future learning is likely to be accelerated. There is no evident formula for calculating how often courses or other teaching methods must be used in order to produce the desired enhancing effect on formal retraining. This apparently depends on many factors, including the adaptability and past experiences of the individual and the difficulty of the material he must learn. In general, some kind of vigorous mental exercise at least once every two years does not appear to be excessive for most people, and even more than that would be valuable for technical and professional workers.

To some extent, exposure to formal training will come whether management intends it as a strategy to facilitate new learning or not. The rate at which jobs obsolesce and the need to preserve employability will see to that. But job-retraining courses are unlikely to be sufficiently close together in time to have a facilitating effect upon each other. The half-life of jobs may be getting shorter, but it is not likely to get so short that retraining acquires the kind of velocity that would be needed for enhancement to occur. Yet performance in formal retraining courses is, after all, what we are trying to enhance.

Some kind of additional stimulation between courses, as it were, is therefore needed to help insure that men entering formal training will not be too rusty or too set in their ways. In fact, one can foresee that the investment in retraining (and in all subsequent retraining) will eventually become so great that it would be prohibitively expensive *not* to take steps between training periods that can enhance the payout from training itself. Other changes can also be foreseen. Industrial education may very well grow to such proportions that a thorough revision of all educational scheduling and funding may be necessary.

Many people may receive less education in early life and more education in later life than is common today. The demands on educational facilities and personnel will become so great that a more rational allocation will be needed, and the present tendency to overeducate young people to the relative neglect of the educational needs of older people will have to be corrected. Coping with problems of this magnitude will call for imaginative new methods. But that topic is vast enough to deserve a book of its own; in this book we must return to a consideration of competence loss, this time of the type that results from an actual decrease in what the individual is capable of accomplishing.

Thus far we have dealt with forms of competence loss that are the result of a lack of exercise with respect to learning. In its more severe forms, this can lead to an actual handicap in which the individual becomes considerably less able to adapt to a new occupation than he may once have been. However, these are only potential losses, rather than real ones, until some circumstance comes along that demands learning. If the individual is spared that demand, his loss may never become apparent.

Competence loss can also occur *within* an occupation; that is, where no new learning is required. There are relatively few facts to guide us here, so we will have to feel our way into the subject as best we can by means of some informed guesswork. One reason for the scarcity of facts regarding individual competence loss is that it is quite difficult to establish for certain that it has really happened. We seldom have a suitable "before" measure of productivity with which to compare productivity "after" we begin to suspect that competence loss may have occurred.

Many jobs do not lend themselves to simple measure-ments of productivity anyway; and when measuring *can* be done, it is frequently difficult to determine what part to attribute to the individual and what part to other factors tools, materials, supervision, and so on. Despite these difficulties, there is no shortage of opinions on the subject, and sometimes these are so unanimous that they are seldom questioned. Probably the most widespread bit of unsupported "common knowledge" about competence loss is that advancing age brings with it a physical and mental decline which eventually renders the individual unable to compete with younger, presumably more vigorous co-workers.

What little we know about the longevity of abilities indicates that most of them decline slowly, if at all, with age; that wisdom and maturity usually increase with age and can therefore offset — sometimes more than offset — any decline in ability; and above all that there is more variability in productivity *within* any age group than there is *between* any two age groups. The latter is perhaps the hardest fact we have to guide us. It strongly suggests that increasing age, in itself, has only a minor tendency to bring about competence loss. Other causes, possibly including some that we haven't even identified yet, are surely more important.

Most physical and mental abilities seem to continue growing until some time during the third decade of life, after which they remain relatively stable or decline slowly until some time during the sixth decade, when a steeper decline may commence. This is true of visual acuity, hearing, muscular strength and coordination, manual dexterity, verbal intelligence, memory, and reasoning. Somewhat faster declines seem to occur in reaction speeds and in learning complex relationships. Yet for every one of these statements it is necessary to add that they refer to averages, not to everyone, and that there is so much variation around those averages that generalizations are dangerous.

Probably the wisest guess that can be made at present about individual competence loss is that it is *abnormal,* rather than a natural result of aging, and that it is caused either by a failure of wisdom to develop at a rate faster than the rate at which strength declines or by some kind of physical or emotional damage. As for the failure of wisdom to accumulate rapidly enough to offset losses of strength, this may result from a lack of "learning exercise," from a lack of learning motivation (which usually dates from childhood, and sometimes reflects the values of the community in which an individual was raised), or from low intelligence. Physical damage includes not only obvious forms, such as blindness and deafness, but subtler forms — such as cerebral arteriosclerosis, or "hardening of the arteries" in the brain — whose impact on job effectiveness sometimes begins long before the individual comes to the attention of a physi-cian. Emotional damage includes the fairly common "unsettled" periods that occur in midlife when some men must finally face the fact that their youthful ambitions are not going to be realized. These problems are worth a textbook in their own right, but they cannot be pursued here except for one note of caution.

One of the toughest problems a manager ever faces is whether to refer an employee to a neurologist or a psychiatrist. Sometimes, symptoms of potentially serious ailments become apparent in work behaviour before they are obvious to relatives or friends off the job. Forgetfulness, tendencies to repeat oneself, inattentiveness, and other early outcroppings of what could become serious problems are all more likely to be noticed on the job than elsewhere, because they can directly affect productivity.

But they could also have trivial causes, and indeed it is not easy for most laymen to be certain that a man with whom they work has actually become more forgetful, or less attentive, than he used to be. Further, a man who is in fact going through the early stages of a neurologic or psychiatric illness is likely to be at least dimly aware himself that something is wrong, and more often than not he will be frightened by it. To suggest to such a person that he ought to be examined professionally is likely to produce an angry reaction, because the suggestion only reinforces a fear he is probably trying desperately to deny.

There are plenty of good reasons why managers should not play amateur psychiatrist. On the other hand, when competence loss has occurred management needs to know whether it can be corrected or arrested. For that matter, not only the individual's employment security but his own health and safety may be at stake. So the decision as to whether to seek an examination is always a difficult one. Obviously, there can be no hard and fast rules here. But it does make sense for management to review such cases with competent medical consultants who can at least evaluate the evidence, suggest what else to look for, and then advise about the wisdom or the lack of it in asking the individual to be examined. Of course, the entire problem is obviated in companies that provide routine check-ups for employees above a certain age.

Any action that is intended to remedy individual competence loss must be aimed at the root cause, not just the symptom. Consequently, the first requirement for effective action is an accurate diagnosis. This does not necessarily have to be made by a professional, but it does demand a mind that can deal with subtleties and that has no need to oversimplify. Human beings, even when they are foolish or unsophisticated, are exquisitely complex; therefore their behaviour can never be understood by simply labeling it. To say that a man "just can't handle his job any more" is not a diagnosis but a confession of failure to search beyond the symptom for its cause. Diagnosing the reasons for individual competence loss demands a willingness to gather facts and an unwillingness to leap to "obvious" conclusions.

Once a diagnosis has been reached that is a reasonable match for the available facts, a tentative plan of action can be prepared. (It has to be tentative, because until it is tried we don't know whether the diagnosis was right.) If the trouble seems to stem from a lack of learning exercise — that is, if the individual is set in his ways — at least one attempt at getting him to change his ways through retraining is usually worthwhile. This is not because the learning attitude is easy to restore (it is not), but because it is easy to overestimate the degree to which someone really is set in his ways.

It must be remembered that any individual who has drifted into the habit of *not* learning for any extended period is probably going to be handicapped with respect to new learning. The man whom the years make merely older — not wiser — is in danger of becoming a psychological cripple who will not be able to function effectively outside his own accustomed environment. He needs special treatment in re-education for the same reason that a physically handicapped person needs special treatment: He cannot learn what he has to learn without it. Specifically, he needs more time, more explanation, and more practice than the person with the same basic intelligence who has been using his more steadily. He needs emotional support too: He should not have to compete with younger or abler trainees, and it should be made clear that the function of his instructors is to teach him, not to pass judgment on him. The judgment, if one is necessary, can come later in the environment where he can defend himself best — on the job. Judgments are passed much too casually about such people, anyway. It is too easy to dismiss them as having brought their inflexibility upon themselves, when in reality their work has been so unvaried and over learned that the necessity of learning has been absent from their lives for years.

When people are capable of learning, but have not done so because they have not been motivated to learn, the cause may lie in one or both of two circumstances. First, they may have learned, usually in childhood, the advantages of *not* learning. This is paradoxical only to people who grew up in communities where learning was the passport to self-respect and therefore to prestige. In communities where people have learned not to expect to achieve self-respect -where they expect, in other words, to be victimized by their environment regardless of what they do to escape it learning is a passport to frustration and ridicule. It takes a much stronger character to resist the pressures against learning in a depressed community than it does to accept the pressures for learning in one that is not depressed, which is the main reason successful learners emerge so rarely from depressed comm-unities in the first place.

Second, the lack of motivation to learn may have its roots in private defeats in the individual's own past which are not necessarily the common experience of the community from which he comes. He may, in other words, have had more trouble than he could handle during the years when his attitudes toward the learning process were being formed. For example, he may have encountered disparagement, incom-petent teaching, or family tensions that overshadowed whatever the school was trying to teach him. Any of these not uncommon experiences, or a combination of them, could turn a basically intelligent child away from learning if they struck too hard or too often.

No matter how someone learns that it is wiser not to learn that is, that it hurts less to abandon the effort than to persevere he is for all practical purposes a badly handicapped person. The basic motivational problem is to find a way to change his perception of learning itself to have him see it as both possible and worthwhile if *that* is possible. And it must be said that it isn't always possible. But if the change is to be made at all, it has to be done on the basis of a convincing demonstration. You cannot exhort, promise, or inspire intelligent people to commit themselves to something which their entire experience has taught them to avoid. To be convincing, a demonstration must be dramatic, it probably must be repeated fairly often, and above all it must not fail and thereby reinforce the very resistances that need to be loosened.

It is precisely because the requirements of a convincing demonstration are so exacting that the salvage of people who have learned not to learn is sometimes impossible. Whenever someone learns a way to avoid something he wants very much to avoid, that way that technique of avoidance — acquires an enormous inertia which at best is costly and difficult to overcome. In short, the cards need to be stacked so heavily *in favour* of the individual that the possibility of failure is very nearly ruled out. Consequently, the rehabilitation of anyone with a learning motivation problem is both expensive and risky, to the point where some may wonder whether the uncertain payoff is worth the sums that have to be gambled. The answer depends largely on the intelligence with which those sums are used.

Basically, the motivationally damaged adult needs a chance to take small steps slowly. This means expensive forms of training: small classes; ample time for repetition and for "hands on" training, if that is appropriate; and plenty of personal attention from the instructor. Such labour-saving educational devices as programmed instruction, or even old-fashioned reading assignments, would probably be inappropriate for this type of person, at least until the back of the motivational problem itself has been broken. This is simply because any technique which requires the individual to provide his own motivation would be self-defeating with a person whose intuitive reaction to study is to avoid it.

Breaking the back of a motivational block can take a long time. In addition to demonstrating to the individual that he *can* learn, it is also necessary to show him that learning pays off. Sometimes this can be done effectively, if not elegantly, by making it clear that failure to make the transition successfully could lead to a downgrading in pay or even to being laid off. But "motivation" that is essentially a threat works best with people who are goaded, not routed, by threats.

The kind of person we have been describing is more likely to accept defeats passively, as if they were inevitable, than to make a good hard try to avoid them. This is why motivational problems of this type can seldom be attacked successfully unless job security can, for all practical purposes, be taken for granted. Thus the payoff for learning must consist of something extra, something over and above the mere preservation of employability. Some possible extra rewards would be more attractive or more prestige ful work or the possibility of higher pay. The practical problems of imple-menting such a motivational policy for costly, high-risk training programs are both obvious and severe. And that is why the scrap heap is where so many basically good minds end up minds that have been frightened, for one reason or another, of taking on the challenge of learning.

Sometimes wisdom fails to accumulate because the individual is poorly equipped to accumulate it; that is, he is not adequately endowed with that marvelous and ill-understood something that psychologists call "intelligence. " Although this faculty that most people (and some other animals too) have for benefiting from their experience has had more concentrated study than any other aspect of behaviour, we can still do little more than describe it. We don't really know, except in a gross way, what it is or what causes it. But we do know that it is a potential, in the same sense that the energy of water stored behind a dam is a potential until it is fed into penstocks. There is, in other words, a certain amount of leeway in dealing with intelligence: People are seldom using all they have.

The problem, in brief, is to "feed it into the penstocks" to get people to use more of the intelligence they were born with. Another thing we know about intelligence is that it has both biological and social roots. Some people are evidently born with more of this potential than others, but the extent to which they actually use it seems to depend largely on the kinds of experiences to which they have been exposed, especially in early life. In addition, there are certain kinds of diseases and injuries which can have the effect of reducing the potential, but these need not detain us here.

To say that a person has low intelligence is actually to make a rather complex statement, and therefore it should never be made lightly. We have to ask, "Low relative to what?" and, "What do you mean by 'intelligence'?"

In this case, the only answers that really make sense are, "Low relative to the minimum level at which people can be employed economically in this particular occupation," and, "In this context, intelligence is the ability to minimize errors and maximize productivity on the basis of on-the-job experience. " In spite of this complexity, the diagnosis of low intelligence is often made entirely too lightly. For example, people are written off as "just not having it" (presumably "it" means intelligence) for reasons more often casual than profound.

Thus to fail to grasp a point immediately when it may have been foggily made, to persist in errors that have never been clearly pointed out as errors, or to disagree with ideas whose premises have never been clearly spelled out — any of these can lead to the rather unintelligent decision that a man who is not a mind-reader is not intelligent. But the "diagnosis," once made, tends to persist, and for this reason the decision to write off a man's chances of regaining a satisfactory competence level because he "isn't intelligent enough" is always suspect.

As with every other aspect of competence loss, the first two stratagems here are to challenge the diagnosis and then, if the diagnosis survives, to try to minimize its effects by moving the individual closer to the top of his own capabilities. A sizable number of seeming problems can be cleared up through a combination of this kind of skepticism and insistence on more-than-ordinary efficiency. But after both stratagems have had their day, there will still be quite a few people who are not so easily salvaged, because they really are limited in their ability to turn their experience into wisdom. And the salvage of these people rests on the successful redesign of both the jobs they are assigned to do and the ways in which they are trained to do them.

Because people who are intellectually handicapped are obviously unable to handle complex assignments, there is a tendency for management to overcompensate for their deficiencies by assigning them to work that is well below the limits of even their modest abilities. But people who are not as bright as most can become just as bored as most other people when their work fails to challenge them. The main difference is likely to be a less intelligent reaction to the boredom. Instead of striking at the roots of their problem by trying to alter the job, they are likely to rebel against it and find ways of doing it *less* efficiently. Thus they may compound the felony; yet they were innocent of the felony itself. No solution to problems of this kind is likely to be lasting if it tries to cope with such people at their own level by attempting, in other words, to suppress their reaction with threats or other pressures.

When it becomes necessary to reassign such a person or to restructure his job because, presumably, he has fallen below the rising level of acceptable competence in his original job — it is vitally important not to commit the felony of underutili-zing him. On the other hand, it is always wise to allow a margin for error in setting the difficulty level of a redesigned job. Thus the question arises as to whether it is wiser to make the first approximation on the high side, so that any adjustments are likely to be in the direction of less difficulty, or on the low side, so that any adjustments are likely to involve increasing the difficulty level. In general, the latter course is probably wiser, if only to avoid the discouragement that a further downgrading could bring.

Training methods for the less intelligent worker should emphasize supervised practical experience, as opposed to classroom teaching and textbook study. The necessity for remembering material that will not be used frequently should be obviated, whenever possible, by eliminating the non-repetitive aspects of the job. The conditions under which the worker would be expected to alter his routine behaviour (for example, to turn off a machine or to summon his supervisor) should be few in number and easily identified. There should be plenty of stress on rote memory and on over learning that is, repetition to the point where the correct response becomes almost automatic, requiring little if any memory-search or decision making. Above all, ample time should be allowed for training.

This prescription for training the mentally handicapped worker is in many respects diametrically opposed to what we have been preaching throughout this book: that most people are more effectively motivated when more is expected of them than when their assigned work is well within the limits of what they know they can do. But most people are not mentally handicapped; and right there, in that almost absurdly obvious little truism, lies the crux of one of management's most serious motivational problems. Most jobs should not be designed in ways that minimize the exercise of intelligence. With the exception of those relatively few people for whom mental exercise leads rapidly to overexertion, it is much wiser to design difficulty, variety, and challenge into most jobs. The result will not necessarily be "happy" workers, but in most cases they will be more involved in and more committed to their work than they can be when their jobs are too easy for them.

Sometimes problems which are essentially motivational, rather than educational or intellectual, can bring about a condition of competence loss which is as temporary or as permanent as the motivational problem itself. These range considerably in both variety and severity. Three of the more common types of motivationally induced competence loss are the problem of the chronic "underachiever"; the attitude that there is nothing to be gained by preserving one's competence level; and what might be called "reactive incompetence" — that is, a catastrophic loss of effectiveness resulting from some extreme form of stress.

One of the likeliest victims of rising competence levels is the person who has never been entirely convinced of his own competence in the first place. Any success at all takes such people by surprise, and sometimes success is not enough to erase their own doubts about their abilities. When new demands are placed on those abilities — for example, when their jobs are to be upgraded

— they may shrink from attempting it. Or more likely, they may become so well prepared, mentally, for the "inevitable" failure that it seems futile to try very hard to avoid it.

By continually discounting their own chances in this manner, such people manage to accomplish considerably less than they are actually capable of. Sometimes their problem will be obvious, as in the case of the highly trained student who never manages to put his training to productive use. But many other underachievers are unsuspected, because the world accepts their own greatly diminished concept of their potentialities. They seem, in other words, to be properly positioned, and they give no indication of possessing untapped reservoirs of ability.

Thus the fact that they are functioning well below the level of their capacity is masked and may not become apparent until they start falling behind the normal pace of growth.

Problems of this kind tend to be chronic, going back a long way into the individual's history. That is why they are very hard to deal with. Professional counseling sometimes helps. For management, the most important consideration is a prompt diagnosis. When this type of person is at the point of failure that is, when he has been presented with the challenge of growth and has not responded to it he is-commencing a retreat which, if not checked, can turn into a rout.

He may be prepared, in other words, to abandon the plateau of competence on which he had been resting and withdraw to a lower plateau, rather than hazard the climb to a higher one. Checking the retreat is primarily a matter of getting some personalized help and reassurance to him in a hurry, before his pattern of overestimating challenges and underestimating his ability has had time to harden. This is easier said than done. That is why, as the pace of technological change continues, many more underachievers will be discovered resting comfortably on competence plateaus well below the level of their real abilities.

Sometimes a man may see little advantage in increasing, or even in preserving, his competence level. This may happen when the penalty for failing to grow is not particularly severe — as, for example, in the case of people whose incomes are protected and who therefore are not dependent on their personal earning power. It may also happen when the reward for increased competence seems too remote. If a man does not really expect to be employed in a particular trade — because jobs are scarce, or because he considers himself unable to compete for them, or because he expects to be victimized by discrimination — he probably won't try very hard to learn that trade.

Sometimes, upgrading one's employment also means uprooting one's way of life — relocating, changing hours, or even just submitting to the disciplines of regular employment — and these changes may actually make an upgraded job seem less attractive than an underpaid, underutilized status quo. But perhaps the most important reason why men may profess to see little gain in adding to their competence is rationaliza-tion: They are trying to convince themselves that they don't really want the thing they fear they cannot get or could not accept if they did get it. Most people in these situations are likely to be considered lazy, and "laziness" is one of those poorly thought-out labels that have acquired the ring of finality. Someone who is lazy is presumably incorrigibly addicted to not exerting himself. But laziness is no more inherent in man than diligence.

From the standpoint of motivation, men are lazy or diligent for essentially the same reason it seems to them advantageous to be one or the other. Both are habits; both are learned. The ease or difficulty of changing them therefore depends on how strong the habits are, and that in turn depends largely on how long they have been habits. Thus the attitude that "there's nothing in it for me" ("it" being a competence gain) is most easily combated in the young or the recently discouraged and is much more difficult to deal with when it has become ingrained.

Sometimes life deals harder blows than a man is prepared to withstand. When this happens—especially when a number of these misfortunes occur more or less simultaneously — it may trigger a decline in productivity. This is especially likely when one of the blows was dealt by the job itself, as in the case of a demotion or a dismissal.

The essential motivational message of such an event is that somebody in the environment does not have confidence in you. If that kind of message reaches a man whose own confidence has already been shaken perhaps by events in his private life the combination may be enough to disorganize his customary ideas about himself. He is then compelled to seek out a less demanding role for himself, one that can be more easily sustained than the one which his experience had invalidated. The result is likely to be a more timid and tentative approach to work. In all probability, his productivity will fall away sharply.

Whether this sort of reactive incompetence is temporary or permanent depends on whether the man's original self-concept can be restored, or to put it more simply, on whether he can regain his original confidence. The best guarantee that he will is the possession of a basically strong character that can reknit and rebuild itself once an abnormal period of adversity has passed.

Since not everyone is built that way, the next best guarantee of recovery is a management that can deliver a blow to a man's ego without shattering it. What is needed, in other words, is a sufficiently open relationship with a man to allow for telling him convincingly that, while the action taken against him was justified, it by no means precludes a readvancement if he is determined to earn it.

However, management of such quality is rather rare, and for that reason the most common approach to reactive incompetence is to leave the individual to work his own way out of it as best he can. Unfortunately, he may only work his way more deeply into it. That is why it is so important, whenever a man's effectiveness declines sharply after some kind of blow to his self-esteem, to reassure him that his future performance has not been prejudged. Failure to do that — and to mean it — is tantamount to writing off an asset that might otherwise have had considerable value.

11

Income Statement

INTRODUCTION

The income statement summarizes the results of a firm's operations for a period of time. Four major types of items appear on income statements: revenues, expenses, gains, and losses. *Revenues* are inflows of assets (or reductions in liabilities) that result from providing goods and services to customers; they arise from a firm's ongoing operations. Sales of inventory to customers, for example, generate assets (cash or accounts receivable) and constitute revenues. *Expenses* arise from consuming resources in order to generate revenues. The cost of inventory sold to customers shows an expense.

Gains, as with revenues, increase assets or decrease liabilities, yet they arise from activities that are not central to a firm's major operations. For example, a gain would result from selling land for more than its carrying (book) value. *Losses* are similar to expenses in that they decrease assets or increase liabilities, but they are not central to a firm's major activities. The sale of land at an amount less than its carrying value would result in a loss.

AN ILLUSTRATED INCOME STATEMENT

The 1997 income statement for Altron Incorporated, a manufacturer of component parts used in advanced electronics equipment. The income statement is for the year ended January 3, 1998. Although most firms use a calendar year–end of December 31, Altron uses a 52-week year and prepares its financial statements as of the Saturday closest to December 31. A 52-week year enhances comparisons across quarterly reports because each quarter will have 13 weeks. Some firms use a natural year-end instead of a calendar year-end. That is, the financial statements are prepared shortly after the firm's busy season. Wal-Mart, for example, prepares its annual financial statements on January 31, which is a good fiscal year-end for them because December is their busiest time of year. By the end of January, Wal-Mart has completed its busy season; it has made any exchanges or refunds, and its inventory levels are probably rather low. This is a good time to tally results.

EXHIBIT **Multiple Step Income Statement**

Altron Incorporated
Income Statement
For the Year Ended January 3, 1998
(Dollars in thousands)

Net sales	₹172,428
Cost of sales	134,373
Gross profit	38,055
Selling, general and administrative expenses	14,844
Income from operations	23,211
Other income	1,503
Interest expense	31
Income before provision for income taxes	24,683
Provision for income taxes	10,016
Net income	₹14,667

Altron's income statement, similar to the income statements of many corporations, is highly condensed. It contains two revenue items, four expense items, and no gains or losses. However, Altron almost certainly did experience gains and losses, but their relative sizes were probably so small that they were combined with other items on the income statement. This is an application of the materiality principle, which states that separate disclosure is not required if an item is so small that knowledge of it would not affect the decision of a reasonable financial statement reader.

This principle can actually improve the usefulness of financial statements by eliminating the disclosure of inconsequential items, which helps analysts concentrate on items of importance.

The major revenue line on Altron's income statement is labeled Net sales. Note that the terms sales and revenue are used interchangeably by many firms, while the term net implies that certain items have been deducted from the gross (or full) sales price. For example, most firms allow their customers to return merchandise within a specified period, and customers are usually offered a full refund upon returning the merchandise.

The original sales amount is included in gross sales. The refund amount is termed a sales return, and it is subtracted from gross sales in calculating net sales. Even if the term net is omitted, reported sales on the income statement are usually net sales. Cost of sales is often referred to as cost of goods sold. It reflects the cost to Altron of the goods sold to its customers. The difference between sales and cost of goods sold is called gross profit or gross margin.

Altron has elected to combine selling, general, and administrative expenses, although some companies report separate figures. Selling expenses include advertising costs, commissions to salespersons, depreciation of equipment used in the selling function, and a number of other items. General and administrative expenses consist of senior managers' salaries, accounting and auditing costs, insurance, depreciation of administrative offices, and so on. Operating income equals sales minus all costs and expenses incurred by normal operations. Operating income is a primary indicator of how well a firm has managed its operations and serves as a basis for comparing firms within the same industry.

Altron's income statement contains several other items. Other income can arise from a variety of sources, such as interest on investments. Interest expense reflects the firm's cost of borrowing money from creditors. Income taxes are imposed by the federal government, state and local governments, and foreign jurisdictions. Neither interest nor income taxes directly relate to a firm's operations. For example, interest expense is largely a function of how much the firm has borrowed to finance its operations. Differences in interest expense between firms are determined primarily by choices the firms have made in financing their businesses. Some firms elect to borrow heavily, which results in large interest charges.

Other firms rely on investments by owners; Interest charges are not paid on these funds and, because of this, interest expense is deducted after operating income is calculated. The bottom line of the income statement is called net income, earnings, or profit. Although interest and income tax expenses do not affect operating income, they are appropriate deductions in the calculation of overall profitability. Because net income reflects the increase in net assets from all profit-oriented activities, it is the focus of much scrutiny by analysts, investors, and other financial statement readers. Keep in mind the difference between revenue and profit.

Revenue refers to the total inflow of assets (or reduction in liabilities) from customers. Profit is the net increase in a firm's recorded wealth after deducting expenses from revenue. Altron's income statement presented is in the multiple-step format. Multiple-step income statements calculate certain subtotals for the reader. Altron's statement contains subtotals for gross profit and operating income. In contrast, income statements using the single-step format summarize all revenues in one section and all expenses in another. A single-step income statement. Whereas the single-step approach is simpler, the multiple-step approach provides more information.

USES OF THE INCOME STATEMENT

A major purpose of the income statement is to show a firm's profitability, yet it also provides a number of additional performance measures. Revenue, for example, is a key measure of growth that reflects a firm's success in expanding its market. Additionally, comparisons of expense numbers from year to year indicate a firm's success in controlling costs.

Operating income measures managers' performance in conducting a firm's operations. Income statement information provides the basis for a variety of decisions. Because earnings underlie a firm's ability to generate cash flows for dividends and growth, equity investors are interested in the income statement. Lenders are also interested in the income statement because a firm's ability to pay principal and interest in a timely manner ultimately depends on its profitability. A firm's management can use income statement information to make a variety of decisions.

For example, managers must constantly evaluate the prices they set for the firm's products and services. Pricing affects both profitability and growth. The income statement tells managers and investors how well the firm's pricing strategy has accomplished stated objectives.

Corporations always strive to reduce the costs of their operations, and the income statement can also measure the success of cost-cutting initiatives. However, costcutting, such as employee layoffs, do not ensure increased profitability.

Apple Computer Inc. cut thousands of jobs in 1996 and 1997, yet continued to post losses. Continued competition from industry rivals and the loss of human talent are issues that must also be addressed.

EXHIBIT Single-Step Income Statement

Altron Incorporated
Income Statement
For the Year Ended January 3, 1998
(Dollars in thousands)

Revenues		
Net sales	₹172,428	
Other income	1,503	
		₹173,931
Expenses		
Cost of sales	134,373	
Selling, general and administrative expenses	14,844	
Interest expense	31	
Provision for income taxes	10,016	
		159,264
Net income		₹14,667

As a final illustration, managers often use the income statement when setting dividends. Net income is a primary measure of a firm's ability to pay dividends. In fact, some firms set a dividend target equal to a certain percentage of net income.

REVENUE RECOGNITION

A firm's earnings process often takes place over an extended period of time. A manufacturer's typical earnings process entails purchasing raw materials, manufacturing, storing and selling the finished product, and collecting cash from the customer. The manufacturer creates value through all these steps, but for accounting purposes, firms usually select a discrete point in time to recognize (record) revenue.

GENERAL RULE

The revenue recognition principle states that revenue should be recognized in the accounting records when:

- The earnings process is substantially complete, and
- The amount to be collected is reasonably determinable.

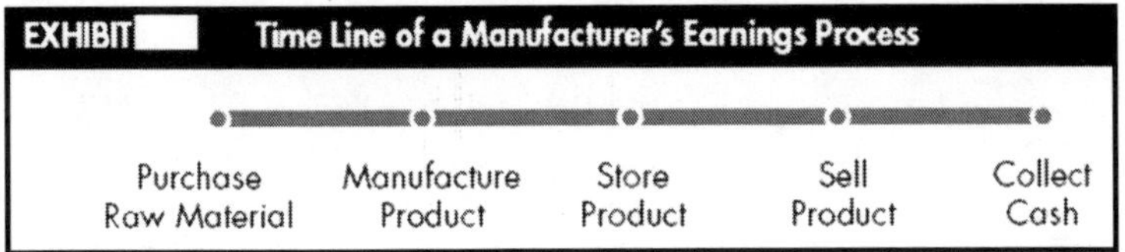

The first criterion prevents the recognition of revenue before a firm has fulfilled its obligation to the customer. The second criterion indicates that the sales price has been set and that the customer will probably pay the amount due. Both criteria ensure that revenue is not recognized prematurely. If revenue is recognized too soon, the income statement will indicate that the firm has accomplished activities that it has not, which would mislead financial statement users. In most situations, these criteria are met at the point of sale, that is, when a product is delivered or a service is rendered to a customer.

Even if payment is not immediately received, a claim to cash (an account receivable) has been obtained, and revenue recognition is proper. Two additional comments need to be made about revenue recognition at the point of sale. First, many sellers guarantee their products' performance for a period of time. If a product malfunctions, the seller is obligated to incur the cost of correcting the problem. Does the existence of such a warranty indicate that the earnings process is not substantially complete at the time of sale? No, it does not. For most sellers, the warranty cost is relatively minor.

Thus, the earnings process is substantially complete at the time of sale. Second, when accounts receivable are obtained at the point of sale, can we be certain that cash will ultimately be collected? In most cases, absolute assurance cannot be obtained, but if the seller has done a good job of checking customers' credit histories, a reasonable estimate of worthless accounts receivable can be made. This estimate is used to adjust both the income statement and the balance sheet.

EXCEPTIONS

A number of exceptions exist to the general rule of thumb that revenue is recognized at the point of sale. One exception deals with the collectibility of receivables. If the seller is highly uncertain about the collectibility of a receivable, revenue recognition should be delayed beyond the point of sale to the point when cash is actually collected. This approach is sometimes used in the real estate industry. Another exception deals with long-term construction contracts (for bridges, highways, and so on).

These projects can take several years to complete. If revenue recognition is delayed until the earnings process is substantially complete, no revenue is recognized in any contract year except the final one, at which point all the revenue is recognized. Such an uneven pattern of revenue recognition would contrast with the actual earnings process, which takes place throughout the life of the contract.

Accordingly, if

- A binding contract exists between the buyer and the seller and
- The seller can reasonably estimate the costs to complete the project, then revenue, the related costs, and the resultant profit should be estimated and recognized each year by the percentage of completion method.

This method recognizes a portion of the revenue, cost, and profit each year just as to the percentage of the job completed. A similar situation exists with some service contracts. For example, consider a health club that sells one-year memberships for an immediate payment of ₹600. Revenue recognition at the point of sale is inappropriate because the earnings process has barely begun.

However, delaying revenue recognition until the twelfth month, when the earnings process is substantially complete, is also inadvisable. GAAP permits proportional revenue recognition each month over the contract's life. Most firms describe their revenue recognition policies in a note to the financial statements. Because the earnings process has just begun at that point, the magazine records a liability instead of revenue. Recording a liability recognizes that Reader's Digest has an obligation to provide its customers something of value: either the magazine or a refund. Revenue is recognized as the magazines are mailed to the customers.

EXPENSE RECOGNITION

The matching principle governs expense recognition. It states that all costs that were incurred to generate the revenue appearing on a given period's income statement should appear as an expense on the same income statement. In other words, we should match expenses against revenues. Revenues are first recognized and expenses are then matched with those revenues. By doing this, the income statement contains measures of both accomplishment (revenue) and effort (expenses), thereby enabling an assessment of firm performance. The matching principle is implemented in one of three ways.

ASSOCIATING CAUSE AND EFFECT

One method of implementing the matching principle is known as associating cause and effect. This implies that a clear and direct relationship exists between the expense and the associated revenue. Cost of goods sold is a good example. A retail store certainly cannot generate sales revenue without consuming inventory. Salespersons' commissions are another example. Because commissions are usually paid as a percentage of sales revenue, commission expense is tied directly to revenue.

SYSTEMATIC AND RATIONAL ALLOCATION

Another method used to implement the matching principle is systematic and rational allocation. Many costs cannot be directly linked to specific revenue transactions. They can, however, be tied to a span of years and allocated as an expense to each of those years. Sales equipment, as an example, is essential to generate revenue.

However, linking the cost of each display case, piece of furniture, and the like to specific sales transactions is difficult. Instead, the equipment's cost is systematically allocated as depreciation expense to the years during which the equipment helps generate revenue.

IMMEDIATE RECOGNITION

The final method of applying the matching principle is immediate recognition. Some expenditures have no discernible future benefit. In these cases, the expenditure is expensed immediately. Officers' salaries, utilities, and interest are treated in this manner.

A CLOSER LOOK AT THE INCOME STATEMENT

As indicated earlier, income statements summarize past transactions and events. Many users of income statements are interested in the past only to the extent that it can help predict the future. Financial statement users are concerned about earnings sustainability, which refers to the likelihood that earnings will persist in the future.

Historical income statements will be less useful for predicting the future if the results of ongoing operations are combined with the effects of events that are unusual or are not expected to recur in the future. Consequently, GAAP requires that income statements separately report certain items. This part describes these items and shows how they are displayed on the income statement.

DISCONTINUED OPERATIONS

If a firm ceases to operate (or plans to cease operating) a major segment of its business, separate income statement disclosure is required of its (1) continuing operations and (2) discontinued operations. The income statement of Hahn Automotive Warehouse, Inc., which sells replacement auto parts. Hahn traditionally had sold to both commercial concerns, such as automotive repair shops, and to retail customers (do-it-yourselfers) via its AUTOWORKS retail division, which Hahn decided to dispose of in 1997 because of poor profitability.

EXHIBIT **Income Statement with Discontinued Operations**

Hahn Automotive Warehouse, Inc.
Statement of Operations
For the Year Ended September 30, 1997
(Dollars in thousands)

Net sales	₹142,242
Cost of products sold	86,967
Gross profit	55,275
Selling, general and administrative expense	46,717
Depreciation and amortization	2,005
Income from operations	6,553
Interest expense	(4,670)
Other income	719
Income before provision for income taxes	2,602
Provision for income taxes	1,011
Income from continuing operations	1,591
Loss from discontinued operations:	
Write-down of investment, net of tax benefit	(18,789)
Loss from discontinued operations, net of tax benefit	(3,937)
Total loss from discontinued operations	(22,726)
Net loss	(₹21,135)

The first 11 lines of Hahn's income statement reflect the results of continuing operations. The discontinued operations part contains two line items; the first line reports the loss from the AUTOWORKS division, and the second line indicates the results of operating the segment. In making predictions about future earnings, most analysts would ignore the effects of these items by focusing on income from continuing operations. To qualify for separate reporting, the discontinued operation must represent an entire major line of business.

Many divestitures do not qualify as an entire line of business and do not necessitate separate reporting. For example, a Wall Street Journal substance stated: "HCA-Hospital Corporation of America, bowing to weakness in the psychiatric hospital industry, said it will sell 22 hospitals and take an after-tax charge of as much as ₹300 million in the third quarter." The charge reflects operating losses and anticipated losses on the sale. Because HCA retained ownership of 26 psychiatric hospitals and 73 general hospitals, it did not dispose of an entire line of business. Treatment as a discontinued operation would be inappropriate.

The ₹300 million charge would be included in continuing operations. Thus, financial statement readers must be aware that continuing operations might contain revenues, expenses, gains, and losses that will not persist in the future. Some analysts would prefer to remove the ₹300 million charge from the current quarter's earnings when making projections about the future. On the other hand, some analysts might view HCA's sale of hospitals as a normally recurring modification of the firm's strategy. Because these modifications are expected to occur periodically, these analysts would not remove the ₹300 million from reported earnings.

EXTRAORDINARY ITEMS

Extraordinary items are events and transactions that are unusual in nature and infrequent in occurrence. Unusual in nature implies that the event or transaction is, at most, incidentally related to a firm's typical operations. Infrequent in occurrence suggests that the item is not expected to recur in the foreseeable future. Extraordinary items usually include natural disasters and actions by foreign governments, such as expropriation of assets. Separate disclosure of extraordinary items enables analysts to make better projections of a firm's future operations.

A partial income statement for a California-based company, American Enterprises, Inc. (AE) and an accompanying note. It shows that AE lost a building in an earthquake, which meets the criterion of being unusual in nature. A question arises as to whether they are expected to recur in the foreseeable future. In California, earthquakes continue to occur with some regularity. This is another accounting situation that requires judgment. Evidently, AE and its auditors feel that earthquakes in their area occur with sufficient irregularity that they are not expected to recur in the foreseeable future. Based on the footnote disclosures, analysts can exercise their own judgment about reported extraordinary items.

EXHIBIT ■ Partial Income Statement

American Enterprises, Inc.
Partial Income Statement
For the Year Ended October 31, 2001
(Dollars in thousands)

Income before extraordinary gain	₹9,846
Extraordinary gain (net of income taxes of ₹1,047)	1,387
Net income	₹11,233

Note: The company's former headquarters building in San Francisco was severely damaged by an earthquake. After the sttlement with the insurers, the company retired the building and recognized an extraordinary gain of ₹1,387,000, net of income taxes of ₹1,047,000.

Note also that AE recognized a gain. A gain arose because the proceeds from the insurance settlement exceeded the carrying value of the building. Buildings are carried in the accounting records at depreciated historical cost, which does not reflect current market values. When making predictions about AE's future income levels, most analysts would remove the extraordinary gain from AE's reported net income:

Reported net income	₹11,233,000
Less extraordinary gain	1,387,000
Adjusted net income	₹9,846,000

INCOME TAXES

Given that many income statements have several major parts (continuing operations, discontinued operations, and extraordinary items), a decision must be made about where to report income tax expense. GAAP takes the reasonable position that taxes should be allocated to each major part. Consider again; one item listed is provision for income taxes. This is not Hahn's total income tax expense, however. It is the income tax associated with continuing operations. The tax effects associated with discontinued operations are included in the calculation of those reported losses. This format shows discontinued operations net of tax. Note that discontinued operations generated a loss and that the tax effect is labeled a tax benefit. Losses yield tax benefits because they lower the taxes a firm must pay. Consider a simple example. In 2001, Crimp Corporation earned, before taxes, a profit of ₹10,000 on continuing operations. It also incurred a ₹2,000 loss on discontinued operations. Assume a tax rate of 30%. Had the ₹2,000 loss not been incurred, Crimp's total tax expense would have been ₹3,000:

$$\text{Total tax expense} = ₹10{,}000 \times .3 = ₹3{,}000$$

However, given that Crimp did incur the ₹2,000 loss, its total tax expense is ₹2,400:

$$\text{Total tax expense} = (₹10{,}000 - ₹2{,}000) \times .3 = ₹24{,}00$$

Thus, the loss from discontinued operations reduced income tax expense by ₹600. The tax expense allocated to continuing operations is ₹3,000, and the tax benefit allocated to discontinued operations is ₹600. A partial income statement would appear as follows:

Crimp Corporation
Partial Income Statement
For the Year Ended December 31, 2001

Earnings before taxes	₹10,000
Income tax expense	3,000
Net earnings from continuing operations	7,000
Loss from discontinued operations (less income tax benefit of ₹600)	1,400
Net income	₹5,600

EARNINGS PER SHARE

Many financial numbers are stated on a per-share basis. Price per share and dividends per share are widely quoted in the financial press. Because a share of stock is the basic ownership unit in corporations, this mode of expression is quite useful. Consequently, GAAP requires that publicly held companies state net income on a per-share basis. In general terms, this requires dividing net income by the average number of shares of stock outstanding. The result is earnings per share (EPS):

$$\text{EPS} = \frac{\text{Net income}}{\text{Shares outstanding}}$$

Per-share amounts make it easier to relate the dividends, prices, and earnings of a given firm.

ANALYZING THE INCOME STATEMENT

As you've seen by now, the income statement contains a great deal of useful information about a firm. This part shows how to extract and interpret that information. The income statements of OshKosh B'Gosh, Inc. (OB) for the years 1997 and 1996, which are summarized in serve as the basis for this part. One item on OB's income statement deserves special mention. In 1996, OB incurred a ₹32,900,000 special charge.

The charge includes costs to close facilities, write down assets, and lay off employees. Because OB did not discontinue an entire line of business, these changes do not qualify as a discontinued operation, yet this charge might not recur in the near future. Consequently, some analysts would delete this ₹32,900,000 loss in calculating ratios and evaluating trends.

VERTICAL ANALYSIS

Vertical analysis examines relationships within a given year. To do this with the income statement, divide each line by the first item, net sales. Net sales are a summary measure of a firm's total activities, so evaluating each income statement item relative to net sales makes sense. The result yields common-size income statements in percentage terms. OB's common-size statements appear in.

The first line of a common-size income statement is always 100% because the net sales figure is divided by itself.

EXHIBIT Income Statements for 1997 and 1996

OshKosh B'Gosh, Inc.
Income Statements
(Dollars in thousands)

	Year Ended December 31, 1997	1996
Net sales	₹395,196	₹444,766
Cost of products sold	250,815	300,495
Gross profit	144,381	144,271
Selling, general, and administrative expenses	115,439	122,055
Special charges and plant closings	—	32,900
Royalty income, net	(7,945)	(6,100)
Operating income (loss)	36,887	(4,584)
Interest expense	(305)	(1,088)
Other income	1,605	1,575
Income (loss) before taxes	38,187	(4,097)
Income taxes (benefit)	15,629	(5,216)
Net income	₹22,558	₹1,119

Note: During 1996, the company recorded special charges of ₹32,900,000 to close facilities, discontinue the company's Genuine kids retail store chain, and wind down th company's Europenan subsidiaries. Special charges (net of income tax benefit) reduced net income by ₹15,200,000 (₹1.23 per share) in 1996.

The second line of the common-size income statement, cost of products sold divided by net sales, is referred to as the cost of goods sold percentage. For a firm that is a merchandiser, one that simply buys and resells goods without changing their shape or form, this percentage reflects the relationship between the price the firm pays for the goods and the price it charges customers. For a manufacturer, a firm that buys raw materials and component parts and reshapes them into a finished product, the cost of goods sold percentage can also indicate the efficiency of the manufacturing process.

In assessing a firm's ability to generate cash flows, low costs and consequently low cost of goods sold percentages are desirable. This provides a larger profit per item sold. For every dollar of revenue in 1997, OB paid about ₹0.64 to manufacture the associated clothing.

The third line, gross profit (or gross margin) percentage, is calculated either by dividing gross profit by net sales or by subtracting the cost of goods sold percentage from 100%. It reflects the percentage of the sales price that exceeds the cost of goods sold. It measures the percentage of revenue that is available to cover expenses other than cost of goods sold and to contribute towards profits.

In 1997, about ₹0.36 of every OB sales dollar was available for these purposes. Given that a lower cost of goods sold percentage is desirable, a higher gross profit percentage is preferable.

Two basic strategies exist to increase the gross profit percentage (or, in other words, to decrease the cost of goods sold percentage).

- *First,* unit selling prices could be increased. This option is limited because of competition from other companies in the firm's industry.
- *Second,* efforts can be made to reduce the cost of goods sold. This can be done, for example, through more astute purchasing (such as buying in bulk to obtain a discount) or a more efficient manufacturing process. The fourth line of OB's common-size income statement reflects the relationship between selling, general, and administrative expenses and net sales.

Managers have substantial control over these costs, and percentages that increase over time are usually viewed with disfavour. Of the remaining items in The two most important are the operating income percentage and the net income percentage.

The operating income percentage is an indicator of management's success in operating the firm. The numerator, operating income (or loss), excludes both interest expense and taxes.

Because these expenses are not directly affected by operating (buying and selling) decisions, the operating income percentage is a better reflection of how management handles the day-to-day affairs of the firm. The net income percentage reflects the firm's overall profitability, after interest and taxes, relative to its level of activity (net sales). Both ratios are indicators of a firm's financial success. Graphically depicts the information contained in Exhibit.

EXHIBIT Common-Size Income Statements

OshKosh B'Gosh
Common-Size Income Statements

	Year Ended December 31,	
	1997	1996
Net sales	100.0%	100.0%
Cost of products sold	63.5	67.6
Gross profit	36.5	32.4
Selling, general, and administrative expenses	29.2	27.4
Special charges and plant closings	—	7.4
Royalty income, net	(2.0)	(1.4)
Operating income (loss)	9.3	(1.0)
Interest expense	(.1)	(.2)
Other income	.5	.3
Income (loss) before taxes	9.7	(.9)
Income taxes (benefit)	4.0	(1.2)
Net income	5.7%	.3%

EXHIBIT OshKosh B'Gosh Graphic Depiction of Common-Size Income Statements

	1997		1996
Net Income	5.7%	Net Income	.3%
All Other	1.6%	All Other	4.7%
Selling and Administrative	29.2%	Selling and Administrative	27.4%
Cost of Products Sold	63.5%	Cost of Products Sold	67.6%

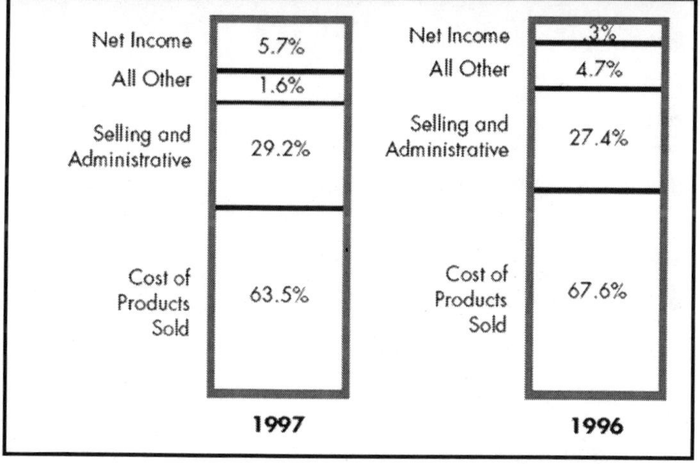

TREND ANALYSIS

Trend analysis involves comparing financial statement numbers over time. One way to implement this is to compare the common-size income statement items over time. The trends in OB's cost of goods sold percentage and its gross profit percentage are favourable. For example, the cost of goods sold percentage decreased from 67.6% in 1996 to 63.5% in 1997. This decrease could reflect decreases in the prices of raw materials, increased demand for its products (allowing an increase in selling prices) or efficiencies in the manufacturing process. The trend in selling, general, and administrative expenses as a percentage of net sales is not favourable. They have increased from 27.4% of sales to 29.2% of sales. However, the total dollar amount of these costs has declined. Both operating income and net income show very desirable trends. However, if OB's special charge is not expected to recur, the operating income percentage and net income percentage should be adjusted for purposes of assessing performance and forecasting future results. To adjust the 1996 operating income percentage, the special charge should be added to operating income because it has already been subtracted in arriving at that number.

$$\text{Adjusted operating income percentagae} = \frac{\text{Operating income} + \text{Special charge}}{\text{Net sales}}$$

$$= \frac{-₹4,584 + ₹32,900}{₹444,766} = 6.4\%$$

Because net income is an after-tax figure, the adjusted net income percentage must be modified on an after-tax basis.

The after-tax effect of the special charge was ₹15,200,000. The after-tax cost is smaller than the pre-tax cost of ₹32,900,000 because it reflects the benefit of a reduction in taxes due to the loss. The adjustment is accomplished by adding the ₹15,200,000 after-tax loss to net income.

$$\text{Adjusted net income percentage} = \frac{\text{Net income} + \text{After-tax special charge}}{\text{Net sales}}$$

$$= \frac{₹1,119 + ₹15,200}{₹444,766} = 3.7\%$$

Using these adjusted percentages for 1996 as a benchmark, OB's performance in 1997 has still improved, but not to the degree as the unadjusted percentages indicated.

HORIZONTAL ANALYSIS

Horizontal analysis is another form of trend analysis. It uses the figures from a prior year's income statement as the basis for calculating percentage increases and decreases over time. A horizontal analysis of OB's income statements. The figures in the exhibit are obtained by dividing the items in the 1997 income statement by their corresponding amounts in the 1996 income statement. The exhibit shows that net sales decreased 11.1% (100%–88.9%) between 1996 and 1997. A decrease in sales is often a cause of major concern. A sales decline could reflect a decrease in sales activity (number of units sold) or a decrease in unit selling prices. Either of these causes could have adverse effects on profitability.

Additional research regarding OB indicates that the sales decline was due primarily to two other factors. *First,* OB intentionally adopted the strategy of reducing its reliance on wholesalers, who are intermediaries that purchase the company's products and resell them to retail vendors, such as department stores. OB concluded that its relationship with certain wholesalers was not sufficiently profitable to warrant continuation. The other major reason for the decline in sales was that OB discontinued its own European operations, which had a negative effect on sales. To replace these operations, however, OB granted a license to another organization that is more familiar with the European market. The license permits this organization to sell OB products in exchange for royalty payments.

Royalty income increased by 30%. Thus, OB's strategy was to trade the profit generated by its own European operations for the royalty income generated by its licensee. The strategies of OB that affected sales should also have impacted expenses. Cost of products sold is the largest single expense item.

This item declined 16.5% (100%–83.5%) from 1996 to 1997. The decrease in cost of products sold is larger than the decrease in sales (11.1%). This suggests that the actions taken by OB will have a positive effect on profitability. The decline in cost of products sold is also attributable to two other reasons; OB was able to find less expensive sources of raw materials, and OB improved the efficiency of its manufacturing operations. The latter was accomplished, in part, by plant closings, the costs of which were contained in the 1996 income statement. Also note that the decline in cost of products sold relative to sales is consistent with the results of the common-size income statements that showed that the cost of products sold had decreased as a percentage of sales.

EXHIBIT Horizontal Analysis of Income Statements

OshKosh B'Gosh
Income Statements—Horizontal Analysis

	Year Ended December 31,	
	1997	**1996**
Net sales	88.9%	100%
Cost of products sold	83.5	100
Gross profit	100.1	100
Selling, general, and administrative expenses	94.6	100
Special charges and plant closings	—	100
Royalty income, net	130.2	100
Operating income	NA	100
Interest expense	28.0	100
Other income	101.9	100
Income before taxes	NA	100
Income taxes	NA	100
Net income	2,015.9%	100%

NA = Not available

The percentage change in operating income for 1997 is not available. This is due to the fact that an operating loss was generated in 1996 and operating income was generated in 1997. Although the 1997 figure can be calculated (36,887/–4,584–805%), care must be exercised when dealing with negative numbers. The negative denominator yields a negative percentage, yet the income in 1997 is much more positive than the 1996 loss. Even if absolute values are used, knowing that the 1997 operating income is eight times as large as the 1996 operating loss is not particularly insightful. Regardless of the difficulties with this calculation, the trend in operating income is extremely favourable.

The trend in net income is also quite favourable. Net income in 1997 is 20 times greater than 1996 net income. This result underscores another pitfall in calculating ratios: the small denominator problem. The large percentage increase is not primarily due to 1997 being so superlative. Rather, the small net income generated in 1996 has the effect of inflating the calculated value. Although net income improved substantially in 1997, a percentage increase of 2,015.9% probably overstates the improvement.

OTHER RATIOS

Several ratios link the income statement and the balance sheet. Return on shareholders' equity (ROE) is of utmost importance to shareholders. To calculate ROE, divide net income by average shareholders' equity:

$$\text{ROE} = \frac{\text{Net income}}{\text{Average shareholder equity}}$$

ROE relates the earnings generated by a firm to the assets invested by its shareholders. It is obviously in the shareholders' best interest to have larger earnings generated on their investments. A potential investor, faced with competing investment choices, will use ROE to help identify the preferred investment. The denominator of ROE is average shareholders' equity. Because net income is earned over the course of a year, it makes sense to use the firm's average shareholders' equity during the year. As a practical matter, average shareholders' equity is usually calculated by averaging beginning and end-of-year shareholders' equity amounts, which are found on the balance sheet. OB's 1997 ROE is:

$$\text{ROE} = \frac{₹22{,}558}{(₹138{,}077 + ₹113{,}157)/2} = 18.0\%$$

A ROE of 18% is very close to OB's industry average. The 1997 ROE compares extremely favourably to the 1996 ROE of.8%.

EXHIBIT **Summary of Selected Information**

OshKosh B'Gosh
Selected Balance Sheet Information
(Dollars in thousands)

	1997	1996
Total shareholders' equity	₹113,157	₹138,077
Total assets	₹217,211	₹229,131

Another important ratio is return on assets (ROA). This ratio relates a firm's earnings to all the assets the firm has available to generate those earnings. ROA differs from ROE in that ROE utilizes only the assets that the shareholders supplied. ROE measures management's success in using the assets invested by shareholders, whereas ROA measures how successfully management utilized all the assets entrusted to it. To calculate ROA, divide net income, adjusted for interest expense, by average total assets:

$$\text{ROA} = \frac{\text{Net income} + \text{Interest expense}(1 - \text{tax rate})}{\text{Average total assets}}$$

Why is interest expense added to net income in the numerator? A firm can acquire assets from two sources: owners and creditors. Interest expense is a cost incurred to acquire assets from creditors (*e.g.*, interest expense on bank borrowings). It arises from a financing decision (obtaining funds from creditors rather than owners), not an operating decision (utilizing assets). Because ROA is designed to measure managers' success in utilizing assets, interest expense is irrelevant. Its effect on net income should be eliminated when calculating ROA.

Interest expense has direct and indirect effects on net income, and both effects should be eliminated. Regarding the direct effect, because interest expense has already been subtracted in calculating net income, it is now added back. The indirect effect relates to taxes. Because interest expense is a deduction for tax purposes, tax expense is lower and net income is higher by an amount equal to interest expense multiplied by the tax rate.

Therefore, to adjust fully for the elimination of interest expense, net income must be increased by interest expense and decreased by interest expense multiplied by the tax rate. The difference between these two amounts is interest expense multiplied by 1 minus the tax rate):

$$\begin{array}{rl} + & \text{Interest expense} \\ - & \text{Interest expense} \times \text{tax rate} \\ \hline & \text{Interest expense} \times (1 - \text{tax rate}) \end{array}$$

Eliminating the effects of interest expense facilitates the comparison of asset utilization across firms that have different amounts of debt. Financial statements disclose, in the notes, firms' tax rates. OB's effective rate in 1997 was 40.9% and its ROA for 1997 was

$$\text{ROE} = \frac{₹22,558 + ₹305(1 - .409)}{(₹196,033 + ₹174,788)/2} = 12.3\%$$

OB's 1997 ROA greatly exceeds its performance in 1996. The dramatic improvements in OB's ROE and ROA reflect the success of its operational changes. The final ratio discussed in this part is times interest earned. Because profits ultimately are a source of cash, and because cash is necessary for the payment of interest charges, creditors are concerned about the relationship between profits and interest expense. The times interest earned ratio shows how many times interest expense is covered by resources generated from operations, and creditors prefer higher times interest earned ratios. It is calculated by dividing earnings before interest and taxes by interest expense:

$$\text{Time interest earned} = \frac{\text{Earning before interest and taxes}}{\text{Interest expense}}$$

Earnings before interest and taxes, not net income, is used in the numerator. Because interest expense is already deducted in calculating net income, net income understates the resources available to cover interest expense. Tax expense should not reduce the numerator because, in a worst case scenario, as income declines, taxes would be eliminated. OB's income statement does not contain a line item for income before interest and taxes. The easiest way to calculate this figure, given OB's income statement format, is to add interest expense to income before taxes. In 1997, OB's income before interest and taxes would be determined as follows:

Income before taxes	₹38,187,000
Interest expense	305,000
Income before interest and taxes	₹38,492,000

OB's 1997 times interest earned ratio is 126.2:

$$\text{Times interest earned} = \frac{₹38,492}{₹305} = 126.2$$

This ratio indicates that interest expense is covered 126.2 times at present income levels. This is an outstanding ratio and reflects that OB has little outstanding debt. Given that potential creditors would look very favourably on a ratio this large, OB would likely have little problem securing additional financing, if it so desires.

LIMITATIONS OF ACCOUNTING INCOME

Although financial statement readers find reported accounting income very useful, it does have several limitations. Conceptually, we often think of income as an increase in wealth. If our bank account grows by ₹100 because of interest, we feel as though our income is ₹100. For many assets, however, accounting does not recognize an increase in value when it occurs. Instead, the value increase and the associated income are recognized at the time of the asset's disposal. Sometimes the difference between historical cost and current value can be quite large. Consider Hiroshi Fujishige, who owns a 58-acre farm across the street from Disneyland. The farm was purchased in 1953 for ₹2,500. Southern California real estate experts estimate its value to be ₹55,000,000.

In spite of this estimate, the Fujishige Farm balance sheet reflects the land at ₹2,500, and the increase in value has not appeared on any of Fujishige's income statements. In general, to recognize a value increase, accounting rules require the occurrence of a transaction for verification purposes. Financial statements do not reflect still other accomplishments of a firm. For example, the Wall Street Journal reported that the Food and Drug Administration planned to approve an anticlotting drug developed by COR Therapeutics, Inc. This was extremely good news for COR; in fact, its stock soared 79% on the news.

However, this event was not included in its accounting records when the announcement was made. At that time, COR had not engaged in any transaction; no sales had been made. The financial statement effects of the drug sales will be recognized in the accounting records as they occur. Accounting's conservatism principle can also limit the extent to which accounting income reflects changes in wealth. This principle states that when doubt exists about the accounting treatment for a given transaction, a conservative alternative should be selected. In other words, select the alternative that reports lower asset values and lower net income. For example, expenditures for research and development are immediately expensed, even when they result in valuable products or patents. Spending on employee training is expensed immediately, even though its objective is to create a more highly skilled workforce.

These examples suggest that the balance sheets of some companies may have undervalued or unrecorded assets; this, of course, implies that the net income figure on the income statement does not necessarily reflect changes in wealth. On the other hand, most accountants support the conservatism principle because it helps avoid overly optimistic financial statements. In summary, to ensure that reliable and verifiable financial statements emerge from the accounting process, GAAP precludes the recognition of certain potential value changes. Because of this, accounting income does not strictly measure changes in wealth. However, it is a very useful performance measure on which the business community relies heavily.

ACCOUNTING INCOME AND ECONOMIC CONSEQUENCES

The managers of many publicly-held corporations receive bonuses that are based on reported accounting net income. These bonus plans typically include a floor and a ceiling. The floor requires that net income must reach a certain level before the bonus is activated, while the ceiling places a limit on the size of the bonus. That is, the bonus is not increased as net income increases above the ceiling.

Thus, managers prefer that net income falls at the high end of the range between the floor and the ceiling. Bonuses can motivate managers to undertake actions that will improve the operations of the firm, thereby increasing profits. Unfortunately, bonuses can also motivate managers to make accounting-related decisions that do not affect the underlying profitability of the firm, but that do affect reported accounting income.

For example, firms occasionally engage in big baths. These are accounting decisions that result in large losses in a single year. If reported earnings would otherwise have been below a bonus plan's floor, such losses have no effect on the current year's bonus. Moreover, by taking the losses all at one time, subsequent periods are relieved of those charges, and the chances of higher reported profits and bonuses in the future are maximized. The actions taken by Waste Management are within the bounds of allowable managerial discretion.

Other corporations, however, have been accused of much more questionable actions. For example, Miniscribe, a bankrupt disk-drive manufacturer, is alleged to have recognized revenue prematurely on shipments that customers had not ordered, improperly estimated uncollectible accounts receivable, and falsified inventory. The application of GAAP requires the exercise of judgment. At the same time, manager's self-interest is affected by reported accounting income. Accordingly, financial statement users should not be surprised that managers' self-interests influence their accounting policy judgments. As a result, financial statements may not be unbiased reflections about the underlying economic activities of firms.

12

The Balance Sheet

INTRODUCTION

This stage focuses solely on the balance sheet, which is often called the statement of financial position. Beginning with formal definitions of the basic elements of the balance sheet, the discussion describes the types of assets, liabilities, and owners' equity that are found on the balance sheets of most business firms. A variety of balance sheet ratios are presented to show how managers and investors use balance sheet information in making decisions.

ELEMENTS OF THE BALANCE SHEET

The previous two stages introduced you to the three basic financial statements. They showed how transactions and other events affecting business firms cause changes in the elements reported in the financial statements. This stage focuses solely on the balance sheet, which is often called the statement of financial position. At any given date, the balance sheet shows the sources from which the firm has obtained its resources and the ways in which those resources are currently employed. The basic accounting equation:

ASSETS = LIABILITIES + OWNERS' EQUITY

Another way to state this relationship is,

Uses of resources = Sources of resources

In other words, liabilities and owners' equity are the sources from which the firm has obtained its funds, and the listing of assets shows the way in which the firm's managers have put those funds to work. This relationship is showed as follows, based on the balance sheet for Sample Company at the end of 2000.

Uses of resources	=	Sources of resources
Assets	=	Liabilities + Owners' Equity
₹2,057,000	=	₹1,199,000 + ₹858,000
₹2,057,000	=	₹2,057,000

Viewed in this manner, there is no mystery to the fact that both sides of the balance sheet have the same total; they are merely two sides of a single coin, or two ways of describing the total wealth of the firm. The firm's wealth can be viewed in terms of sources of financing (from creditors and owners) and in terms of uses of resources (owning or controlling assets).

EXHIBIT A Balance Sheet

Sample Company Balance Sheet
at December 31,2000

Assets			Liabilities and Owners' Equity		
Current assets			Current liabilities		
Case	₹110,000		Accounts payable	₹260,000	
Accounts Receivable	466,000		Notes payable	225,000	
Inventories	812,000		Warranry obligations	112,000	
Prepaid expenses	32,000		Accrued expenses	75,000	
Total current assets		₹1,420,000	Taxes payable	27,000	
Noncurrent assets			Total current liabilities		₹ 699,000
Land	₹ 85,000		Noncurrent liabilities		
Buildings and equipment			Bond payable	₹350,000	
(net of accumulated			Martgage payable	150,000	
depreciation of			Total noncurrent		
₹313,000)	552,000		liabilities		500,000
			Total liabilities		₹1,199,000
Total noncurrent assets		637,000	Shareholders' equity		
			Paid-in capital	₹600,000	
			Retained earnings	258,000	
			Total shareholders' equity		858,000
Total assets		₹2,057,000	Total liabilities and Shareholders' equity		₹2,057,000

Another useful way to view the balance sheet is as the cumulative result of the firm's past activities. Liabilities represent the total amount the firm has borrowed during its existence, minus the amounts that have been repaid to date. The owners' equity items show the total amount invested by owners, plus the total profits earned by the firm during previous periods, minus any amounts that have been distributed to owners. Similarly, the assets of the firm represent the total resources obtained by the firm from lenders and owners, minus those that have been consumed in the firm's operations, repaid to lenders, or distributed to owners.

DEFINITIONS OF ASSETS, LIABILITIES, AND OWNERS' EQUITY

The Financial Accounting Standards Board (FASB) has identified the essential characteristics of assets, liabilities, and owners' equity. The FASB definitions, "The Basic Concepts of Financial Accounting," and are summarized in Exhibit, provide a frame of reference that helps accountants identify the items to be included in the balance sheet. For now, note that just as to the FASB's definitions, assets represent future benefits, liabilities represent future sacrifices, and owners' equity is the residual amount, or difference, between assets and liabilities. The following sides introduce you to the types of individual assets, liabilities, and owners' equity to be found on the balance sheets of most business firms. In studying these individual balance sheet items, keep in mind the FASB's definitions shown in Exhibit.

FASB DEFINITIONS OF ASSETS, LIABILITIES, AND OWNERS' EQUITY

Assets are probable future economic benefits obtained or controlled by a particaular entity as a result of past transaction or events. Liabilities are probable future sacrifices of economic benefits arising from present obligation of a particular entity or provide services to other entities in the future as a result of past transaction or events. Equity is the residual interest in the assets of an entity that remains after deducting liabities. In a business enterprise, the equity is the ownership interest.

Source: Statement of Financial Accounting Concepts No. 6, "Elements of Financial Statements" (Stamford, CT: FASB, 1980).

ASSETS

Assets represent "probable future economic benefits obtained or controlled by a particular entity as a result of past transactions or events." Future economic benefits come in many forms. For example, cash is an asset because it represents purchasing power; the firm can use cash to acquire goods and services, to repay debts, or to make distributions to owners. Inventories are assets because they are merchandise intended for sale to customers for cash and other assets.

The firm's buildings and equipment are assets because they enable the firm to perform its operations and to earn profits in the future. Assets typically represent tangible economic resources, such as cash, buildings, and trucks. On the other hand, some economic resources are intangible, such as patent rights and copyrights to a text or musical score. Assets may also be represented by promises of future payments from customers who bought goods or services on credit. Assets can be created by contract or acquisition of property rights, and yet they may not be visible to the human eye. All assets, however, have a common characteristic in that they represent probable future economic benefits to the firm.

Asset Classifications

Assets are classified into two overall categories: current assets and non–current assets. This distinction is based on the length of time before the asset is expected to be consumed or converted to cash. Current assets include cash and other assets that will typically become cash or be consumed in one year or one operating cycle, whichever is longer. Current assets are used quickly and repeatedly during a firm's normal operations.

This notion of using assets on a cyclical basis corresponds to a concept called turnover. Current assets turn over quickly, anywhere from daily to annually, and are usually generated in the normal course of business operations.

The notion of turnover is used to differentiate current assets from other asset categories that are used (turn over) much more slowly over a number of years. To show, Sample Company's balance sheet shows that the firm's total assets of ₹2,057,000 are comprised of ₹1,420,000 in current assets and ₹637,000 in non-current assets. The balance sheet equation is easily expanded to show this additional detail:

Assets		=	Liabilities	+	Owners's Equity
Current	Non–current				
₹1,420,000 +	₹637,000	=	₹ 1,199,000	+	₹ 858,000
₹–2,057,000		=	₹2,057,000		

This classification of assets is useful to the analyst concerned with the liquidity of the firm. Liquidity reflects the ability of the firm to generate sufficient cash to meet its operating cash needs and to pay its obligations as they become due. This focus on liquidity will become clear as we discuss the ordering and valuation of individual current assets in the next part.

Current Assets

Current assets are listed in the order in which they are expected to be consumed or converted to cash. For example, Sample Company's current assets are listed in the following typical order of maturity or collectibility:

- Cash and cash equivalents,
- Accounts receivable,
- Inventories, and
- Prepaid expenses.

Cash and cash equivalents include currency, bank deposits, and various marketable securities that can be turned into cash on short notice merely by contacting a bank or broker. These amounts are presently available to meet the firm's cash payment requirements. Note that only securities that are purchased within 90 days of their maturity dates, or are scheduled to be converted to cash within the next 90 days, may be classified as cash equivalents. Accounts receivable represent credit sales that have not been collected yet. They are converted into cash as soon as the customers or clients pay their bills (their accounts). Accounts receivable should turn over, or be collected, within the firm's normal collection period, which is usually 30 or 60 days. A slower accounts receivable turnover embodies more risk to the organization because the probability of nonpayment usually increases as turnover decreases.

Overdue accounts may imply that the customer is either unable to pay or is unwilling to pay because of disagreement over the amounts billed. Both cases imply that the amount of cash that will ultimately be collected is less than the amount originally billed to the customer. Managers are interested less in the total amount of accounts receivable than in the estimated cash to be generated from collections of the accounts. For this reason, accounts receivable are listed on the balance sheet at the amounts estimated to be actually collectible. This amount is termed the net realizable value of the receivables. For example, if management estimates that some portion of the amounts billed to customers will ultimately be uncollectible, then the estimated uncollectible portion will be deducted in valuing the accounts receivable on the balance sheet.

The uncollectible portion of the receivables is termed an allowance account, "Current Assets". Inventory represents items that have been purchased or manufactured for sale to customers. That is, inventory can either be created through the manufacturing and assembly efforts of the organization or be acquired from others and held for resale. Inventory is the "stuff of commerce" dating back to merchants on camels and pirates raiding the high seas looking for bounty. Inventory can be as prosaic as black tea or salt, or it can be as glamorous as gold bullion or silver coins. Today, inventory is often "high tech," such as silicon wafers, memory chips, or disk drives.

Should the company discover that some of its inventory is unsalable, or marketable only at a greatly reduced price, the reported value of the inventory should be reduced accordingly. Prepaid expenses, the final category of current assets, represents unexpired assets such as insurance premiums. Insurance policies, for example, are frequently paid ahead on an annual basis. The unexpired portion, the portion of the policy paid for but not yet used, is shown as part of prepaid expenses, which are interpreted as current assets. Prepaids are usually minor elements of the balance sheet, and, in the usual course of events, prepaids will not be converted or turned into cash. Instead, the rights to future benefits will be used up in future periods.

The Operating Cycle and Liquidity

Manufacturing and merchandising firms' operating cycles include turning inventory into cash. Using three of the current assets discussed earlier, the operating cycle evolves from the purchase of inventory, to the exchange of inventory for a promised payment by a customer (an account receivable), and finally to the conversion of the receivable into cash. Operating cycles may vary in length from just a few days (in the case of food retailers) to months (consumer appliance sellers) or even years (defence contractors). The operating cycle.

The more quickly this cycle is completed, the more quickly the inventory is turned into cash, and liquidity is higher. When the operating cycle becomes longer, the firm's liquidity usually is lower.

Should the operating cycle become too long, the firm will be forced to incur debt in order to pay its suppliers of inventory. To some extent, the length of the operating cycle is outside management's control. The length of time permitted customers to pay their accounts, for example, may be governed by industry practice. To attract and retain customers, the firm may need to offer credit terms as liberal as those offered by its competitors.

Likewise, the amount of inventory that the firm keeps on hand may be related to the length of its "production pipeline". Some products require a lengthy production process that entails a substantial investment in inventory at various stages of completion. On the other hand, the turnover of accounts receivable and inventory may be influenced by management.

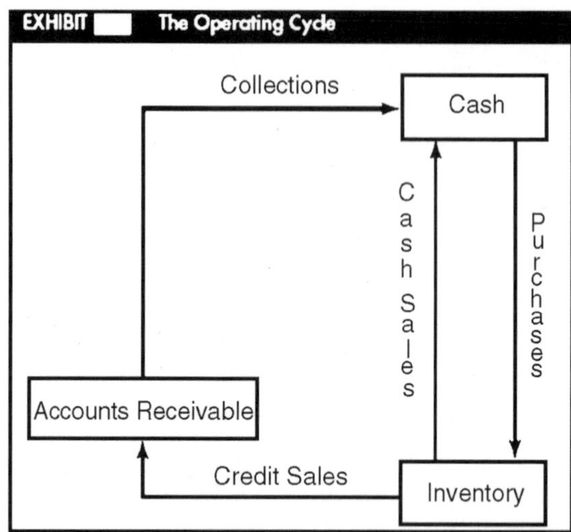

For instance, managers may have considerable leeway in of fering credit terms to customers or in deciding how much inventory to keep on hand. The analyst, in attempting to assess the firm's liquidity, needs to understand these underlying factors that cause differences in the amounts of accounts receivable and inventories across firms and industries. The composition of current assets differs for two firms engaged in different industries.

Non–current Assets

Non-current assets are long-term assets that are used in the conduct of the business. Whereas current assets are liquid and turn over in relatively short time periods, non-current assets usually turn over very slowly, on the order of once in several years. In other words, while the operating cycle for current assets is usually less than a year, the replacement cycle for non-current assets is longer than a year.

In a high-tech organization, however, some non-current assets may be replaced more frequently. All non-current assets are recorded on the balance sheet at their historical acquisition costs. The disadvantage of this is that as time passes the historical costs of many non-current assets become out of date relative to their current market values.

Consequently, they indicate little about the market value of the organization and about the future resources necessary to replace the assets. However, the historical costs listed on the balance sheet do represent the costs of these assets that will eventually be consumed by future operations.

Property, Plant, and Equipment

For most firms, non-current assets consist mainly of property, plant, and equipment. These assets are widely referred to as fixed assets. Property usually represents the land on which the firm's offices, factories, and other facilities are located. In most cases, property is a relatively minor portion of the total non-current assets, yet in some cases, such as firms engaged in mining, logging, or oil and gas exploration, property constitutes a major operating asset. Property is also valued on the balance sheet at its historical acquisition cost, and because property is usually one of the oldest assets held by an organization, its recorded historical cost is often the most out of date in terms of current market values.

Buildings and equipment represent the largest category of non-current assets. Buildings or plant may be office, retail, or factory buildings; warehouses or supply depots; or hospitals or health clinics.

Equipment includes office desks and chairs, tools, drill presses, robots, computers, X-ray and other scanners, podiums, and so on. In other words, buildings and equipment are the primary productive assets of many organizations.

Whether widgets or rings are produced, whether knowledge or health is improved, buildings and equipment are necessary to produce most goods and services. Because buildings and equipment are long-lived assets, it would not make sense to treat their entire cost as expenses in the year they are acquired. On the other hand, because buildings and equipment gradually lose their economic value over time, it does not make sense to wait until the end of their service lives to recognize their declining usefulness to the firm. As a consequence, accountants gradually and systematically reduce the reported values of buildings and equipment on successive balance sheets in order to allocate expenses to individual years of asset use.

The reduction in the reported value of buildings and equipment during a period is called depreciation expense. On the balance sheet, the total amount of depreciation expense recognized to that date is called accumulated depreciation. It is subtracted from the initial cost of the asset. The resulting carrying value is referred to as the net book value of the asset. In The net book value of ₹552,000 for buildings and equipment is calculated by subtracting the ₹313,000 of accumulated depreciation from the original cost of ₹865,000:

Building and equipment	₹865,000
Less: Accumulated depreciation	–313,000
Net book value	₹552,000

In other words, of the original cost of ₹865,000, a total of ₹313,000 has been expensed, or written off, in previous periods. The net book value of these assets is unlikely to reflect their current resale value because of changes in technology, price inflation, and many other factors.

Accumulated depreciation is not an attempt to adjust carrying values to current resale values. It also does not represent any cash or other investments that the company has set aside for replacing the buildings and equipment. Rather, depreciating an asset is an attempt to apportion or allocate its original cost as an expense to the periods that benefit from the asset's use. The net book value of buildings and equipment can be used to estimate the remaining productive capacity of the organization. For example, Sample Company's buildings and equipment are about 36% depreciated (₹313,000 accumulated depreciation divided by ₹865,000 initial cost). If Sample Company does not purchase additional buildings and equipment, then each successive balance sheet will show a lower net book value for these assets.

Such a declining net book value will signal to analysts that Sample Company is not replenishing its productive capacity on a regular basis. As a practical matter, most firms regularly invest in new plant and equipment and, as a result, the net book value of these assets usually increases over time.

The percentage relationships between the initial cost and the accumulated depreciation of these assets may give analysts a rough gauge of the overall age of the firm's productive capacity. However, the analyst must usually refer to other disclosures in the financial statements to evaluate the firm's productive capacity.

Other Non-current Assets

In addition to property, plant, and equipment, many firms possess other non-current assets such as intangibles. Intangibles are non-current assets that lack physical substance and yet are important resources in the regular operations of a business. Intangibles often consist of legal rights, such as patents or copyrights. Such legal rights are vital to the operations of many firms and, in some cases, may be the most valuable resources owned by the organization. Consider, for example, the importance of copyrights to computer software developers or book publishers. The value of such firms depends almost entirely on the value of the copyrights that protect their legal rights to the products they have developed.

Accounting for intangible assets is similar to that of buildings and equipment because the initial costs are systematically recognized as expenses over the years that benefit from the use of the assets. Intangible assets are valued on the balance sheet at their historical costs, minus any amounts subsequently recognized as expenses. The term amortization is used in place of depreciation when referring to the consumption of intangible assets. Another important type of intangible asset is goodwill. Goodwill is a general label used by accountants to denote the economic value of an acquired firm in excess of the value of its identifiable net assets (assets minus liabilities).

Goodwill reflects the adage that "the value of the whole differs from the sum of its parts." This economic value is largely due to factors such as customer loyalty, employee competence and morale, management expertise, and so on. In other words, the value of a successful business firm is usually much greater than the total values of its individual assets. The balance sheet recognition of good will depends on whether the firm's goodwill is internally generated or externally acquired. Internally generated goodwill evolves gradually as the firm develops a good reputation and customer base.

It also evolves as the firm cultivates successful relationships with its suppliers, trains and retains a skilled labour force, and conducts other value-enhancing activities. The costs incurred in generating this goodwill are generally not recorded as assets by the firm and instead are recognized as expenses when incurred.

The argument used to support the immediate expensing of these costs is the uncertainty and subjectivity involved in identifying future benefits. Externally acquired goodwill, on the other hand, usually arises when one business firm acquires another.

In this case, the amount that the purchaser is paying for the goodwill of the seller can be more objectively determined by appraisers. "Reporting Issues for Affiliated and International Companies," which deals with various business combinations. The composition of non-current assets, and the relative amounts of current to non-current assets, varies across industries. Non-current assets differ between two firms in different industries.

Assets: Summary and Evaluation

Before leaving the asset side of the balance sheet, it is helpful to summarize the conventions used by accountants to define and value the firm's assets. We also identify here some of the limitations faced by analysts who must use asset values shown in the balance sheet to evaluate the firm's liquidity and productive capacity. As we have seen, accountants classify assets into two broad groups: current and non-current. In reporting current assets, the focus is on liquidity. For this reason, current assets are generally valued at the lower of their acquisition costs or present resale values. An exception to this rule is made for investments in the securities of other firms. These practices are useful to the analyst concerned with the ability of the firm to meet its short-term cash needs.

Non-current assets, on the other hand, are generally valued at their acquisition costs minus amounts that have been recognized as expenses in previous periods. These previously recognized expenses will have been shown as depreciation of buildings and equipment or as amortization of intangibles such as patents or good will.

In reporting non-current assets, the focus is on the operating capacity of the firm; that is, the firm must focus on the structure of its long-lived assets, both tangible and intangible, which are necessary in order for the firm to produce goods or services. The carrying values of these non-current assets represent the portion of their original acquisition costs that will be recognized as expenses in future periods. The carrying values of non-current assets rarely reflect their market values because inflation has usually caused asset replacement costs to increase beyond their reported values.

The experienced financial statement analyst is alert to two central issues in examining a firm's asset structure as reported on the balance sheet:

- Different valuation methods are used for various types of assets (cost, market values, lower of cost or market value).
- Many assets that are critical to the firm's successful operations are not shown on the balance sheet.

With respect to these "missing" assets, chief executive officers (CEOs) are fond of proclaiming:

- "Our employees are our most important resource."
- "Research today provides profits tomorrow."
- "Our reputation for quality ensures our success."

Regardless of these lofty statements, resources such as employee morale, productivity, research and development expertise, and a loyal and satisfied network of customers and suppliers are absent from the balance sheet. Accountants justify these omissions either because these valuable resources do not meet the conditions stated in the FASB's definition of assets or because there is no reliable method for measuring or valuing such resources.

LIABILITIES

Liabilities represent "probable future sacrifices of economic benefits" that are the result of past transactions or events. Many times they entail cash payments to other entities, such as repayment to lenders of amounts that have been previously borrowed.

The concept of a liability is somewhat broader than this. Liabilities include any probable obligation that the firm has incurred as a consequence of its past activities. For example, many firms warranty their products and consequently are obliged to perform repairs or pay refunds when defects are later uncovered, so, as you can see, not all liabilities require that the firm repay specific dollar amounts on specified dates. Moreover, some liabilities require estimation and judgment in order to determine their amounts. All liabilities, however, have a common characteristic: They represent probable future economic sacrifices by the firm.

Liability Classifications

Just as with assets, liabilities are classified into two overall categories: current liabilities and non-current liabilities. The distinction is based on the length of time before the liability is expected to be repaid or otherwise satisfied by the firm and on whether payment will require the use of assets that are classified as current. Current liabilities are short-term obligations that are expected to utilize cash or other current assets within a year or an operating cycle, whichever is longer. Non-current liabilities represent obligations that generally require payment over periods longer than a year. To show, Sample Company's balance sheet shows that the firm's total liabilities of ₹1,199,000 are comprised of ₹699,000 in current liabilities and ₹500,000 in non-current liabilities. The following balance sheet equation shows this additional detail:

Assets		=	Liabilities		+	Owners' Equity
Current	Non–current		Current	Non–current		
₹1,420,000 +	₹637,000	=	₹699,000 +	₹500,000	+	₹858,000
₹2,057,000		=	₹2,057,000			

Current Liabilities

The current liabilities of Sample Company, consist of accounts payable, notes payable, warranty obligations, accrued expenses, and taxes payable. These liabilities represent various claims against the firm's economic resources. Accounts payable usually represents debts that the firm incurs in purchasing inventories and supplies for manufacturing or resale purposes. Accounts payable also includes amounts that the firm owes for other services used in its operations, such as rentals, insurance, utilities, and so on. Accounts payable are often called trade debt because they represent debt that occurs in the normal course of any trade or business.

Notes payable, the next current liability are more formal current liabilities than the accounts payable. A note may be signed on the borrowing of cash from a local bank. The note represents a legal document that a court can force the firm to satisfy. Warranty obligations represent the firm's estimated future costs to fulfill its obligations for repair or refund guarantees. These obligations refer to any products sold or services provided prior to the balance sheet date. Unlike accounts and notes payable, the exact amount of the firm's obligations for warranties cannot be determined by referring to purchase documents, formal contracts, or similar evidence.

Instead, the amount reported for the warranty obligation is based on management's judgment about future claims for repairs and refunds that may arise from past sales. The amount reported is an estimate, based in part on the past experience of the firm and its competitors.

The FASB defines liabilities in terms of "probable future economic sacrifices". If Sample Company's products have required warranty repairs in the past, then it is probable that items sold recently will also require warranty repairs in the future. Because the sales have already occurred, the obligation exists at the balance sheet date, and these estimated amounts must be reported as liabilities. The next item listed among Sample Company's current liabilities is accrued expenses, which represent liabilities for services already consumed but not yet paid for or included elsewhere in liabilities. These accrued liabilities usually constitute only a minor part of current liabilities.

Taxes payable comprise the final account listed among the current liabilities of Sample Company. Taxes payable represents unpaid taxes that are owed to the government and will be paid within a year. Taxes payable may include employee withholding taxes, unemployment taxes, employer income taxes, or any number of other taxes that are incurred in the normal course of operations. Taxes payable are typically a relatively minor portion of current liabilities because governmental units require that taxes be paid on a timely basis.

The current liabilities of Sample Company are a representative sample of many short-term liabilities. Businesses engage in many credit-based transactions; most sales to businesses involve accounts receivable, and most purchases by businesses correspondingly involve accounts payable. As a result, the largest of the current liabilities usually consists of trade accounts payable. The other liability items, although less significant in dollar amount, also represent common business transactions and circumstances.

Non-current Liabilities

Non-current liabilities generally have longer maturities than the current liabilities discussed in the preceding part. Their maturity date is more than one year. Most non-current liabilities represent contracts to repay debts at specified future dates. In addition, these borrowing agreements often place some restrictions on the activities of the firm until the debt is fully repaid. We discuss a variety of different borrowing arrangements that are widely used. Sample Company has two types of non-current liabilities: bonds payable and mortgage payable. These liabilities are similar because they require Sample Company to make future payments of interest and principal. Yet they differ in terms of the collateral that Sample Company used to obtain the loan. Bonds payable are a major source of funds for larger business firms.

They represent liabilities that the firm incurs by selling a contract called a bond. A bond contains the firm's promise to pay interest periodically (usually every six months) and to repay the money originally borrowed (principal) when the bond matures. The amount of money that the firm receives from investors for its bonds depends on investors' views about the riskiness of the firm and the prevailing rate of interest. Investors rely on the ability of the firm to generate sufficient cash flows from its operations to meet the payments as they become due. Mortgage payable is similar to bonds payable because firms must also make principal and interest payments as they are due.

Unlike most bonds, a mortgage represents a pledge of certain assets that will revert to the lender if the debt is not paid. The simplest example of a mortgage is that of a bank holding title to your house until your loan is fully paid. If the loan is not paid, the bank can sell the house and use the proceeds to pay off the debt. Mortgages on factories and hospitals are very similar. The problem in such cases is that there are often very few buyers of specialized assets such as factory buildings and equipment. In such cases, possible mortgage default represents more risk and higher costs to lenders.

It also indicates that most lenders will cooperate with borrowers to find alternative solutions to avoid defaults. From an analytical perspective, the analyst or manager must make sure that mortgage terms are being satisfied and that payments have been promptly remitted. For both bonds and mortgages, analysts will try to discern whether cash flows from operations are sufficient to pay the interest and principal.

Liabilities: Summary and Evaluation

Before leaving the liabilities or "borrowed resources" part of the balance sheet, it is useful to summarize various liabilities and to point out some limitations faced by analysts in assessing the firm's liabilities. Liabilities are classified as either current or non-current, based on their maturity dates. The current liabilities of the firm are closely related to its operations. As examples, trade accounts payable arise as a direct consequence of purchasing inventory; accrued expenses and taxes payable result from the firm's operating and tax expenses; and product warranty obligations occur because the firm has sold products covered by warranties.

For this reason, analysts often refer to these types of obligations as spontaneous or operating liabilities. In contrast, non-current liabilities consist mainly of long-term borrowing contracts that managers have negotiated with investors, banks, and other parties.

This type of borrowing reflects a deliberate decision by managers to obtain funds from lenders, rather than to obtain additional investments from owners. The decision about how much of the firm's resources should be provided by long-term borrowing and how much should be invested by owners is a fundamental issue faced by all firms. Financial statement users are concerned with the firm's ability to pay both its short-term and long-term obligations as they mature.

We discuss some ratios that are useful for making these assessments. The analyst is aware of two important features of liability reporting. First, not all liabilities result from promises by the firm to repay specific amounts at determinable future dates. Instead, many liabilities require estimates of future events, such as the warranty obligations reported in Sample Company's balance sheet. Many other obligations reported by business firms entail similar liability estimates "Accounts Payable, Commitments, Contingencies, and Risks,". Second, the analyst is aware that some potential obligations of business firms either are not reported on the balance sheet or are reported at amounts that do not adequately reflect their potential future claims against the assets of the firm. Consider, for example, lawsuits against the firm.

At present, tobacco firms are disputing a lengthy list of ailments allegedly associated with cigarette smoking. Similarly, large chemical and nuclear industry firms are being sued over toxic wastes.

In these cases, the potential damages awarded to plaintiffs could result in awards of billions of dollars. Although these potentially ruinous lawsuits are based on business activities prior to the current balance sheet date, none of these firms reports significant contingent liabilities because the loss cannot be reliably estimated at this time.

OWNERS' EQUITY

This final element of the balance sheet represents the equity of the firm's owners. The FASB defines owners' equity simply as the "residual interest in the assets of an entity that remains after deducting liabilities." This definition makes it clear that the balance sheet's valuation of owners' equity is determined by its valuations of assets and liabilities. This view of owners' equity as a residual amount is apparent when we rearrange the balance sheet equation in the following way:

Owners' Equity = Assets – Liabilities

Sample Company's balance sheet shows a firm that has been organized as a corporation, which is an entity that is owned by a group of shareholders. Although a corporation's owners' equity may be called shareholders' equity, in Sample Company, it comprises both paid-in capital, which represents direct investments by the owners of the firm, and retained earnings, which represents the earnings of the firm that have been reinvested in the business.

Sample Company's balance sheet shows that owners have paid ₹600,000 for shares of stock of the company. Sample Company has received this invested capital (probably in cash from investors) in exchange for its shares of stock. In addition, the firm has been profitable in the past, and Sample Company has reinvested ₹258,000 of those profits in the business. This ₹258,000 represents Sample's retained earnings. If in the next year, Sample Company reports profits of ₹200,000 and pays dividends to shareholders of ₹75,000, then retained earnings will increase by ₹125,000 (₹200,000–₹75,000). Bear in mind, however, that retained earnings do not represent cash available for the payment of dividends. Rather, retained earnings reflect the amount of resources that a firm has obtained as a result of operations.

The firm has retained this increase for use in its operations, rather than returning it immediately to the investors as dividends. Those resources are presently invested as shown on the asset side of the balance sheet. For this reason, it is possible that a firm may have a large retained earnings balance, but have insufficient cash available for dividends. The reporting of shareholders' equity for two firms, one of which reports a negative (deficit) balance in retained earnings. This discussion of owners' equity completes our tour of Sample Company's balance sheet, and, at this point, you are aware of the typical components of the balance sheets of most business firms. As suggested, generally use the term shareholders' equity, rather than the more generic term owners' equity. The following part shows a variety of balance sheet relationships that are of interest to analysts.

BALANCE SHEET ANALYSIS

Various ratios are used to help interpret and understand financial statements. These ratios are guides to understanding changes in financial performance for one company from year to year and differences in financial performance between two or more companies. Ratios are most useful when comparisons are made, either between time periods or among different companies. Ratios are useful shortcuts that permit the analyst to collapse the myriad details in financial statements into a few simple numbers. But remember that the ratio calculations are not the answers; they just show relationships. The analyst or manager must understand those relationships and make decisions on the basis of a host of information.

Ratios are just one input to those decisions. In other words, ratios are one indicator of financial health and viability, but they do not tell the whole story. Users of financial statements must be careful not to become too enamored of the ratios themselves and should not forget to look for other indicators that will permit better decision–making.

Also, ratios are historical. Judgment is needed to use them for decision–making because future conditions may change. Bear in mind that ratios are only as good as the data that comprise them.

The discussions will help you be aware of differences in accounting policies that can cause differences in ratios. Balance sheet ratios aid the analyst in assessing a firm's liquidity, asset management, and debt management policies, each of which is discussed in this part.

Vertical Analysis

Analysts usually begin with a review of the firm's assets, as well as its liabilities and owners' equity. This review begins with the preparation of a common-size balance sheet, which shows the percentage component of each major part to the grand totals on each side of the balance sheet.

EXHIBIT Vertical Analysis

Sample Company Balance Sheet: Vertical Analysis at December 31, 2000

Assets			**Liabilities and Owners' Equity**		
Current assets			Current liabilities		
Cash	5.3%		Accounts payable	12.6%	
Accounts receivable	22.6		Notes payable	10.9	
Inventories	39.5		Warranty obligations	5.4	
Prepaid expenses	1.6		Accrued expenses	3.6	
Total current assets		69.0%	Taxes payable	1.3	
Noncurrent Assets			Total current liabilities		33.8%
Land	4.1%		Noncurrent liabilities		
Buildings and equipment (net of accumulated depreciation of ₹313,000)	26.9		Bonds payable	17.1%	
			Mortgage payable	7.3	
			Total noncurrent liabilities		24.4
			Total liabilities		58.2%
Total noncurrent assets		31.0	Shareholders' equity		
			Paid-in capital	29.3%	
			Retained earnings	12.5	
			Total shareholders' equity		41.8
Total assets		100.0%	Total liabilities and shareholders' equity		100.0%

This analysis is called vertical analysis, or vertical percentage analysis, because it is based on the percentage relationship of each line in the balance sheet to the total. Exhibit has been revised as showing the vertical percentages for each account on the balance sheet.

These percentages are calculated by dividing each line by the total assets (₹2,057,000). Note that either total assets or total liabilities plus owners' equity can be used as the denominator for this calculation because the number is the same (₹2,057,000).

Liquidity Ratios

Liquidity represents the ability of a company to convert its assets to cash, and liquidity ratios are often calculated from balance sheet data. Although there are many types of liquidity ratios, we focus here on a few of the more basic ones.

Current Ratio

The most popular liquidity ratio is the current ratio. The current ratio is calculated by dividing all current assets by all current liabilities:

$$\text{Current ratio} = \frac{\text{Current assets}}{\text{Current liabilities}}$$

For the data in Exhibit.

$$\text{Current ratio} = \frac{₹1,420,000}{₹699,000} = 2.03$$

Current ratios that represent good liquidity and financial health vary widely across firms and industries. Currently, many companies have a current ratio between 1.3 and 1.5.

Many companies have short-term lines of credit and other borrowing capacities that permit them to operate with a nearly balanced amount of current assets and current liabilities. In any event, the analyst would be worried to find current liabilities substantially in excess of current assets (in other words, when the current ratio is considerably less than 1). Declining trends in the current ratio would also cause concern, especially in conjunction with declining trends in other ratios.

Quick Ratio

Another major liquidity ratio is the quick ratio, which is often called the acid test. In this context, "quick" means close to cash. To calculate this ratio, cash and receivables are added and then divided by all current liabilities. In computing the quick ratio, the net realizable value of the accounts receivable should be used.

The purpose of the quick ratio is to indicate the resources that may be available quickly, in the short term, for repaying the current liabilities.

For this reason, inventory and prepaid expenses are left out. In other words, the quick ratio is a type of "disaster" ratio that is used to indicate a worst case scenario that might apply if no other resources are available to pay the current liabilities that are due within the next year.

$$\text{Quick ratio} = \frac{(\text{Cash} + \text{Receivables})}{\text{Current liabilities}}$$

$$\text{Quick ratio} = \frac{(₹110{,}000 + ₹466{,}000)}{₹699{,}000}$$

$$= .82$$

Values for the quick ratio are often less than 1.0, and a rule of thumb used by some analysts is that the quick ratio should not be less than.30. Again, declining trends should cause the most concern. When comparing two companies, a lower quick ratio and a lower current ratio do not, in and of themselves, indicate that the company with the lower values is in worse financial condition. Lower liquidity may be offset by a variety of other financial indicators, such that the company with lower liquidity ratios could still rank higher on its overall financial stability and financial health.

Asset Management Ratios

Asset management ratios focus on the composition of the firm's assets and on changes in the composition of assets over time (changes between successive balance sheets). A vertical analysis of the left side of the balance sheet allows the analyst to examine the percentages of the total assets devoted to each category. This examination gives some indication of the resources used for current assets relative to those used to provide operating capacity. In reviewing the percentage composition of a firm's assets, the analyst keeps several factors in mind.

First, to a large extent, the composition of assets depends on the industry in which the firm operates. In some cases, comparisons between industries may be meaningless. "Smokestack" industries, for example, such as metal fabrication, require large investments in factory buildings and heavy equipment, such that a major portion of these firms' assets are non-current. On the other hand, merchandising industries, such as department stores, require large amounts of accounts receivable and also substantial investments in inventories available for resale, but relatively minor investment in buildings and equipment.

Financial firms such as banks and insurance companies have relatively little in the way of inventories, factory buildings, and equipment. Instead, the assets of financial firms consist mainly of loans receivable and investments in securities (stocks and bonds) of other firms. A first step for the analyst in assessing a firm's asset composition is to be aware of any peculiar industry norms or special circumstances. In addition to industry characteristics, the analyst knows that managers may have sound business reasons for structuring a firm's assets differently than those of its competitors. For example, some managers may extend liberal credit terms to customers as a way of improving sales and, as a result, may have a large accounts receivable balance. Other managers may carry large inventories for customer convenience or may stockpile inventories in anticipation of rising price or supply bottlenecks. On the other hand, large amounts of accounts receivable may indicate that a firm has difficulty collecting its accounts. Similarly, large inventories may reflect obsolete items or declining product sales. In short, increases or decreases in specific components of a firm's total assets may be either good news or bad news.

Any ratio computations are only the first step for the analyst. The creative art in ratio analysis is understanding the reasons for ratio differences among firms and over time.

DEBT MANAGEMENT RATIOS

The most inclusive and most useful debt management ratios are the composition ratios drawn from a vertical analysis of the right side of the balance sheet. Note the liability and equity composition ratios in the right-hand column of Exhibit. These percentage composition ratios indicate the relative proportions of various forms of debt and owners' equity used to finance the organization. The vertical analysis of Sample Company's sources of funds shows that 33.8% of all financing came from current liabilities.

A smaller amount (24.4%) came from long-term liabilities, and the largest portion (41.8%) came from owners. Of the 41.8% portion that came from owners, 29.3% was in the form of direct investment, and 12.5% was in the form of profits reinvested in the business. The ratio of total debt to total assets, also called the debt-to-assets ratio, is often used as a primary indicator of the firm's debt management. Exhibit shows that Sample Company's total liabilities are equal to 58.2% of total assets.

As this key ratio increases or decreases, it indicates the firm's changing reliance on borrowed resources. The lower the ratio, the lower the firm's risk because the organization will usually be better able to meet its obligations for interest and debt payments. A lower debt-to-assets ratio also suggests a lower risk of default.

Default on a firm's liabilities is a costly event from both a lender's and a borrower's perspective and should be avoided if at all possible. The fact that Sample Company's owners' equity provides 41.8% of the firm's resources suggests that the owners' equity of this firm offers substantial protection to lenders. Suppose, for example, Sample Company was unable to continue its operations and had to liquidate its assets, or, in other words, convert its assets to cash. In such a situation, Sample Company could incur losses of 41.8% of the assets' carrying value, and the cash received would still be sufficient to pay off all the firm's debts. Of course, nothing would then be left for the owners.

Limitations of Balance Sheet Analysis

Although the ratios reviewed in this part provide a useful starting point for assessing a firm's financial management policies, several limitations must be considered. First, ratio calculations are only the initial step in analyzing a firm's condition. They merely provide the analyst with a point of departure for asking further questions. Second, individual financial statements such as the balance sheet are seldom analysed separately from other statements. In fact, many of the most useful ratios used by analysts measure relationships among financial statements, rather than relationships within a single financial statement.

For this reason, as suggested, expand and enrich our study of ratio analysis after first describing the other primary financial statements. Third, information useful for analyzing and clarifying financial statements is contained in other parts of a company's financial reports. An important limitation in comparing financial ratios across firms is the fact that their accounting methods may differ. The varieties of different methods that firms may use in measuring assets, liabilities, shareholders' equity, revenues, and expenses. For now, be aware that financial ratios may be significantly affected by alternative accounting methods. The analyst attempts to adjust for differences caused by accounting methods in order to make valid ratio comparisons among different firms. The notes to the financial statements alert the analyst to the principal methods being used.

13

Statement of Cash Flows

AN OVERVIEW

This Accounting Standard is not mandatory for Small and Medium–Sized Companies, as defined in the Notification. Such companies are however encouraged to comply with the Standard.

OBJECTIVE

Information about the cash flows of an enterprise is useful in providing users of financial statements with a basis to assess the ability of the enterprise to generate cash and cash equivalents and the needs of the enterprise to utilise those cash flows. The economic decisions that are taken by users require an evaluation of the ability of an enterprise to generate cash and cash equivalents and the timing and certainty of their generation. The Standard deals with the provision of information about the historical changes in cash and cash equivalents of an enterprise by means of a cash flow statement which classifies cash flows during the period from operating, investing and financing activities.

SCOPE

An enterprise should prepare a cash flow statement and should present it for each period for which financial statements are presented. Users of an enterprise's financial statements are interested in how the enterprise generates and uses cash and cash equivalents. This is the case regardless of the nature of the enterprise's activities and irrespective of whether cash can be viewed as the product of the enterprise, as may be the case with a financial enterprise. Enterprises need cash for essentially the same reasons, however different their principal revenue-producing activities might be. They need cash to conduct their operations, to pay their obligations, and to provide returns to their investors.

BENEFITS OF CASH FLOW INFORMATION

A cash flow statement, when used in conjunction with the other financial statements, provides information that enables users to evaluate the changes in net assets of an enterprise, its financial structure (including its liquidity and solvency) and its ability to affect the amounts and timing of cash flows in order to adapt to changing circumstances and opportunities. Cash flow information is useful in assessing the ability of the enterprise to generate cash and cash equivalents and enables users to develop models to assess and compare the present value of the future cash flows of different enterprises.

It also enhances the comparability of the reporting of operating performance by different enterprises because it eliminates the effects of using different accounting treatments for the same transactions and events. Historical cash flow information is often used as an indicator of the amount, timing and certainty of future cash flows. It is also useful in checking the accuracy of past assessments of future cash flows and in examining the relationship between profitability and net cash flow and the impact of changing prices.

DEFINITIONS

The following terms are used in this Standard with the meanings specified:

- Cash comprises cash on hand and demand deposits with banks.
- Cash equivalents are short term, highly liquid investments that are readily convertible into known amounts of cash and which are subject to an insignificant risk of changes in value.
- Cash flows are inflows and outflows of cash and cash equivalents.
- Operating activities are the principal revenue-producing activities of the enterprise and other activities that are not investing or financing activities.
- Investing activities are the acquisition and disposal of long-term assets and other investments not included in cash equivalents.
- Financing activities are activities that result in changes in the size and composition of the owners' capital (including preference share capital in the case of a company) and borrowings of the enterprise.

CASH AND CASH EQUIVALENTS

Cash equivalents are held for the purpose of meeting short-term cash commitments rather than for investment or other purposes. For an investment to qualify as a cash equivalent, it must be readily convertible to a known amount of cash and be subject to an insignificant risk of changes in value. Therefore, an investment normally qualifies as a cash equivalent only when it has a short maturity of, say, three months or less from the date of acquisition.

Investments in shares are excluded from cash equivalents unless they are, in substance, cash equivalents; for example, preference shares of a company acquired shortly before their specified redemption date (provided there is only an insignificant risk of failure of the company to repay the amount at maturity). Cash flows exclude movements between items that constitute cash or cash equivalents because these components are part of the cash management of an enterprise rather than part of its operating, investing and financing activities. Cash management includes the investment of excess cash in cash equivalents.

PRESENTATION OF A CASH FLOW STATEMENT

The cash flow statement should report cash flows during the period classified by operating, investing and financing activities. An enterprise presents its cash flows from operating, investing and financing activities in a manner which is most appropriate to its business. Classification by activity provides information that allows users to assess the impact of those activities on the financial position of the enterprise and the amount of its cash and cash equivalents.

This information may also be used to evaluate the relationships among those activities. A single transaction may include cash flows that are classified differently. For example, when the installment paid in respect of a fixed asset acquired on deferred payment basis includes both interest and loan, the interest element is classified under financing activities and the loan element is classified under investing activities.

OPERATING ACTIVITIES

The amount of cash flows arising from operating activities is a key indicator of the extent to which the operations of the enterprise have generated sufficient cash flows to maintain the operating capability of the enterprise, pay dividends, repay loans and make new investments without recourse to external sources of financing. Information about the specific components of historical operating cash flows is useful, in conjunction with other information, in forecasting future operating cash flows. Cash flows from operating activities are primarily derived from the principal revenue-producing activities of the enterprise. Therefore, they generally result from the transactions and other events that enter into the determination of net profit or loss.

Examples of cash flows from operating activities are:

- Cash receipts from the sale of goods and the rendering of services;
- Cash receipts from royalties, fees, commissions and other revenue;
- Cash payments to suppliers for goods and services;
- Cash payments to and on behalf of employees;
- Cash receipts and cash payments of an insurance enterprise for premiums and claims, annuities and other policy benefits;
- Cash payments or refunds of income taxes unless they can be specifically identified with financing and investing activities; and
- Cash receipts and payments relating to futures contracts, forward contracts, option contracts and swap contracts when the contracts are held for dealing or trading purposes.

Some transactions, such as the sale of an item of plant, may give rise to a gain or loss which is included in the determination of net profit or loss. However, the cash flows relating to such transactions are cash flows from investing activities. An enterprise may hold securities and loans for dealing or trading purposes, in which case they are similar to inventory acquired specifically for resale. Therefore, cash flows arising from the purchase and sale of dealing or trading securities are classified as operating activities. Similarly, cash advances and loans made by financial enterprises are usually classified as operating activities since they relate to the main revenue-producing activity of that enterprise.

INVESTING ACTIVITIES

The separate disclosure of cash flows arising from investing activities is important because the cash flows represent the extent to which expenditures have been made for resources intended to generate future income and cash flows.

Examples of cash flows arising from investing activities are:

- Cash payments to acquire fixed assets (including intangibles). These payments include those relating to capitalised research and development costs and self-constructed fixed assets;
- Cash receipts from disposal of fixed assets (including intangibles);
- Cash payments to acquire shares, warrants or debt instruments of other enterprises and interests in joint ventures (other than payments for those instruments considered to be cash equivalents and those held for dealing or trading purposes);
- Cash receipts from disposal of shares, warrants or debt instruments of other enterprises and interests in joint ventures (other than receipts from those instruments considered to be cash equivalents and those held for dealing or trading purposes);
- Cash advances and loans made to third parties (other than advances and loans made by a financial enterprise);
- Cash receipts from the repayment of advances and loans made to third parties (other than advances and loans of a financial enterprise);
- Cash payments for futures contracts, forward contracts, option contracts and swap contracts except when the contracts are held for dealing or trading purposes, or the payments are classified as financing activities; and
- Cash receipts from futures contracts, forward contracts, option contracts and swap contracts except when the contracts are held for dealing or trading purposes, or the receipts are classified as financing activities.

When a contract is accounted for as a hedge of an identifiable position, the cash flows of the contract are classified in the same manner as the cash flows of the position being hedged.

FINANCING ACTIVITIES

The separate disclosure of cash flows arising from financing activities is important because it is useful in predicting claims on future cash flows by providers of funds (both capital and borrowings) to the enterprise.

Examples of cash flows arising from financing activities are:

- Cash proceeds from issuing shares or other similar instruments;
- Cash proceeds from issuing debentures, loans, notes, bonds, and other short or long-term borrowings; and
- Cash repayments of amounts borrowed.

REPORTING CASH FLOWS FROM OPERATING ACTIVITIES

An enterprise should report cash flows from operating activities using either:

- The direct method, whereby major classes of gross cash receipts and gross cash payments are disclosed; or
- The indirect method, whereby net profit or loss is adjusted for the effects of transactions of a non-cash nature, any deferrals or accruals of past or future operating cash receipts or payments, and items of income or expense associated with investing or financing cash flows.

The direct method provides information which may be useful in estimating future cash flows and which is not available under the indirect method and is, therefore, considered more appropriate than the indirect method. Under the direct method, information about major classes of gross cash receipts and gross cash payments may be obtained either:

- From the accounting records of the enterprise; or
- By adjusting sales, cost of sales (interest and similar income and interest expense and similar charges for a financial enterprise) and other items in the statement of profit and loss for:
  - Changes during the period in inventories and operating receivables and payables;
  - Other non-cash items; and
  - Other items for which the cash effects are investing or financing cash flows.

Under the indirect method, the net cash flow from operating activities is determined by adjusting net profit or loss for the effects of:

- Changes during the period in inventories and operating receivables and payables;
- Non-cash items such as depreciation, provisions, deferred taxes, and unrealised foreign exchange gains and losses; and
- All other items for which the cash effects are investing or financing cash flows.

Alternatively, the net cash flow from operating activities may be presented under the indirect method by showing the operating revenues and expenses excluding non-cash items disclosed in the statement of profit and loss and the changes during the period in inventories and operating receivables and payables.

REPORTING CASH FLOWS FROM INVESTING AND FINANCING ACTIVITIES

An enterprise should report separately major classes of gross cash receipts and gross cash payments arising from investing and financing activities, except to the extent that cash flows.

REPORTING CASH FLOWS ON A NET BASIS

Cash flows arising from the following operating, investing or financing activities may be reported on a net basis:

- Cash receipts and payments on behalf of customers when the cash flows reflect the activities of the customer rather than those of the enterprise; and
- Cash receipts and payments for items in which the turnover is quick, the amounts are large, and the maturities are short.

Examples of cash receipts and payments are:

- The acceptance and repayment of demand deposits by a bank;
- Funds held for customers by an investment enterprise; and
- Rents collected on behalf of, and paid over to, the owners of properties.

Examples of cash receipts and payments are advances made for, and the repayments of:

- Principal amounts relating to credit card customers;
- The purchase and sale of investments; and
- Other short-term borrowings, for example, those which have a maturity period of three months or less.

Cash flows arising from each of the following activities of a financial enterprise may be reported on a net basis:

- Cash receipts and payments for the acceptance and repayment of deposits with a fixed maturity date;
- The placement of deposits with and withdrawal of deposits from other financial enterprises; and
- Cash advances and loans made to customers and the repayment of those advances and loans.

FOREIGN CURRENCY CASH FLOWS

Cash flows arising from transactions in a foreign currency should be recorded in an enterprise's reporting currency by applying to the foreign currency amount the exchange rate between the reporting currency and the foreign currency at the date of the cash flow. A rate that approximates the actual rate may be used if the result is substantially the same as would arise if the rates at the dates of the cash flows were used. The effect of changes in exchange rates on cash and cash equivalents held in a foreign currency should be reported as a separate part of the reconciliation of the changes in cash and cash equivalents during the period.

Cash flows denominated in foreign currency are reported in a manner consistent with Accounting Standard (AS) 11, The Effects of Changes in Foreign Exchange Rates. This permits the use of an exchange rate that approximates the actual rate. For example, a weighted average exchange rate for a period may be used for recording foreign currency transactions.

Unrealised gains and losses arising from changes in foreign exchange rates are not cash flows. However, the effect of exchange rate changes on cash and cash equivalents held or due in a foreign currency is reported in the cash flow statement in order to reconcile cash and cash equivalents at the beginning and the end of the period.

This amount is presented separately from cash flows from operating, investing and financing activities and includes the differences, if any, had those cash flows been reported at the end-of period exchange rates.

EXTRAORDINARY ITEMS

The cash flows associated with extraordinary items should be classified as arising from operating, investing or financing activities as appropriate and separately disclosed. The cash flows associated with extraordinary items are disclosed separately as arising from operating, investing or financing activities in the cash flow statement, to enable users to understand their nature and effect on the present and future cash flows of the enterprise. These disclosures are in addition to the separate disclosures of the nature and amount of extraordinary items required by Accounting Standard (AS) 5, Net Profit or Loss for the Period, Prior Period Items and Changes in Accounting Policies.

INTEREST AND DIVIDENDS

Cash flows from interest and dividends received and paid should each be disclosed separately. Cash flows arising from interest paid and interest and dividends received in the case of a financial enterprise should be classified as cash flows arising from operating activities. In the case of other enterprises, cash flows arising from interest paid should be classified as cash flows from financing activities while interest and dividends received should be classified as cash flows from investing activities. Dividends paid should be classified as cash flows from financing activities.

The total amount of interest paid during the period is disclosed in the cash flow statement whether it has been recognised as an expense in the statement of profit and loss or capitalised in accordance with Accounting Standard (AS) 10, Accounting for Fixed Assets. Interest paid and interest and dividends received are usually classified as operating cash flows for a financial enterprise. However, there is no consensus on the classification of these cash flows for other enterprises. Some argue that interest paid and interest and dividends received may be classified as operating cash flows because they enter into the determination of net profit or loss. However, it is more appropriate that interest paid and interest and dividends received are classified as financing cash flows and investing cash flows respectively, because they are cost of obtaining financial resources or returns on investments.

Some argue that dividends paid may be classified as a component of cash flows from operating activities in order to assist users to determine the ability of an enterprise to pay dividends out of operating cash flows. However, it is considered more appropriate that dividends paid should be classified as cash flows from financing activities because they are cost of obtaining financial resources.

TAXES ON INCOME

Cash flows arising from taxes on income should be separately disclosed and should be classified as cash flows from operating activities unless they can be specifically identified with financing and investing activities.

Taxes on income arise on transactions that give rise to cash flows that are classified as operating, investing or financing activities in a cash flow statement. While tax expense may be readily identifiable with investing or financing activities, the related tax cash flows are often impracticable to identify and may arise in a different period from the cash flows of the underlying transactions. Therefore, taxes paid are usually classified as cash flows from operating activities. However, when it is practicable to identify the tax cash flow with an individual transaction that gives rise to cash flows that are classified as investing or financing activities, the tax cash flow is classified as an investing or financing activity as appropriate. When tax cash flow are allocated over more than one class of activity, the total amount of taxes paid is disclosed.

INVESTMENTS IN SUBSIDIARIES, ASSOCIATES AND JOINT VENTURES

When accounting for an investment in an associate or a subsidiary or a joint venture, an investor restricts its reporting in the cash flow statement to the cash flows between itself and the investee/joint venture, for example, cash flows relating to dividends and advances.

ACQUISITIONS AND DISPOSALS OF SUBSIDIARIES AND OTHER BUSINESS UNITS

The aggregate cash flows arising from acquisitions and from disposals of subsidiaries or other business units should be presented separately and classified as investing activities. An enterprise should disclose, in aggregate, in respect of both acquisition and disposal of subsidiaries or other business units during the period each of the following:

- The total purchase or disposal consideration; and
- The portion of the purchase or disposal consideration discharged by means of cash and cash equivalents.

The separate presentation of the cash flow effects of acquisitions and disposals of subsidiaries and other business units as single line items helps to distinguish those cash flows from other cash flows. The cash flow effects of disposals are not deducted from those of acquisitions.

NON-CASH TRANSACTIONS

Investing and financing transactions that do not require the use of cash or cash equivalents should be excluded from a cash flow statement.

Such transactions should be disclosed elsewhere in the financial statements in a way that provides all the relevant information about these investing and financing activities. Many investing and financing activities do not have a direct impact on current cash flows although they do affect the capital and asset structure of an enterprise. The exclusion of non-cash transactions from the cash flow statement is consistent with the objective of a cash flow statement as these items do not involve cash flows in the current period.

Examples of non-cash transactions are:

- The acquisition of assets by assuming directly related liabilities;
- The acquisition of an enterprise by means of issue of shares; and
- The conversion of debt to equity.

COMPONENTS OF CASH AND CASH EQUIVALENTS

An enterprise should disclose the components of cash and cash equivalents and should present a reconciliation of the amounts in its cash flow statement with the equivalent items reported in the balance sheet. In view of the variety of cash management practices, an enterprise discloses the policy which it adopts in determining the composition of cash and cash equivalents. The effect of any change in the policy for determining components of cash and cash equivalents is reported in accordance with Accounting Standard (AS) 5, Net Profit or Loss for the Period, Prior Period Items and Changes in Accounting Policies.

OTHER DISCLOSURES

An enterprise should disclose, together with a commentary by management, the amount of significant cash and cash equivalent balances held by the enterprise that are not available for use by it. There are various circumstances in which cash and cash equivalent balances held by an enterprise are not available for use by it. Examples include cash and cash equivalent balances held by a branch of the enterprise that operates in a country where exchange controls or other legal restrictions apply as a result of which the balances are not available for use by the enterprise. Additional information may be relevant to users in understanding the financial position and liquidity of an enterprise.

Disclosure of this information, together with a commentary by management, is encouraged and may include:

- The amount of undrawn borrowing facilities that may be available for future operating activities and to settle capital commitments, indicating any restrictions on the use of these facilities; and
- The aggregate amount of cash flows that represent increases in operating capacity separately from those cash flows that are required to maintain operating capacity.

The separate disclosure of cash flows that represent increases in operating capacity and cash flows that are required to maintain operating capacity is useful in enabling the user to determine whether the enterprise is investing adequately in the maintenance of its operating capacity. An enterprise that does not invest adequately in the maintenance of its operating capacity may be prejudicing future profitability for the sake of current liquidity and distributions to owners.

Index